GROUNDWORK
OF COMMERCE

H. L. JONES
M.A. (Manch.), M.Ed.(Manch.)

R. P. JONES
B.A., A.C.I.S., A.I.B.

Fifth Edition

BOOK 2

Edward Arnold

© 1973 H. L. Jones and R. P. Jones

First published 1937
by Edward Arnold (Publishers) Ltd,
25 Hill Street, London W1X 8LL

Reprinted 1939, 1944, 1945
Revised Edition 1952
Reprinted 1955, 1957, 1959, 1960, 1961
Third Edition 1964
Reprinted 1965, 1967, 1968
Fourth Edition 1969
Reprinted 1970 (twice)
Reprinted 1971, 1972
Fifth Edition 1973
Reprinted 1974, 1976 (twice)

ISBN: 0 7131 1775 3

Printed Offset Litho in Great Britain by
Cox & Wyman Ltd, London, Fakenham and Reading

PREFACE TO THE FIFTH EDITION

Groundwork of Commerce provides a text-book on Commerce and Introductory Economics suitable for the examination syllabus of the Royal Society of Arts, the London Chamber of Commerce, the Commerce syllabuses of the numerous Examination Boards, and for the various professional and other examining bodies. The topics cover the essential requirements of divergent syllabuses; Book I contains a full first-year course, suitable for Day and Evening Courses in both Schools and Colleges of Further Education, whilst Book 2 covers the requirements of more advanced examinations, including the National Diploma in Business Studies, the National Certificate in Business Studies and the General Certificate of Education.

Great changes have been taking place in Commerce since this book was first published; the world has witnessed remarkable advances in scientific knowledge and its application to industrial and commercial uses. It has therefore become necessary to revise various sections of this book, in order to give a more accurate picture of present-day conditions. Britain's entry to the European Economic Community and the measures introduced to control the supply of money are but two of the far reaching decisions recently made that will affect the economic scene for many years. Throughout this edition therefore, statistics have been brought up-to-date, changes in organisation described in some detail, whilst the use of diagrams, photographs and charts has been adopted wherever desirable.

In this edition, the general scope and character of the book has been improved to present the subject in a modern style; a slightly greater emphasis has been given to the economic aspects and implications of the subject in order to cater for modern trends and also to give the purely descriptive element greater understanding; it is for this reason that the subject-matter has been arranged under headings, and each chapter is complete in itself. The teacher or lecturer may, of course, vary the order of presentation to meet the requirements of any examination syllabus.

A selection of questions from recent examination papers has been added to each chapter. These have been carefully chosen to give opportunity for original thought and research by the student as distinct from the mere copying of notes and text.

The author is indebted to the Controller of H.M. Stationery Office for permission to use information from official publications, and to the Associated Examining Board, the Joint Matriculation Board, The Oxford Delegacy of Local Examinations, both the Royal Society of Arts and the London Chamber of Commerce, the Union of Lancashire and Cheshire Institutes, the Union of Educational Institutions, the University of Cambridge and the University of London who have generously permitted the reproduction of questions taken from previous examination papers. My thanks are also due to Aerofilms Ltd, Bank of England, British Railways Board, British Steel Corporation, District Council of Norwich, Esso Petroleum Company Ltd, Lloyds Bank Ltd, Moura-George Briggs Ltd, Port of London Authority, Simon Engineering Ltd, The Guardian and the Stock Exchange for permission to reproduce copyright photographs.

It is hoped that the book, in its revised form, in addition to meeting examination requirements, will encourage students to further their studies in this field and enable them to have a better understanding of the age in which they live.

R.P.J.

1973

CONTENTS

Chapter 1

The Branches of Production

In Britain, about 26 million men and women are engaged day by day in a large variety of occupations. They perform their work because they all have a large number of wants which they require to satisfy. The most urgent of these are for food, shelter and clothing, but people are not satisfied when they have provided for these fundamental needs. They require food which not only satisfies their appetites, but also provides them with a varied diet; their clothing must serve not only as a protection to the body, it must give them comfort and adornment. Similarly, man is not satisfied with shelters which merely give protection from the weather; they must provide for personal comfort by being decorated and furnished in as artistic a manner as possible. For their leisure hours, men and women demand facilities for amusement, recreation and social relaxation, and call upon the services of large numbers of other people in order to satisfy these demands. Human wants are unlimited in number, for as existing wants are satisfied, new ones appear.

In the early days of history, man satisfied his wants directly: he grew his own food, built his own shelter, and made full use of the natural products around him. Nowadays, he satisfies his own wants by satisfying those of others; men specialise in performing some particular service, and by means of money exchange their services. The wants of man are therefore satisfied today in a *roundabout* manner: every country in the world specialises in making that article or rendering that service for which it has some peculiar advantage, and exchanges its surplus goods or services for the goods or services of other countries. Britain for example imports principally food and raw materials and in exchange exports manufactured products and services to the rest of the world. This exchange has been facilitated by the improvements in transport and communications over the past hundred years.

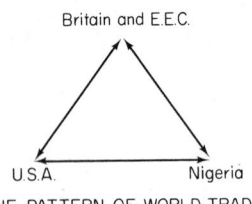

THE PATTERN OF WORLD TRADE

The *satisfaction of wants* is therefore the cause of all productive activity and millions of people throughout the world follow their daily occupations in order to satisfy their own wants by satisfying the wants of others.

2. THE MEANING OF PRODUCTION

The wants of man are varied, but in order to show the meaning of production, we may classify them into the following groups:

(a) Material Wants that are satisfied by using the gifts of nature, for we are dependent on these for all material things. Man cannot create matter, he can only make it more useful in three ways:

(1) *Change of Form*. The gifts of nature are not always in the form desired by man; in their original state, as in say clay, we speak of them as raw material. This may be changed in form by processes of manufacture, in order to be made more useful to man and become say bricks.

(2) *Change of Place*. Nature has not always provided our materials in the place where they are most useful; on account of geological and climatic reasons, many are abundant in particular countries of the world. Man increases their utility or usefulness by transporting them from the places where they are abundant to places where they are scarce or non-existent.

Similarly, he increases the usefulness of minerals such as diamonds, metal ores, oil, etc., by bringing them to the surface, and distributing them to the various countries of the world.

(3) *Change of Ownership.* Many individuals and firms possess a greater supply of a commodity than they require for their own use. This may be due to specialisation, since a greater output is obtained by means of large-scale production. Specialists in distribution, known as *middle-men*, are therefore necessary to transfer the surplus goods from the owner who possesses too much of a commodity to persons who lack supplies. By this change of ownership, the goods are made more useful to the community as a whole.

(b) Immaterial Wants. In addition to our material wants, we all have a large number of wants that can only be satisfied by personal services. We need, for example, protection, education, and amusement. These wants may be satisfied by direct personal services, such as those of a doctor or a shopkeeper, or they may be satisfied collectively, as is the case when we visit a theatre or watch television. But all services which satisfy our wants must be regarded as being productive, just as much as those services which provide us with material goods.

Production, basically may be defined as the satisfaction of human wants by creating new utilities; any article or service which satisfies a human want is said to possess utility or usefulness. All occupations are engaged in rendering services either to material things or to people, and must therefore be regarded as taking part in production.

3. THE BRANCHES OF PRODUCTION

We have seen that the term Production includes all those occupations which are engaged, directly or indirectly, in adding utility to the gifts of nature. In this way, human wants are satisfied. It is as well to remember at an early stage though that from the *Economists* point of view no act of production is complete until the finished article is in the hands of the consumer.

If we consider the complete process of production, we see that *there stages* are necessary:

(*a*) The raw material must be obtained and changed in form, or combined with other raw material in order to satisfy human wants.

(*b*) The finished articles must be distributed to the persons who wish to purchase them.

(*c*) A large number of personal services, such as those performed by the doctor or teacher, contribute to the efficiency of the first two stages, although not directly connected with either.

There are thus three branches of production:

(a) Industry is that branch engaged in obtaining the raw materials; manufacturing the raw material into the finished articles, of constructing the final product from both.

(b) Commerce is that branch of production engaged in the *distribution* of goods; commercial occupations distribute the raw materials from where they are obtained to the places of manufacture, and similarly distribute the finished product from the manufacturer to the consumer.

(c) Direct Services are rendered, not to material goods as in Industry and Commerce, but to other persons. These services are a branch of production since they increase its efficiency, and possess utility as they satisfy human wants.

4. THE DIVISIONS OF INDUSTRY

Industry consists of all those occupations that are engaged in obtaining the raw material, or in changing its form to satisfy the needs of man. Industry may therefore be divided into:

(a) Extractive Industries, which are engaged in obtaining the raw material. Examples of extractive industries are agriculture, mining, quarrying and fishing. These industries are fundamental, since we depend on them for all material goods; the manufacturer depends on them for his supplies of raw material which he changes into a form to satisfy our wants. These were the earliest form of human activity, and are still the foundation stone upon which all other occupations are built.

(b) Manufacturing Industries include all those occupations engaged in changing the form of the gifts of nature: they work on the raw materials provided by the extractive industries and change them into the form desired by man. In the manufacturing industries, capital in the form of plant and machinery is of great importance; machinery has taken over a large part of the work formerly done by hand. The division of labour has been carried to an advanced stage, which has led to large-scale production in the manufacturing industries.

Throughout the greater part of the nineteenth century Britain was the only important country carrying on manufacturing industries on a large scale, but with the industrial development of such countries as the United States, Russia, Germany and Japan, Britain has ceased to be the only workshop of the world.

Shipbuilding in Scotland on the river Clyde

(c) Constructive Industries consist of those occupations which take the finished products of the manufacturers and build them up into an organised whole.

This can readily be seen in the shipbuilding and motor vehicle industries. The various parts of a motor vehicle are manufactured from the raw material at a number of different factories. The engines, tyres, bodies, instruments, etc., are then transported to an assembly point where an organised unit is constructed.

The constructive industries have become important during the present century on account of the progress of engineering. In addition, the higher standard of living throughout the world has resulted in a greater demand for mass-produced articles. It is because of the need to satisfy this demand and produce an article as cheaply as possible that much of the modern construction industry uses standardised parts.

5. DIVISIONS OF COMMERCE

Specialisation within industry whereby a man specialises in one process is a common feature today. The same degree of specialisation can be related to commercial occupations when we consider the work of the commercial man.

The raw materials necessary for the production of an article may be the products of a number of countries. These must be purchased, stored, graded and distributed to the point of manufacture. Ultimately the article will be sold to the consumer after passing through the hands of other commercial specialists. This whole process is known as the *Roundabout Methods of Production*.

If we take the motor vehicle industry as an example:

(*a*) The numerous raw materials such as rubber, wool, steel, etc, are purchased by buyers on both the home and foreign markets.

(*b*) The foreign-produced material is transported to Britain from all parts of the world. Together with the home-produced material it is stored by the commercial man until required by the manufacturer.

(*c*) It is sold to the manufacturer in bulk.

(d) The manufactured or semi-manufactured article is sold and transported to the next stage of assembly.

(e) The completed article is stored by the commercial man and later sold to the consumer on both the home and foreign markets.

(f) Various other commercial specialists play their part in the process of production. They will have made the necessary arrangements for the payment, insurance and advertising of the products.

The term *Commerce* therefore covers a large variety of occupations, all engaged in the movement of goods. Notice that the commercial man makes no material alteration to the goods, but he increases its utility or usefulness.

There are six divisions of commerce:

(a) Trade consists of all those occupations engaged in the buying and selling of goods: it includes therefore the wholesale and retail traders, who buy goods in order to sell them again. A trader handles the goods in which he deals and becomes the owner of them for a period of time. This exchange of commodities is the essential part of commerce; the other branches of commerce—transport, warehousing, banking, insurance and advertising—are auxiliaries to trade, since they facilitate the distribution of goods over the world.

(b) Transport occupations form a part of commerce, since they are engaged in the movement of goods from place to place, and so increase their utility. By means of transport, the surplus goods of each nation are distributed to other countries, whose supplies of certain commodities are inadequate.

Great improvements in transport have taken place during the present century. The development of road, rail, air and water transport has led to the rapid movement of goods over vast distances. In addition containerised transport has enabled the consignor to despatch his goods with the minimum of delay whether the consignee is on the home or foreign markets.

As a result of these improvements in transport, the gifts of nature are collected and distributed over a wider area, and the standard of life in most countries of the world has been raised.

(c) Warehousing, or the storage of commodities, is an important branch of commerce. Supplies of raw materials and foodstuffs arrive irregularly in this country, but are in regular demand. Large stocks therefore must be stored in order that essential commodities may be available at all times. Goods are stored in the warehouses of manufacturers or of wholesale dealers to whom the manufacturer has sold his finished products. At the principal ports (London, Liverpool, Southampton, etc.) are bonded warehouses, where dutiable articles are stored until the duty is paid on them.

Warehousing enables production to be ahead of demand, and avoids the fluctuations in prices which would occur if the entire supply were placed on the market as soon as it arrived.

(d) **Banking** facilitates the distribution of commodities by making arrangements for the payment for goods: in the home trade, the method of payment by cheque or bank giro has developed, whilst in foreign trade, the foreign bill of exchange and documentary credit is used. Because of the work of banks, relatively very little money in the form of notes and coin is used in settling indebtedness either at home or abroad. Banks also collect together large deposits of money, and are thus able to finance commercial transactions by making loans to traders for short periods.

(e) **Insurance** has developed to overcome the risks of trade, which have increased in number since the world has become one market.

There are four principal groups: Fire, Life, Accident and Marine through which the businessman or private individual may guard against possible loss. Insurance companies have drawn up statistical tables, based on past experience, and are therefore able to calculate the frequency of the various risks. Small premiums are collected from a large number of traders out of which a fund is created. From this claims can be paid to compensate the trader upon whom the loss has fallen.

(f) **Advertising.** In order that the manufacturer or retailer can increase his turnover, he must devise means to make his products known to the consumer. This can be achieved by an advertising campaign which may be directed towards a national, local, general or specialist market. Various methods may be used ranging from television and the Press to free samples and gift schemes.

The principal objects will be:

(1) to inform and persuade the consumer to buy.

(2) to create and maintain a demand for that product.

There are many specialist firms engaged in the techniques of advertising and it is estimated that at the present time about £500 million is spent annually on advertising in Britain.

6. DIVISIONS OF TRADE

The exchange of commodities, which the word 'trade' signifies, is the essential part of commerce. The volume of the world's trade has grown enormously during the last hundred years, on account of the increase in population, the improvement in standards of living, the use of machinery and the improvements in transport and communication. Each country of the world is now able to specialise in the production of that commodity for which it has some special advantage, and it is the function of the trader to distribute the surplus goods of each country to other places where supplies are lacking.

Trade may be divided into the following groups:

(a) Home Trade is the internal trade of a country, and therefore refers to the buying and selling of commodities by the inhabitants themselves. We are apt to underestimate the importance of the home trade, and to forget that it embraces a large part of the trade of the United Kingdom.

The Home Trade consists of two branches:

(1) *The Wholesale Trade,* which purchases raw materials and manufactured goods in large quantities, and sells in smaller quantities to the manufacturer or retailer.

(2) *The Retail Trade* which deals in smaller quantities and sells direct to the consumer. This trade forms the last link in the chain of production, and it is the function of the retailer to hand over the finished article to the consumer.

This process can be illustrated by the following diagram:

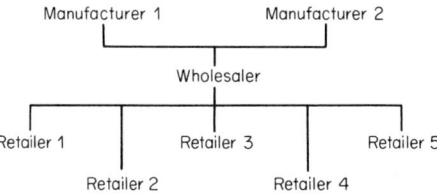

(b) Foreign Trade is the external trade of a country, and consists therefore of the exchange of commodities between the peoples of different countries. Foreign Trade is of great importance to Britain, since we depend on other countries for at least half of our food supply for the population of 56 millions, and for the greater part of the raw material for our manufacturing industries.

Foreign Trade consists of two branches:

(1) *Import Trade*, which includes all trade engaged in bringing goods from abroad to this country. This consists of food, raw materials, semi-manufactured and manufactured goods from all parts of the world. Goods are stored in warehouses until required, and agents or brokers frequently act on behalf of foreign traders in marketing the goods in this country.

(2) *The Export Trade* covers all trade engaged in sending goods from this country for sale abroad. Britain exports her manufactures in payment for her imports or raw materials and foodstuffs, etc. This country also performs a great many financial and other services for other countries that are known as Invisible Exports.

The branches of Production may be illustrated by the following diagram:

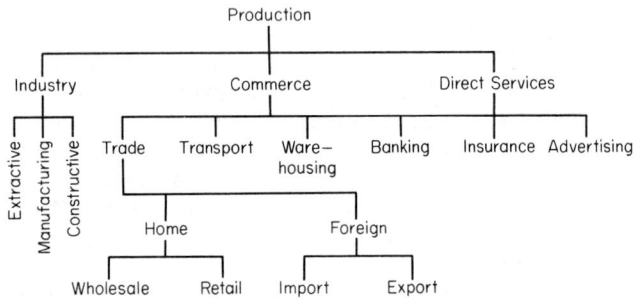

7. THE IMPORTANCE OF CAPITAL

Land (including the seabed) and Labour are the essential Agents of Production, since raw materials must be obtained and made more useful to man by human labour. From the earliest days, however, some form of capital has been used; the simple tools made by primitive man made his work more productive, and therefore were part of his capital. Capital has taken many forms in different stages of industrial development, but in all the stages, capital represents wealth which has been put aside for the production of further wealth.

The following diagram relates to the sources and application of funds found in a typical business organisation:

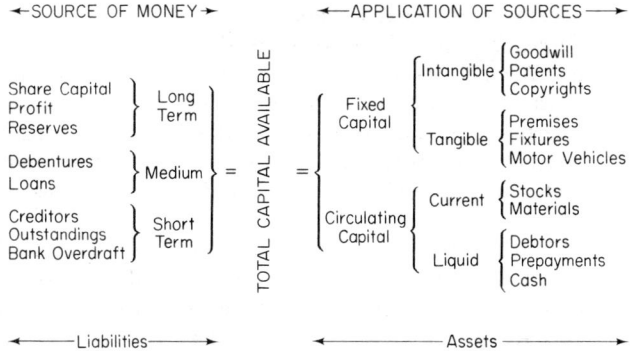

Capital may be considered from two points of view:

(a) **Economic.** The economist regards capital as man-made material things which are not immediately consumed, but are devoted to the production of further wealth; goods which have been produced are used in two ways—some are required to satisfy immediate wants, whilst the remainder is kept in reserve. The latter class of goods is known as Capital. In primitive civilisations, the goods themselves were stored for future use, but with the development of money, men postpone the enjoyment of part of their income by depositing it in a bank, or investing it elsewhere. Money therefore facilitates the transfer of capital, since the bank is able to make loans in order to finance industry and trade. Capital is often regarded as money, but from the economic point of view, capital consists of material things which are devoted to the production of further goods.

The economist divides capital into two classes:

(1) *Fixed Capital*, which consists of material goods that are used over and over again in production, such as the premises and machinery of a factory, or the fixtures and fittings of a retail shop. The amount of Fixed Capital depends on the type and size of the business; a jeweller, for example, will have more Fixed Capital than a newsagent or a greengrocer, and similarly, a department store has more Fixed Capital than a small retailer. The total of the fixed capital (or fixed assets) in the balance sheet on page 14 is £15,000.

(2) *Circulating (or Floating) Capital*, consists of material goods which are used only once in production. Examples of this form of Capital are the stock of a retail or wholesale business, and the raw material of a manufacturing concern: the stock and the raw material, when manufactured, are sold again, and further supplies are purchased.

In addition note must be taken of the money owed to the business for goods sold or services rendered (debtors) and cash. The circulating capital is the monetary value of the current assets in the balance sheet on page 14, i.e. £6,000.

The above terms are not mutually exclusive: whether an article is fixed or circulating capital depends upon the use to which it is put. If it is to be retained as part of the equipment of a firm, it becomes part of that firm's fixed capital, but if it has been purchased with the intention of selling it again, the same article is circulating capital. For example, the motor van used by a garage to deliver spare parts is part of the fixed capital, whilst the vans offered for sale in the shop are circulating capital.

(b) Business Capital. The businessman measures the value of the material things he possesses in terms of money, and expresses the amount of his capital in the monetary unit of the country in which he lives. He should distinguish, however, between the amount of capital *owned* from the amount of capital *employed*.

(1) *Capital owned by a Firm.* The Capital owned by a firm is

found by deducting the current liabilities from the total assets: thus the total of capital shown in a Balance Sheet is the total of capital *owned* by a firm.

The assets may include cash, prepayments, debts due to the firm (debtors), stock, furniture, fixtures, premises, etc.; the liabilities are the amounts owing by the firm to others and may include loans from the bank, bills of exchange payable by the firm, debts owing by the firm (creditors), payments in arrears, etc. The surplus of the total assets over the current liabilities represents the capital *owned* by the firm at that particular date. From the balance sheet on page 14, the capital owned can be calculated thus:

Total assets (£21,000) — Loan (£5,000) + Current liabilities
(£2,000)
= £14,000.

(2) *Capital employed (or invested)* by a Firm. The capital employed by a firm may be greater or less than the capital actually owned by the firm. A firm may increase its capital employed temporarily by a loan from a bank, etc. The greater the amount borrowed by the firm, the greater will be the amount of capital employed.

The amount of capital *employed* will be the total value of all the assets less the debtors. The debtors are excluded since this is in effect money lent by the firm to customers from sales and is not being put to use within the firm.

The capital employed in the balance sheet on page 14 is therefore:

Total Assets (£21,000) — Debtors (£2,400) = £18,600.

The student should realise however that there is some controversy over the meaning of the term capital employed, especially when used by Accountants to interpret the profitability of a business. It is usual in these circumstances to relate the profit earned in a year to the capital employed.

If in the above example the profit at the end of the year was £3,720, this would represent a return of 20 per cent on the capital employed. Similar calculations may be made in respect of profit to capital owned, sales, etc., which are of interest to the Accountant.

    (3) *Working Capital.* Is the amount of capital that remains in the business for day to day working. It is the total current assets minus the total current liabilities, i.e. £6,000 — £2,000 = £4,000. The amount required varies a great deal between businesses, but any firm with little or no working capital is in a vulnerable position should its creditors press for payment.

The following balance sheet will illustrate the points mentioned in this section:

BALANCE SHEET A. TRADER AS AT DECEMBER 31ST 19..

Liabilities		£			*Assets* £
Capital			*Fixed Assets:*		
(including Net Profit			Premises	9,000	
for the year)		14,000	Fixtures and		
			Fittings	2,900	
Loan		5,000	Motor Vehicles	3,100	15,000
Current Liabilities:			*Current Assets:*		
Creditors	1,800		Stock in Trade	3,000	
Bills of Exchange			Debtors	2,400	
payable	200	2,000	Cash at bank	600	6,000
		21,000			21,000

    (a) Fixed Capital   = £15,000   (d) Capital Employed = £18,600
    (b) Circulating Capital = £ 6,000   (e) Working Capital   = £ 4,000
    (c) Capital Owned   = £14,000

QUESTIONS

    1. 'The work of the wholesaler and of the retailer is just as productive as the work of the manufacturer.' Explain this statement fully.   (U.L.C.I.)

    2. Discuss the several meanings that may be attached to the concept 'capital', and explain the difference between the capital owned by a firm of retailers and the capital employed by the firm in its business.   (R.S.A.)

    3. 'Business consists of the production of goods and commodities, and also of their transportation and exchange.' Examine this

statement, and use it to help you to draw up a classification of occupations in general. (R.S.A.)

4. British Industries can be classified into the following groups:
   Fuel and Power;
   Metals and Engineering and Allied Industries;
   Textiles and Clothing;
   Chemicals;
   Food, Drink and Tobacco;
   Other Industries.

Select any *one* group and write a description showing how important it is in the economy of the country. (R.S.A.)

5. *Either* 'Commerce is necessary as the result of specialisation by individuals and nations'. Explain this statement.

Or Suppose you were a house decorator. How would your business be connected with commerce? (Cambridge G.C.E.)

6. What are the functions of the commercial occupations in the working of the British economy? (London G.C.E.)

7. 'Modern industrial production depends for its success on specialisation and mass methods.' Explain the effects of this on commerce. (R.S.A.)

8. 'Production is not complete until goods are in the hands of the consumer.' Explain what this statement means with particular reference to the part played by commerce in production. (J.M.B.)

9. Name six different occupations in which people are engaged near your home and state the characteristics of two of them.

(R.S.A.)

10. (*a*) Name *three* manufacturing industries and *one* extractive industry which are of importance in the Midlands or your own area. In each case name *two* occupations of productive workers employed in that industry.

(*b*) Write an account of *one* of the industries you have chosen and attempt to assess its importance to the economy of the country (U.E.I.)

11. 'Working capital is calculated by deducting the *current liabilities* from the *current assets*. A good margin of working capital show a strong *liquid* position; insufficient capital can lead to *over-trading*.'

Explain the four terms italicised in the above quotation.

(Oxford G.C.E.)

Chapter 2

Inland Transport

I. IMPORTANCE OF TRANSPORT

The development of the internal transport of a country corresponds to the various stages in its industrial progress. In the early days of history, man used the rivers as a means of transport, but with the growth of a system of exchange, roads and tracks were made to assist communication between various groups of people living in the same land. The need for roads, however, was not urgent in English history, since each community was almost self-sufficing until the end of the Middle Ages. Even the splendid military roads of Roman days were allowed to fall into disuse, so that it was during the eighteenth century that industrial progress made improved means of transport necessary.

Improvements in transport are closely connected with scientific progress. The following table will give the student some idea of the relative improvement in transport over the years taking the London–Edinburgh route as an example:

YEAR	MODE	TIME TAKEN
1701	Pack Horse	12 Days
1801	Stage Coach	3 Days
1901	Rail	$8\frac{1}{2}$ Hours
1971	Aircraft	1 Hour

During the eighteenth century many new canals and roads were constructed, whilst in the following century, railways revolutionised methods of inland transport. Today the roads have received renewed attention on account of the development of that form of transport, and in addition, air transport has become of increasing importance. The improvements of the last two hundred years are largely due to the invention of the steam engine, the internal combustion engine, and the jet engine which the progress of science has made possible. Those that have taken place have created an interdependent world in place of self-sufficing communities, and are perhaps the most important factor in determining the mode of life at the present day.

In Britain the dense passenger and freight traffic presents particular problems to the planners especially in view of the complex system and interests already established. Most of the commercial traffic is carried by road and rail, although coastal shipping and to a lesser extent inland waterways and pipelines are important, whilst a relatively small but increasing volume of traffic is sent by air.

The Transport Division of the Department of Trade and Industry has powers relating to inland transport throughout Britain, including certain statutory duties concerning railways, roads, road transport and inland waterways.

The main functions of the Division are:

(a) To carry out the wishes of Parliament in relation to the transport services.

(b) To co-ordinate inland transport working through the appropriate channels as set up by the Transport Act.

(c) To appoint members of the nationalised transport undertakings under its control and to give direction as to their jurisdiction.

(d) To allocate funds provided by Parliament.

(e) Responsibility for general policy in connection with the development of British ports.

2. REORGANISATION OF BRITISH TRANSPORT

The present role and structure of the nationalised transport undertakings are the result of a series of legislative measures, starting with the 1947 Transport Act, which brought them under public ownership. Subsequent Acts have varied the structure from time to time culminating in the 1968 Transport Act that had far reaching effects.

The Transport Act (1968). The principal aim of this act has been to reorganise Britain's road and rail transport into an integrated system, meeting both economic and social needs as efficiently as possible. Other sectors were only slightly affected in connection with administration and control.

The chief objects of the Act were:

(1) To offer a more efficient freight service together with an economic door-to-door road/rail service exploiting the use of containers.

(2) The elimination of wasteful and inefficient competition between publicly owned road and rail services for the same traffic.

(3) To use existing road and rail assets more efficiently by the adoption of new techniques and the co-ordination of new investment.

(4) Making the maximum economic use of both road and rail by promoting the transfer of suitable traffic from the congested roads to the railway.

(5) Making the full benefits of the freightliner system to British industry and commerce.

(6) To improve the safety and efficiency of the road haulage industry by means of revised licensing arrangements, vehicle testing and control of drivers' hours of work.

(7) To associate the transport workers more closely with management in order to reap the maximum benefit from the national asset.

In order to implement the objects a number of Corporations, Executives and Authorities were established as follows:

National Freight Corporation. A State undertaking set up to integrate the *publicly owned* freight services. On its formation it took over from the Transport Holding Company (which has been abolished) all of its road haulage and shipping services. From the British Railways Board it took over depots, vehicles and warehouses (but not the actual trains).

The Freight Corporation is thus responsible for movements of freight *originating by road*. It is therefore a 'retailer' of transport space as compared with say British Rail being the 'wholesaler'. Thus its subsidiary company—Freightliners Ltd— charters trains from British Rail and sells the space to the Freight Corporation's other subsidiaries and private hauliers. Alternatively the Freight Corporation may if more economic or practicable make arrangements to send the goods by road using the services of say National Carriers or British Road Services.

A subsidiary to the Freight Corporation is the **Freightliner Company** owned jointly by the Corporation and the Railways Board. This company is responsible for the marketing and management of freightliners, and the profit is equally divided between the Corporation and the Board.

Further amendments in the Act related to the establishment of Passenger Transport Authorities, a Freight Integration Council and a review of the licensing requirements for road transport undertakings. These are dealt with more fully later in the chapter.

3. RIVERS

These have been a means of communication from an early date. Rivers such as the Thames, Severn, Mersey, Tyne, Clyde, etc., are an important means of both communication and commerce throughout the community. Also a closer examination shows how the estuaries are usually the sites of important ports, and the rivers made navigable far inland.

The following are the principal commercial rivers in Britain:

(a) *The Thames* is the oldest and one of the most important commercial rivers in Britain. It is under the control of the *Port of London Authority* from the sea to Teddington Lock, and the Regional Water Authorities from Teddington to Cricklade in Wiltshire, a distance of over 300 kilometres; all these bodies are statutory authorities, composed of representatives of the various local interests. The river is navigable as far as London Bridge for ships up to 3,000 tonnes. Barges are extensively used to transport cargo from the docks to other parts of the river.

The principal duties of the Port of London Authority covers

the control of the docks, the maintenance and improvement of navigation, and the regulation of craft using the river.

(b) *The Mersey* is also a most important waterway being the principal waterway for the industries of the North-West of England and North Midlands. It is linked to the inland port of Manchester by the Ship Canal and other ports on the river include Liverpool, Birkenhead, Stanlow and Runcorn.

(c) *The Severn* under the control of a Regional Water Authority, is the artery of the industries of the South Midlands and the South-West of England. In the Bristol Channel a canal has been constructed from Sharpness to Gloucester to avoid the bends at the mouth of the river. The river is navigable for a further 67 kilometres from Gloucester to Stourport. Vessels of up to 450 tonnes are able to navigate as far as Worcester, the principal commodities carried being oil and general cargo.

(d) *The Trent* with the Trent Navigation is navigable from the mouth of the Humber to Gainsborough, Lincolnshire. It connects the manufacturing districts of the East Midlands with the North Sea ports of Goole and Hull. The main traffic is petroleum and general cargo.

The rivers Humber, Clyde, Tyne and Tees are also very important British rivers, and are extensively used for the purpose of both industry and commerce. On the continent of Europe the Seine, Scheldt, Rhine, Elbe and the Danube are further outstanding examples of the importance of river transport.

The control of water resources and supplies in England and Wales is vested in the following authorities:

(a) *National Water Council*—a policy-making body concerned with the water interests attached to both national and social needs. Its main function is to co-ordinate the work of the Water Authorities in order to ensure adequate supplies and storage facilities.

(b) *The Regional Water Authorities*—concerned with the more local integration of river management schemes, water supply and sewage disposal. The Authorities acting under the National Water Council have power to transfer water from one authority to another according to national needs.

4. CANALS

Canals were constructed in Britain in the eighteenth century, in order to reduce the cost of carrying coal to the then new industrial centres.

Over 95 per cent of the total yearly commercial traffic, amounting to about 7 million tonnes, is carried on about 650 kilometres of broad waterways, most of the cargo is coal but other goods include oil, grain, timber and metals. The principal commercial canals in use today are:

Aire and Calder Navigation. Links the ports of the river Humber with the industrial area of the West Riding of Yorkshire. It can accommodate ships up to 250 tonnes for the whole of its length of 100 kilometres. The principal traffic is coal.

Sheffield and South Yorkshire Navigation. Serves the steel industry of the Sheffield and Rotherham areas. Is 68 kilometres in length providing an outlet to the Humber ports.

Trent Navigation. Extends from Gainsborough, Lincolnshire to the river Humber a distance of 108 kilometres. The usual traffic is petroleum and general merchandise.

Weaver Navigation. Links the chemical industry of Northwich, Cheshire with the ports of the river Mersey, a distance of 32 kilometres. It can accommodate ships of about 500 tonnes.

Gloucester and Sharpness Canal. Extends for 25 kilometres from Sharpness to Gloucester, with a lock at either end for passage into the river Severn. Sea-going vessels of up to 750 tonnes can use the canal whose principal traffic is petroleum and general merchandise.

Lee Navigation. The 21 kilometres between the river Thames and Enfield is the most important commercially. A substantial tonnage of cargo is carried, including timber, general merchandise, coal and liquids.

Grand Union Canal (below Uxbridge). Is the section between its junction with the river Thames at Brentford and Uxbridge a distance of 19 kilometres, together with a further section of 35 kilometres from Southall to the Regent's Canal Docks. The principal cargo is general merchandise, coal and liquids.

Crinan Canal. Is 14 kilometres long extending from Ardishaig to Crinan on the west coast of Scotland. It provides a short, sheltered passage for small ships, particularly fishing vessels, saving a lengthy journey round the exposed route of the Mull of Kintyre.

Caledonian Canal. Runs south-westwards across the Highlands from Inverness to Fort William, a distance of 96 kilometres. It provides a convenient passage for coasters and small tankers between the North Sea and the Atlantic, enabling them to save over 320 kilometres on the journey round the north of Scotland. Traffic passing through the canal includes coal, oil, grain, timber, etc. Some of this traffic is consigned from Scandinavian countries to the ports on Britain's west coast or Ireland.

The *Manchester Ship Canal*, opened in 1894, one-third of the capital subscribed by the Manchester Corporation. The canal is 58 kilometres in length; its width is 36·5 metres for the greater part of the course. The entrance to the canal is at Eastham, 30·5 kilometres from the bar of the Mersey, and its depth of 8·5 metres allows ocean-going vessels of up to 15,000 tonnes to reach the port of Manchester. There are works and factories of various kinds throughout its length, and at Ellesmere Port, Runcorn, Stanlow and Eastham there are docks, storage tanks and warehouse accommodation.

The Ship Canal Company is also the owner of the Bridgewater Canal, and it is connected with the Shropshire Union Canal, the river Weaver and the river Irwell. The Canal Company is the Port Authority for the Port of Manchester which is among the largest ports in Britain in terms of tonnage handled.

The decline in importance of canals has been most marked in the present century; about 1880, 35 million tonnes were carried each year, but by 1972 the tonnage had fallen to under 5 millions. The decline is also due to (a) the superior transport of railways for long distances (b) improved means and methods of road transport over any distance and (c) the relatively high cost of canal upkeep. In addition the tempo of modern life has increased so that the businessman will often consider canal transport only as a last resort.

Advantages of Canals. Advocates of canal transport point out the following advantages:

(1) It is cheaper than road or rail when assessing the cost per tonne kilometre.

(2) The speed of canal transport is sufficient for bulky materials, especially as the saving of a few hours in transit is not important in this instance.

(3) It is possible for canal barges to load or unload anywhere on the waterway, whereas railway goods depots are often a long way apart. These cargoes usually are ultimately transferred to lorries or vans with the attendant risk of damage in transit.

(4) At ports, it is possible to receive or discharge cargoes direct to or from the ships. Raw materials, for example, are often transferred from a ship to a barge, and taken by canal direct to a factory.

(5) There is very little risk to cargoes sent by canal thus reducing insurance charges. For this reason, canals are widely used in the Midlands, the Potteries, and elsewhere for the movement of raw materials, earthenware, fuel etc.

Disadvantages of Canals:

(1) They lack speed, compared with their competitors: their comparative slowness is not a serious matter when heavy bulky materials are being carried, but in the case of perishable goods, other forms of transport have a distinct advantage.

(2) They serve a limited area, are liable to be frozen in winter, and to suffer from drought in summer.

(3) It is impossible to arrange through traffic over any great distance.

(4) Canals frequently pass through built-up areas, where warehouses line their banks, as in Birmingham and Manchester. Improvement of the canals by widening or increasing their depth is therefore impractical.

(5) Road transport has lighter maintenance charges than either the canal or the railway, since there is no permanent way to provide.

5. PIPELINES

The development of pipelines in Britain has been one of slow growth principally because of the high cost of installation and maintenance. This form of transport is only suitable for certain types of traffic over any distance, namely gas and liquid products. In addition to the water, North Sea gas and petrochemical lines mostly owned by public corporations, the oil companies have constructed a number of lines from deep sea harbours to refineries as for example between Finnart on the Clyde and Grangemouth. Pipelines are also in operation between the refineries and the chief consumers as between Fawley and Heathrow airport. There is also a line of 394 kilometres carrying refined products from the Thames and Mersey refineries to the Midlands area.

Pipelines have the advantage of providing all weather links between given terminals, and by using specialised techniques it is possible to pump more than one type of product through the line during the course of a day. This is extremely advantageous and cost saving especially where branch lines and storage facilities are available.

6. ROADS

Commercial Importance. During the eighteenth century, the improvements in industry aroused an interest in the roads for the first time since Roman days, and many good roads were constructed by Telford, Macadam and Metcalfe. From about 1770 to 1840, numerous attempts were made to adapt the steam engine to transport purposes, both in Britain and abroad, but the heavier road tolls favoured the continued use of the coach.

The internal combustion engine invented in 1884 by Daimler, led to the development of the motor vehicle, especially for commercial purposes after 1918. In 1911 only 175,000 motor vehicles were licensed in Britain as compared with over 16 million today. The growth of this form of transport has given a new importance to roads, which has had far-reaching effects on both rail and canal traffic.

Classification of Roads. In 1972 Britain had over 335,000 kilometres of public highways, which are classified according to their traffic value, those of purely local traffic importance being unclassified.

The following are the categories in order of importance:

(a) *Motorways* forming part of a programme to provide a national network of modern through routes. It is planned that over 3,200 kilometres of motorways should be completed by the early 1980's. By 1972 about half of this had been built and was in use. The cost of construction and upkeep is provided by the Government.

(b) *Trunk Roads.* About 14,500 kilometres of trunk roads have been built and like the motorways are the main arteries of national traffic. The whole cost of their upkeep is met from Government sources.

(c) *Classified Roads* or principal roads for which the Government makes grants towards upkeep, etc. There are about 34,000 kilometres of principal roads in Britain, the highway authority being the local authority in whose area the roads lie.

On maps and signposts the trunk and principal roads can usually be identified by the letter 'A' in front of a route number.

(d) *Unclassified Roads.* Over 288,000 kilometres of road fall into this category and these are entirely the responsibility of the local authority.

Finance. Taxes on motor vehicles are collected by the central taxation authority and the proceeds are paid to the Exchequer. Public expenditure on new and improved roads in Britain is estimated to be over £1,000 million *per annum* and further growth is planned. This represents a high percentage of Government expenditure.

Road Carriers There are two principal types of carriers by road in both the public and private sectors:

(a) *Local Carriers*, that operate in all towns and villages, and who transport all types of goods over a limited area. They frequently connect centres of population with neighbouring communities, perhaps bringing agricultural produce to the market or delivering both domestic and manufactured goods to local industry and the local population.

(b) *General Carriers.* Numerous organisations collect and

deliver goods by road all over Britain. Such firms in both the public and private spheres have depots and agents in large towns and deal with consignments varying in size from a single package to the output of a factory.

Some specialise in the class of goods carried and provide specially constructed vehicles for certain types of goods. They are thus able to make contracts with manufacturing and wholesale firms to provide all their transport requirements, and relieve them of the necessity of maintaining their own transport department.

A few provide a specialised international service for goods between Britain and Europe, using the special ferries at Dover, Harwich, Southampton, etc. This method of transport is of particular importance to the fulfilment of trading contracts with the European Economic Community. Regular through shipment of goods by road or rail with little delay is provided by operators on both sides of the Channel to various destinations. The British road operators are members of either the Freight Transport Association or the Road Haulage Association which with their European counterparts have drawn up acceptable international regulations. These are the TIR (Transports Internationale Routiers) rules which include guarantees to customs and licensing authorities, financial stability of operators, security of loads, roadworthiness of vehicles etc. Certificates of approval are given to the operators, renewable every two years, and TIR plates are fitted to the front and rear of the operators' vehicles for customs clearance etc.

The work of General Carriers includes many of the following services over any distance:

(a) Collection and delivery of all types of goods.
(b) Heavy Haulage (e.g. machinery, girders) and awkward loads.
(c) Tank Haulage (e.g. petrol, milk).
(d) Removals and Storage.
(e) Transport of Livestock, Meat, Provisions, etc.

(c) *Firms Undertaking their own transport.* Many organisations, large and small, undertake the collection and delivery of their goods, and possess a number of vehicles suitable for the size of their businesses. This method of transport organisation has many advantages: the firm is independent of other agencies, and has direct contact with its customers. By this means, the business area may be extended, specially fitted vans and the use of pallets reduce the cost of packing. In addition, the vehicle may be used with advantage as an advertisement for the firm.

Road Rates. A smaller amount of capital is required by a road transport concern than for say a railway as the latter must provide its own permanent way, whereas roads are almost everywhere and open to all. Road transport has a further advantage since the amount of its fixed capital is relatively small, and the number of vehicles can be reduced or increased from year to year to meet trade requirements. Unlike a railway, interest on capital is only a small proportion of its charges. In the case of road transport therefore the running expenses form the greater part of the cost.

Road transport companies do not issue any classification of goods. The rates charged depend to a large extent on the following factors:

(1) The weight of the goods, and distance to be carried.
(2) The liability of the goods to damage.
(3) The likelihood of obtaining a return load.
(4) Any special arrangement which may be made between the consignor and consignee.

Carrier Licensing. A new system of carrier licensing was introduced by the Transport Act (1968) based upon trunk route transport costs and safety considerations as follows:

(1) Transport vehicles under $1\frac{1}{2}$ tonnes unladen are free from all forms of *carrier* licence. The carrier can transport the goods of other tradesmen for reward, in addition to his own over any distance.

(2) Operators of goods vehicles of over $1\frac{1}{2}$ tonnes are required to hold a *quality licence*, satisfying the licensing authority that:

(a) they can and will provide or secure adequate maintenance facilities for their vehicles, keep proper control over their loading and arrange satisfactory checks on the hours worked by their drivers.

(b) their financial resources, and where appropriate the amount of business in prospect, are sufficient to enable them to maintain their vehicles properly.

The licensing authority grant the individual licences so long as no objection is raised by the Transport Trade Unions and Associations, the Police or the Local Authorities, all appeals being heard by the Transport Tribunal. The object of the system is to ensure the economic use of all transport resources.

State-owned Services. By the Transport Act (1968) the *National Freight Corporation* took over all the depots, vehicles and other equipment formerly owned by the State road haulage undertakings. The Corporation is thus now responsible for all freight movements originating by road in the public sector.

In addition a *Freight Integration Council* was established consisting of representatives from the nationalised and private sectors of the industry together with a spokesman from the trade unions under an independent chairman. The chief function of the council is to co-ordinate the activities of the Railways Board and Freight Corporation with a view to gaining the optimum efficiency.

Passenger Transport Authorities. The Transport Act (1968) authorised the Minister for Transport Industries to set up a passenger transport authority in any area where it is considered necessary for the effective organisation and planning of public transport. The integration of road and rail services is particularly necessary in the larger conurbations and the first authorities outside London are at Tyneside, Merseyside, the West Midlands, and South East Lancashire.

The Minister and relevant Local Authorities have appointed a committee for each area, which controls policy and finance and appoints a professional executive responsible for the day-to-day management.

The executive committee having drawn up a plan, operate

the services within the area by entering into agreements with the *National Bus Company* (formerly the municipal and some private bus undertakings), British Rail and other operators so that all the services are fully integrated.

London Transport

The 1968 Transport Act established the *London Transport Executive* whose members are appointed by the Greater London Council. The operational area is that of the Greater London Council and the executive is responsible for both bus and underground services—fares are fixed by the GLC. The executive works in close collaboration with the commuter services of British Rail. The Greater London Council is also the highway authority for all principal roads in London, and has wide powers to deal with the problems attached to traffic management.

London's transport operations cover an area of about 3,200 square kilometres, with a population of about 10 millions. To carry traffic over this area, the Executive owns about 6,400 buses, 4,400 underground railway carriages, and employs a total staff of about 60,000. The network also includes over 8,000 privately owned taxicabs licensed by the Metropolitan Police, nearly 300 railway stations in addition to numerous ancillary services necessary for such a large organisation.

Advantages of Road Transport

(1) It is more flexible than other forms of transport, as the latter are usually limited to places on the line of route, whereas roads lead everywhere and goods can be carried from door to door.

(2) Railways depend on thickly populated areas for their custom, but road vehicles can go where there is traffic to be obtained.

(3) Road transport is both quicker and cheaper for short distances: there is no loss of time due to carting the goods to the station, and as no time-table is necessary for road transport, vehicles can be sent off at any time.

(4) Road transport involves no transhipments, and there is therefore less likelihood of pilferage.

(5) With most classes of goods, the railways have to charge

a high rate in order to cover cost of track, equipment, etc. These do not enter into the road haulier's calculations, and he is able to quote a better price.

(6) Road transport is particularly suitable for the conveyance of perishable goods, where rapid transport is necessary. Specially constructed vehicles are provided for the carriage of milk, fish, fruit, etc., and packing costs are thus reduced.

(7) In road transport, the same chassis can be used for the conveyance of passengers and goods by changing the body of the vehicle. As a result, the capital charges in construction are reduced.

Disadvantages

(1) It has not the speed of railways for long-distance traffic, especially when consignments are sent by freightliner or passenger train.

(2) It cannot handle bulky materials such as coal, iron ore, cement, etc., as cheaply as railways.

(3) Road transport has a limited capacity for a load, and heavy lorries are slow on long distances.

(4) The charge for conveyance may include the expenses of a driver who is away from home for a few days.

(5) Railways have powerful locomotives which can haul many tonnes. For bulky materials therefore the cost per tonne/kilometre is less than by road.

(6) A road vehicle has often to return empty to its destination thus adding to the cost of operation.

(7) Road transport is more easily disrupted by weather conditions during the winter months than rail transport.

7. RAILWAYS

Importance of Railways. In 1825, the first public railway in the world operated by steam locomotives was opened between Stockton and Darlington. This country was a pioneer in the construction of railways, and the success led other countries to follow suit in the second half of the nineteenth century. Railways played an important part in the industrial development of this country, whilst abroad they have enabled the interiors of continents to be opened up to produce supplies of raw materials and foodstuffs for distribution all over the world.

In Britain the 1947 Transport Act brought the railways under public ownership as a single enterprise grouped into a number of regional divisions. Subsequent Acts have dealt with the financial and administrative problems which beset large undertakings, culminating in the 1968 Transport Act that made a number of far-reaching changes.

The *British Railways Board* has the sole responsibility of managing the railway system through the following area or regional boards:

| Eastern | Western | Southern |
| Midland | Scottish | |

These provide a greater degree of decentralisation and a more

British Rail's advanced passenger train.

Britain's railway network.

efficient use of the railways system as local problems can be solved more quickly and easily. In addition greater integration with other regions, the Freightliner Company, National Freight Corporation and Passenger Transport Authorities, etc., is possible.

Modernisation of Railways. Because of economic difficulties, the modernisation of the system has been spread over many years and has meant the spending of many millions of pounds. Long distance passenger services in particular have improved with inter-city services connecting the main centres. The introduction of advanced techniques of passenger travel have recaptured some of the traffic previously lost to competitors. The emphasis today is largely centred on speed, reliability and comfort for the passenger with other services such as restaurant, Pullman and Hotel accommodation as required.

The increased use of mechanisation in the freight division and the introduction of express freight services (freightliners) to link all the main industrial areas has also improved rail transport facilities.

The greater efficiency of the railways is further emphasised by the large projects which have been undertaken. Speeds of up to 150 kilometre/hour are permitted on certain tracks. Electrification of the London–Manchester/Liverpool, London–Southampton and Bournemouth lines have been completed among many others.

Freight services in addition have been improved as new and modern vehicles enter into service. Fully automated marshalling yards assist a speedier service together with a saving on labour costs.

Long-term contracts have been made with a number of manufacturers, to move their goods by special trains. Oil, for example, is moved from refineries to storage depots by *company trains* and coal is fed direct from collieries to power stations in *merry go round* trains on which coal is loaded and discharged automatically from specially designed high capacity wagons. Other contracts include the transport of cars, china clay, fertilisers, milk, grain, cement and newspapers to point of manufacture or distribution centre.

Freightliners.

The Freightliner Company is a subsidiary of the state-owned National Freight Corporation and the British Railways Board. It is responsible for the management and promotion of the freightliner service in Britain. Freightliners, or liner trains are high-speed, long distance trains made up entirely of standardised containers, loaded on specially built wagons. They are permanently coupled in sets, are capable of running at sustained high speed and can accommodate containers of various lengths. Today there are over twenty specially designed freightliner terminals in the principal cities of Britain, linking the industrial centres of this country with the ports and the European freightliner network. The manufacturer or business-man in say Birmingham may therefore dispatch his goods to say Newcastle or Brussels with the minimum delay, maximum safety and quick delivery.

In addition to the standard freight containers, there are insulated containers for perishable foods, special containers for steel coil, timber and paper, and demountable air pressure and gravity discharge tanks for liquids and powders. Goods travelling by the standard containers include scientific instruments, glassware, whisky, biscuits, television sets, etc.

At Tilbury, Liverpool, Hull, Harwich and Southampton there are fully integrated ship, road and rail container berths and terminal complexes. A door-to-door service is provided from all these and other centres between Britain and numerous foreign centres. The large international freight terminal at Stratford, London, in particular links the Midlands and the South East with the continental freightliner trains.

Similar facilities are in operation at the principal ports of Britain dealing with the arrival and dispatch of containers on specially built ships plying between Britain, North America, Australasia, Africa and the Far East. They are capable of a quick turn round and are scheduled to make regular voyages. This is assisted by the construction of container berths together with specialised port and shore installations both in Britain and at the port of disembarkation.

Parcels Service.

The national delivery of numerous small parcels has always

presented a problem to the transport operators. British Rail have attempted to overcome this by offering an express service guaranteeing delivery the same day or following morning over specified routes. Known as the *Red Star* service the arrangement offers direct transit between certain centres on through trains. The consignor delivers the goods to the station where they are placed on a *nominated* train and he advises the consignee of arrival time at the destination. Here the recipient is able to collect the goods using his own transport with the minimum of delay.

Alternatively the businessman may use the *Rail Express Parcels Service* that incorporates door to door collection, transit and delivery to customers premises. Parcels expresses travelling point to point at express passenger train speed ensure rapid delivery, the extent of the service being gauged by the fact that British Rail handle over 2 million parcels per week.

Advantages of Rail Transport.

(1) Is particularly suitable for the carriage of goods in bulk over large distances.

(2) The freightliner service and 'company trains' guarantee delivery of goods at their destination in this country the following day.

(3) Is less affected than other forms of transport by extremes in the weather.

(4) In the large centres of population a good railway system relieves the pressure of passenger traffic on the already congested roads.

Disadvantages.

(1) The use of a fixed track and terminals together with the high capital cost of upkeep means that the railways tend to be more inflexible and in some cases dearer than their competitors.

(2) By the normal goods train, goods are outside the control of the manufacturer. As a result there is a greater chance of pilferage, and there are frequent delays in transit especially on cross-country routes.

(3) Single cross-country consignments require special treatment in the form of a transhipment, etc. This often leads to further delay and possible damage.

QUESTIONS

1. What considerations ought to determine the mode of transport to be adopted in the following cases: (a) Distribution of goods from wholesale warehouse to retailers' shops, (b) Distribution to consumer from retail shop? (R.S.A.)

2. Discuss the several modes of transport available to manufacturers when delivering their products to distributors at home. (R.S.A.)

3. What matters need to be considered in assessing the type of transport to be used when goods are to be sent from point A to point B? Illustrate your answer by referring to two very dissimilar commodities. (London G.C.E.)

4. Compare rail transport and canal transport for the movement of freight, explaining how a business would decide whether to use the one or the other for a particular consignment. (London G.C.E.)

5. Discuss the advantages and disadvantages of road and rail services from the point of view of quality, convenience and cost. (R.S.A.)

6. A business which sells its goods over the whole of England has so far relied on road or rail transport services for sending its goods to customers. What do you think would be the advantages and disadvantages of changing to a system of delivering goods in its own vehicles? (Oxford G.C.E.)

7. What are the reasons for the decline of canal transport after the development of the railways in Britain? Give two examples of cases where canal transport might still be used in preference to rail of road transport. (Oxford G.C.E.)

Chapter 3

Transport by Sea and Air

I. IMPORTANCE OF BRITISH SHIPPING

Transport by sea is important to Britain, since being an island, the majority of the foreign trade depends upon the merchant marine. This transports the supplies of raw materials and food-stuffs for home consumption, and distributes the manufactures to all parts of the world. Until the beginning of the twentieth century, Britain was supreme in the world of shipping. The total tonnage of British shipping up to about 1900 was greater than the rest of the world put together. Since 1914, the decline has been rapid, as the following table shows:

	Percentage of World Tonnage
1914	44
1930	34
1950	22
1961	18
1972	9

The reasons for the decline of British shipping are:

(*a*) Britain suffered heavily from ship losses during two World Wars.

(*b*) Other countries have increased the number of their merchant ships, much of the trade carried exclusively in British ships has therefore been lost to foreign competitors.

(*c*) Some foreign countries adopt a policy of subsidising their shipping out of government funds. In Britain the *Ship Mortgage Finance Corporation* endeavours to overcome some of the financial difficulties experienced by British shipowners. It is financed by both Government and private enterprise making long-term loans to British ship-owners for the purchase of new ships *built in British shipyards*.

(*d*) The British shipping industry is exposed to severe international competition by the prevalence among competitors of such practices as *flag discrimination* and the use of *'flags of convenience'*. Liberia, for instance, is a country with little seaborne trade and yet has as large a tonnage under its flag as any of the traditional maritime nations.

(*e*) The increased tempo of modern life has resulted in speed being of paramount importance, particularly to the businessman. In the passenger trade, safe, long-distance, high-speed and reliable air travel at competitive prices has taken the place of the more leisurely sea voyage especially on the North Atlantic route. It is interesting to note that of the travellers arriving in this country, the seaborne trade accounts for less than 10 per cent of the total.

The British merchant fleet of about 25 million tonnes, however, makes a large contribution to Britain's foreign exchange earnings. This tonnage includes the world's second largest oil tanker fleet and the fourth largest ore and bulk carrier fleet. The principal concern of the fleet is (in addition to the coastal trade):

(*a*) Carrying goods between Britain and the various ports of Europe and the Commonwealth.

(*b*) Taking cargoes between Britain and the rest of the world.

(*c*) Transporting merchandise and material between other foreign countries often not touching British shores.

2. CLASSIFICATION OF SHIPPING

Most of the British registered ships are owned by large companies who operate wide networks throughout the world. These consist of the following classifications:

(*a*) **Passenger Liners** which carry passengers, surface mails, and only a relatively small amount of cargo: the latter consists of consignments of small bulk whose value can bear the higher rates of liner transport. These ships sail on a fixed route at regular intervals, and therefore must sail whether or not they have a full cargo. There has been a sharp decline in this trade particularly since the development of the high speed long range aircraft traffic. The decline in the North Atlantic traffic, especially has led to many ships being purpose built for the lucrative cruising trade to the West Indies and South Africa.

(b) **Cargo Ships** have replaced the tramp steamer to some extent during recent years. They usually operate on fixed routes, and are often fitted out for the particular class of cargo of the routes on which they sail. Cargoes of butter, bananas and meat for example require specialist ships with refrigeration capacity. They may carry a few passengers, but the greater part of their space is used for carrying bulky freight.

A number of British shipping companies have set up subsidiaries to undertake **container transport.** Specially designed ships, terminals and dock equipment have enabled the use of containers on the major ocean routes. The principal ports for container traffic include Tilbury, Liverpool, Manchester, Hull, Harwich and Southampton. This has led to a quicker turnround of ships together with a faster delivery to the destination by the use of the rail freightliner services.

(c) **Tramp Ships** may be owned by individual shipowners, by partnerships or by companies. They have no set routes or fixed times, but go wherever they can find a cargo. They usually carry low-grade goods sent in bulk, such as coal, oil and minerals, frequently being chartered by traders for a given period or a particular voyage. Unlike the liners, the freight rates are determined by bargaining at the **Baltic Exchange,** London. There is greater competition for freights on account of the large number of owners who have not combined to the same extent as the liner companies. Tramp ships are particularly susceptible to world conditions. During a depression trade slackens and there is less demand for this type of shipping.

(d) **Tankers.** Over two-thirds of the British tanker fleet is owned by the oil companies, the rest belonging to a few independent tanker-owning companies who lease the ships on charter through the Baltic Exchange.

There has been a tendency for the size of modern tankers to

soar as companies seek to realise the economies of scale whereby the cost of transport per tonne is reduced.

In addition to the above a new type of specialised bulk carrier—the ore carrier—is in use on a large scale. Some of these are partly owned by the British Steel Corporation and operated by the shipping companies, transporting ores from say Norway or Spain etc. for use in the smelting industries in this country.

Coastal Trade. Whilst most public attention is directed towards the ocean-going vessels of the Merchant Navy, many ships are engaged in the important coastal trade. Coastal shipping is a very cheap form of transport, and is especially suited for bulky cargoes. Regular sailings take place between the chief ports of Britain, in order to distribute numerous commodities including oil, liquid fuels, shingle, etc. There is also a growing trade with the continental countries as evidenced by the growth of the 'roll-on', 'roll off' terminals at many ports including Hull, Harwich, Dover, Southampton, Holyhead, in addition to the transport of vegetables etc. to the South Coast ports for the Covent Garden market. The Channel Islands trade also is largely undertaken by coastal shipping transporting flowers, vegetables and tomatoes to Britain.

3. THE PORTS

Britain with its extensive coastline has over 250 ports, many of them long established, providing employment for over 100,000 people. Port authorities are of four main types: (*a*) *nationalised bodies*, owning about one quarter of the total port capacity and include the ports of Southampton, Hull, Swansea, (*b*) *local authority* ports owned by local ratepayers and include the ports of Bristol, Boston and Preston, (*c*) *Public Trusts* made up of the port users including shippers, importers, exporters etc. Included under this heading are the ports of London, Liverpool and Belfast, (*d*) *private companies* owning ports such as Manchester and Felixstowe. Large sums of money are being spent on modernisation and improvement of facilities. The trend to increasing size of ships, particularly tankers, and the greater use of containers, pallets and other unit-loading

Esso Refinery Fawley with the port of Southampton in the background.

devices demand the more rapid and efficient movement of goods.

A brief survey of the principal British ports would include the following:

London (including Tilbury) is the largest port in Britain, and with New York, Antwerp and Rotterdam (Europoort) is one of the largest ports in the world. There are extensive docks, warehouse facilities and container wharves, being one of the principal entrepot ports for Northern Europe.

Liverpool is the second largest British port and the major export cargo outlet for British goods. A great deal of the country's imports of grain, raw cotton and basic materials pass through this port.

Harwich is the fourth most important British port with its extensive container and roll on roll off traffic to continental ports including Zeebrugge, Ostend, Esbjerg and Kristiansand.

Manchester is an inland port, access to which is by the Manchester Ship Canal. The principal trade includes the import of fuel and raw materials for the industries of South East Lancashire.

Southampton is the chief port for ocean passenger traffic, the principal port for imports of deciduous and citrus fruits, and has an extensive container trade with the United States.

Clydeport is the principal Scottish port serving as an import and export outlet for the industial area of central Scotland.

Tanker Terminals. Vast quantities of crude oil are brought to this country from abroad in large tankers. The majority of these are berthed at specially constructed terminals near to the refineries as at Fawley near Southampton, Milford Haven and Shellhaven. Deep water terminals have also been constructed at Finnart on the River Clyde and Stanlow (Cheshire) to accommodate the modern super tankers. These are connected to the refineries at Grangemouth and Heysham respectively by the extensive use of pipelines.

Hull on the Humber estuary principally serves the industrial centres of Yorkshire and the East Midlands. It is the third most important British port in terms of tonnage passing through the dock gates. It is renowned as one of the largest white fish ports in the world.

4. THE CONTROL OF SHIPPING

In Britain commercial shipping is controlled by the shipping division of the **Department of Trade and Industry.** The work of this division may be summarised as follows:

(*a*) *Registration of Ships.* The Certificate of Registry issued by the Department states the name of the vessel, particulars of construction, tonnage, the name of the owners, and bears a number by which the ship is known. The certificate must be displayed on board the ship.

(*b*) *Measurement of Ships.* The tonnage determines the port and canal dues which a ship must pay, and is assessed by measurement. The *gross* tonnage is found by measuring all the covered space and taking 283 cubic metres as the equivalent of one tonne: the *net* tonnage is found from the gross tonnage by making allowances for the space occupied by the engine-room and the crew quarters.

(*c*) *Enforcement of the Plimsoll line* or load line regulations. This is determined by a line painted on the ship to indicate the maximum depth to which it may be allowed to sink in the water so as to prevent overloading.

(*d*) *Miscellaneous duties* of the shipping division include:

(1) Enquiries into shipping losses by Department inspectors.
(2) The issue of certificates to officers and men of the merchant navy after examination.
(3) The enforcement of regulations for the use of radio.
(4) Administration of the Coastguard Service whose duties include the lighting of the coast and the provision of pilots: these duties are delegated to Trinity House.
(5) The making of regulations dealing with oil pollution and the safety of ships, including the provision of life-saving apparatus and the testing of chains and cables, etc.

5. SHIPPING FREIGHTS

These represent the remuneration paid to shipowners for the carriage of goods in their vessels, or for the hire of ships for a period of time.

Chartering of Ships. The *Baltic Mercantile and Shipping Exchange* in London is the chief centre for the chartering of ships and aircraft: London is therefore the largest freight market of the world, and shipowners of every country are represented on the Baltic Exchange. The charterers are the importers and exporters of commodities shipped in bulk, such as oil, coal, grain and minerals and the Baltic Exchange provides a meeting-place for both the owners of vessels and those requiring carrying services.

Prospective charterers inform their agents of their requirements, and indicate the type of ship required, the dates of loading and destination. The agents meet the various brokers who represent the owners of ships on the floor of the Exchange and after bargaining agree upon terms. The contract made between the owners and the charterers is known as the *Charter Party*.

A vessel may be chartered for a *voyage* between named ports, or on a *time* charter for an agreed period, or by a *demise* charter whereby the charterer agrees to maintain the ship as if he were the true owner.

The charter is usually a tramp ship or tanker, and the rates depend upon the demand for or the supply of shipping at any particular time. Increased rates are charged at say harvest-times and in periods of good trade. Likewise when the number of available ships is small, the rates will tend to be high, but when traffic is scarce, low rates will probably be quoted. Unlike the liner freight rates, tramp rates fluctuate considerably and are determined by competition.

Liner Freight Rates. The number of liner companies is relatively small, and the conditions under which they work provide an incentive to combination, as evidenced by many of the well known shipping companies of today. Most of these companies belong to one of over 60 associations set up to protect sea-going trade from unfair competition. These associations are known as *Shipping Conferences* which are national or international in extent. They agree to fixed rates for both passengers and freight in order to secure standardisation and stability, as well as frequent and regular sailings. Each Conference meets from time to time to review and revise existing rates, or to compile new ones.

Calculation of Freight. Is calculated in various ways according to the nature of the goods.

(1) *Weight Basis*. Heavy goods that do not occupy much space, are charged per tonne weight.

(2) *Measurement Basis*. Light, bulky goods are charged according to tonne measurement; a freight tonne is taken as 1,000 kilogrammes or 1 cubic metre.

(3) *Valuables*. Bullion, specie, jewels and other valuable goods are charged a percentage of their value declared on shipment.

Rebates. Regular shippers are encouraged to ship by lines forming the Shipping Conferences by offering them deferred rebates of 5–10 per cent of all freights paid in a year, on condition that they do not ship by other lines outside the Conference.

6. CONTAINER TRANSPORT

Containerisation is perhaps the most important commercial development for the transport of goods that has occurred in recent years. The idea itself is not new as it has been in operation by both road and rail services for a long time. The development has been in the universal acceptance of standard containers, specially constructed cranes, trucks, lorries, port facilities and ships.

Port of London Authority multi-user container terminal at Tilbury.

To the manufacturer and businessman this form of transport has the advantage of an integrated door-to-door delivery service. In addition the contents are undisturbed (except perhaps for customs examination) from factory to destination, and they are protected from weather, damage and pilferage.

As well as the Freightliner Company, several private operators, principally the shipping lines and forwarding agents have co-operated to form a fully integrated service to and from Britain. Greater emphasis is attached to speed of delivery, which has resulted in the investment of large sums of money both in Britain and abroad to provide a containerised service for a large number of products.

Facilities for the handling of containers exist at the principal ports, airports and at selected rail centres throughout Britain.

7. THE MARINE INSURANCE MARKET

Lloyds. May be regarded as the centre of the Marine Insurance Market, although its interests are not confined to the shipping industry.

The house of Lloyd's is named after Edward Lloyd, a coffee-house keeper of the seventeenth century: his customers were drawn from a class interested in shipping, and Edward Lloyd therefore collected news of ships. In 1734, *Lloyd's List and Shipping Gazette* was published and has been continuously printed since that date, being London's oldest daily newspaper. In 1871, Lloyd's was incorporated by Act of Parliament and is now controlled by a series of special Acts of Parliament to permit the transaction of business not contemplated at the outset.

The market itself is controlled by a Committee of 16 members, elected by the underwriters, who serve for four years. After this they must retire for one year before being eligible for re-election. Their duties include the admittance of members, and matters relating to the proper running of the market.

Lloyd's does not do business itself: it is an association of over 6,000 underwriters having unlimited liability and formed into some 300 syndicates. The members of Lloyd's are **under-**

writers, who are so called because they write their names under the amount of risk they are prepared to take. As the public are unable to deal directly with the underwriters, brokers act on behalf of clients, and receive a commission calculated on the amount of premium. If a ship or a cargo is to be insured for say £50,000, the risk would be divided amongst a number of underwriters, each taking perhaps a few thousand pounds of liability. By this means, losses are averaged out.

The risks insured against at Lloyd's are not confined to marine insurance. These are of almost every description except life and financial guarantee, and are accepted by the members *from all over the world*. It is fair to say that no risk is too small and few are too large for Lloyd's which makes a valuable contribution to the 'invisible earnings' of the City of London.

Lloyd's Register of British and Foreign Shipping is an organisation distinct from the society of Lloyd's which gives particulars regarding the construction and characteristics of almost every ship. The register was first published in 1774, and is still voluntarily maintained by shipowners. It is published annually and gives details of all the ships of the world of over 100 tonnes. For each ship, it states (1) the date and place of construction, (2) the materials of which it is built, (3) the dimensions and tonnage, (4) the quality and condition of the ship.

In addition the organisation carries out surveys and gives technical advice on vessels of all flags at regular intervals. A satisfactory Lloyd's classification is a guarantee to an underwriter that he may accept the risk of a vessel. The classification 'A1', which is the highest grading, is an indication that the ship is in first-class condition.

8. MARINE INSURANCE

Since Britain is an island, her exports are usually insured against loss or damage in transit by sea or air. An immense variety of cargoes and parts of cargoes is therefore dealt with at Lloyd's and by insurance companies. The ship is also insured by the owner—either an individual or especially in the case of larger ships, a business organisation—against loss or damage, so that the insured value of one ship with a full cargo may amount to many millions of pounds.

Insurance may only be placed at Lloyd's through the medium of numerous firms of Lloyd's brokers who alone are permitted to place business with the Lloyd's underwriters.

A member of the public is unable to deal with a Lloyd's underwriter, but must employ a broker, because a specialised knowledge of insurance is necessary. This has advantages for the client as the broker is able to negotiate the most advantageous terms and rates with the underwriters who may specialise in a particular class of business.

Brokers have associates, clients and contacts all over the world and form an essential link between the various parties to any Lloyd's policy. It is the broker's duty to advise his client and obtain the most favourable terms, so that he is not retricted to Lloyd's and he can place business with insurance companies who are outside the framework of this market, should the terms be more advantageous.

Procedure. When the broker receives instructions to place an insurance, he approaches a leading underwriter, and finds the terms on which he is willing to accept the risk: the underwriters specialise in particular kinds of risks, and the broker will first approach an underwriter who deals in the type of business in hand. The broker writes on a slip of paper particulars of the insurance, including (a) its nature—i.e. whether for the ship or cargo, (b) the name of the vessel, (c) whether for the voyage or a period of time, (d) the risks insured against. If terms are arranged between the underwriter and the broker, the former writes on the slip of paper the amount he is willing to take. The paper is then taken to other underwriters, who usually accept the terms quoted by the first: this process continues until the full amount of the insurance is made up. If the total is not reached, the balance is offered to a marine insurance company, but in any case, the risk of loss is spread amongst many which is the basis of all forms of insurance.

In due course a policy is issued. If the insurance is underwritten by Lloyd's members, the issue of the policy to the client by way of the broker will be undertaken by the *Lloyd's Policy Signing Office*. This is a department, administered by

the Committee, which checks the slips signed by the syndicates, and incorporates their individual liabilities into *one
policy* bearing the seal of the signing office. Insurance companies outside the framework of Lloyd's will issue separate
policies for the amount of their liability.

The broker receives a commission from the underwirters
depending upon the value of the insurance. This is paid by the
underwriters direct to the broker after the client has paid the
premium.

Types of Policies. The present form of Lloyd's policy dates
from 1779, with the exception of two slight alterations of wording: the phrases employed are antiquated but are retained
since they have a particular legal meaning.

The principal kinds of policies are:

(a) *Voyage Policy*. This policy is issued when goods are
insured from one place to another.

(b) *Time policy*. Under this policy, the insurance is effected
for a period of time. A continuation clause is usually added to
extend the insurance cover for a further period should it expire
whilst the ship is still at sea.

(c) *Floating Policies*. Are used by manufacturers and traders
who regularly dispatch goods: such policies are also known as
Open Policies. Each shipment of goods must be declared, and
the underwriter agrees to accept the risk *up to the amount of
the policy*. The shipper is provided with continuous protection,
and is therefore able to estimate the cost of insurance on shipments during the period of the policy.

(d) *Valued Policies* state the value of the goods insured,
which includes the value of the goods, together with the cost of
freight and an allowance for profits.

(e) *Unvalued Policies* as the name implies do not state the
value of the goods insured: when a loss occurs, the amount to
be paid by the underwriters remains a matter of assessment.

Lloyd's S.G. (Ship and Goods) Policy is the standard on
which all policies of marine insurance is based. The term is
derived from the days when both ship and goods were insured
by the same policy. Although policies are now printed on
separate forms for ship and cargo, the claim form for either is
still termed the 'S.G.' form.

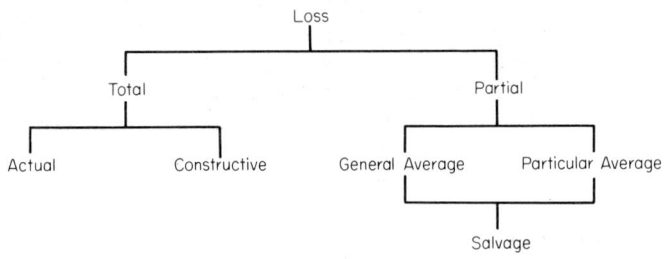

Marine Losses.

Losses by sea fall into two classes—*Total Loss* and *Partial Loss*.

(*a*) *Total Loss* may be further sub-divided into two possibilities—actual or constructive.

    (1) *Actual Total Loss* occurs when the insured goods are either (*a*) wholly destroyed or (*b*) changed in nature so that they cease to be the same as the goods insured, or (*c*) entirely lost to the assurer.

    (2) *Constructive Total Loss* occurs when the goods insured are abandoned because either their total loss seems inevitable, or the expense of recovering or preserving them is excessive.

(*b*) *Partial Loss* may affect the consignment of one individual or of all the persons sending goods by ship. In marine (and fire) insurance, the word 'Average' is used with the meaning of loss or damage: there are two kinds of partial loss—Particular Average and General Average.

    (1) *Particular Average* is a partial loss to the ship or a consignment of goods due to accident, such as damage by sea-water, fire or collision. In such cases, the loss is borne by the person whose property has suffered. The damage must be a certain percentage of the value of the consignment before a claim for particular average can be put forward. Thus a policy taken out by the shipowner or the cargo-owner to cover 'with particular average' will provide against *all* risks at sea. On the other hand a

policy issued 'free of particular average' will be insurance against total loss and general average only.

Damaged goods are surveyed on arrival by an independent assessor, who certifies the damage and states the cause of it as far as possible. The goods are valued later by an expert who settles the amount of loss.

(2) *General Average* is a partial loss which is deliberately made to avoid a common danger.

Examples of general average are:

(a) Fire or a heavy list may make it necessary to throw overboard part of the cargo to save the ship.

(b) It may be necessary to engage a tug in order to prevent a ship becoming a total wreck.

In general average, the losses or additional expenses are shared between the owners of the ship and cargoes in proportion to the interests at stake as it is for their mutual benefit that the ship should be saved. The adjustment of general average is made at the port of arrival. In order to overcome any conflict in the laws of different countries, the *York-Antwerp Rules*, drawn up by international agreement, are usually named in the policy.

The responsibility for making the claim under general average rests upon the shipowner, who usually employs an average adjustor. The latter is an independent person who prepares a statement for presentation to the insurers, and who assesses each claim impartially according to the terms of the policy.

9. TRANSPORT BY AIR

Today air transport is the widely accepted method of travel between most parts of the world where any great distance is involved. It is also increasingly being accepted as the best method between large centres of population within a country.

General responsibility for the development and control of civil aviation in Britain is with the **Civil Aviation Authority.** This includes the licensing control of both the nationalised and independent airlines, passenger safety, air traffic control, aircrew training, airport supervision and accident investigation.

In Britain there are two statutory corporations and a number of independent airline companies that are allowed to operate passenger and cargo services as follows:

(a) British Airways Board have powers of general supervision of the state airline British Airways. It is the co-ordinating factor supervising all forms of capital expenditure for aircraft re-equipment and also route planning. There is also a considerable amount of centralisation and financial integration in the British Airways organisation itself. This affects matters of common interest and concern which for operating purposes covers the following passenger and cargo routes:

(1) The long haul routes providing links between Britain, Europe, North and South America, Africa, Australasia, the Middle East and the Far East.

(2) Domestic flights between Britain and Europe. In addition many internal services are provided in the British Isles some of which cannot be operated on a commercial basis but which meet a vital social need.

British Airways also has a financial interest in a number of associated companies who collaborate with each other in providing a comprehensive network of services.

(b) The Independent Airline Companies operate a wide network of domestic and international services. In addition they provide specialised air-cargo facilities, vehicle ferry services and numerous charter services for service personnel and civilian holiday traffic. There are also a number of companies providing miscellaneous services including crop spraying, aerial surveying and air taxi flights.

Trade by Air. The proportion of Britain's overseas trade has increased steadily over recent years. The chief import items include diamonds for the Hatton Garden diamond market in London, out of season strawberries and other fruits, and numerous containerised pallets containing high value goods.

Goods exported by air include expensive machinery, aircraft and vehicle spares, and electrical products. In addition furs and skins account for a high proportion of the re-export traffic.

Air Freight Facilities. Exporters are rapidly learning the advantages of sending goods by air. Operators have a fleet of vans in a few large cities for the collection of goods and delivery to the airports. Goods from other parts of Britain may be despatched to the airways terminal by road, rail or by internal air services. Air freight rates are dependent on the type of freight, its value, weight and dimensions and its country of destination.

The operators have a number of freighter services on the various routes of the world, making use of containerised transport. Specially designed containers fit into the aircraft, and many airlines offer discounts to companies and agents who use the container service.

Advantages of Air Transport. The great advantage of air transport is its speed. Many passengers and particularly businessmen where 'time is money', are willing to pay slightly higher fares for faster journeys.

For goods traffic, it is usually the urgent or expensive articles that are sent by air on account of the higher costs. Increasing use is being made, however, of the hovercraft for the carriage of goods over relatively short distances. Compared with other forms of transport, the danger of damage to delicate articles is reduced, by air cargo. Also there is less chance of pilferage since there is a shorter travelling time and the goods are only handled at the terminals.

Air transport has a great advantage over large land areas, such as India and the United States, where internal distances are so great that the speed of the aircraft can be fully utilised. In smaller countries too businessmen in particular are making greater use of air travel in order to accomplish their work as evidenced by the numerous internal flights in Britain today.

Limitations of Air Transport. Whilst man achieves greater speeds and larger planes, as far as cargo is concerned air transport still suffers from the handicap of weight in comparison with other forms of transport. The following are the principal disadvantages:

(1) Operating costs and fixed charges are high: machines are costly and a high rate of depreciation must be allowed.

(2) The weight carried is limited: certain articles cannot be accepted, and only goods which can afford a high rate of freight can be sent by air.

(3) Weather conditions interfere with air services to a greater extent than with most other forms of transport.

(4) Whilst considerable time is saved in the flight, the major airports of the world are on the fringe of large cities. A great deal of time is lost in air traffic control over the airport and in the journey from the airport by road.

(5) The increasing frequency of aircraft using the airports together with the larger size of aircraft has heightened the problem of noise.

QUESTIONS

1. Explain the various kinds of policy of marine insurance.

2. What are Shipping Conferences, and how do they seek to control ocean freight rates? (R.S.A.)

3. Explain carefully the circumstances in which a manufacturer might send goods by air rather than by sea. Your answer should stress the reasons for choosing this method of transport. (J.M.B.)

4. Select two of the following and distinguish between the terms:
   (a) Customs and Excise duties.
   (b) Flags of convenience and flag discrimination.
   (c) Charter Party and Bill of Lading. (R.S.A.)

5. Discuss the importance of transport by road, by rail, by inland waterways, and by coastal shipping in the commerce of Britain. (London G.C.E.)

6. When will a businessman prefer to use air transport for the movement of goods? Give reasons. (London G.C.E.)

7. Which form of transport would you expect to be used for each of the following? In each case briefly give your reason and indicate the main document involved.
   (a) Newspapers sent daily from London to Lancaster.
   (b) A large quantity of timber at Quebec to be sent to Liverpool.
   (c) A machine in London to be despatched to Sydney, N.S.W.
   (d) Spare parts of office machinery in London urgently required in Madrid.
   (e) Coal in South Wales to be sent to Cambridge.

(Cambridge G.C.E.)

8. What are the current and future effects of the 'container revolution' in transport? (A.E.B.)

9. Discuss either the development and importance of air transport, or the special services which railways perform for the trader. (R.S.A.)

10. British shipping may be classified into tramp steamers, cargo liners and passenger liners. Discuss the work of each type. (R.S.A.)

11. Assume that the cost of transporting coal amounts to 10 per cent of the final selling price of the coal, and the cost of transporting diamonds amounts to less than 1 per cent of the final selling price of the diamonds. Is it true therefore to say that diamond transport is a more efficient service than coal transport? Explain fully. (R.S.A.)

12. What do you understand by a 'road/rail' transport service? How is it operated and which goods are likely to be moved in this way? (R.S.A.)

13. Discuss the importance and usefulness of the facilities provided by airlines for industry and commerce at the present time. (A.E.B.)

14. Air transport has the great advantage of speed but this is offset by some important drawbacks especially on routes within the British Isles. What are the disadvantages for a business man using the passenger and freight services of internal air routes? How do you think these drawbacks could be overcome?

(Oxford G.C.E.)

Chapter 4

European and Foreign Trade

1. IMPORTANCE OF EXTERNAL TRADE

The relative importance of home and foreign trade varies from country to country. The United States, or Russia, for example, have all the necessary materials that would enable them to feed and clothe their populations, whereas other nations, amongst which Britain is an outstanding example, depend upon others to a great extent for the supply of food and raw materials.

But even those countries which could be self-sufficient would live at a lower standard of life if they did not trade with other nations, since in reality no country can be self-sufficient. Foreign trade is therefore of great importance to every nation and is particularly important to Britain for the following reasons:

(1) With a population of 56 million people, in an area of 244,000 square kilometres, Britain grows less than half of her food supplies. Until the beginning of the nineteenth century, the population was about 12 millions and was almost self-supporting. During the last 150 years, however, the population has increased considerably, and Britain now depends on foreign supplies of foodstuffs to supplement her own agricultural products.

Bearing this important fact in mind, the following table may give the student some idea of the vast social changes involved in population growth in this country over nine centuries.

(2) Home-produced supplies of raw materials are quite inadequate for the productive capacity of this country. Most of our industries today are entirely dependent on foreign supplies

Year	Estimated Population (Thousands)	Year	Estimated Population (Thousands)
1100	2,000	1931	46,038
1801	11,944	1951	50,225
1851	22,259	1961	52,676
1901	38,237	1971	55,526

of raw materials in some form or other. This country's liveli-hood therefore depends, on the smooth flowing of international trade, since the majority of the people depend on foreign lands for their food, clothing *and employment*.

(3) Britain's need to buy food and raw materials makes her the world's largest market for foodstuffs and one of the largest for metals, ores, oil and many other products. Many nations sell their products to Britain in exchange for British manufactures and services. A complete list of these countries would be far too long to give but would include all the European nations, North America, many African and Asian nations and so on. Note particularly that those countries supplying the raw materials and foodstuffs depend to a very great extent on the prosperity of trade as much as industrial countries, such as Britain, the United States, West Germany and Japan. If manufacturing countries are not working or are on short time, the demand for raw materials will be less, and thus every part of the world economy acts and reacts on the others.

(4) The European and foreign trade of Britain also provides employment for those not directly engaged in the manufacture of goods. Our merchant ships carry the products of most countries of the world, whilst the banks and financial houses of the City have made London the monetary centre of the world.

(5) As a member of the European Economic Community, Britain is able to trade with the member countries on advan-tageous terms. In addition London is an important distributing and entrepôt centre for the whole of north-west Europe.

British ships bring the products of the world to London in bulk where they are sold in smaller lots on the commodity markets which are attended by buyers from the Continent. Large quantities of raw materials and foodstuffs are therefore re-exported after purchase by buyers from abroad.

2. THE GROWTH OF EXTERNAL TRADE

The twentieth century has witnessed a world upsurge of commercial activity. This is partly due to the increase in demand for manufactured goods, coupled with rising standards of living. A world wide increase in the demand for raw materials has occurred which can no longer be satisfied by home supplies. Greater reliance is therefore placed upon imported foreign supplies.

External trade has many difficulties which are not so apparent in the home trade. It has to overcome the geographical difficulties and cost of distance, differences of language, money, weights and measures. In the earlier days, this trade was confined to articles which had great value but small bulk, such as jewels and precious stones. Nowadays, because of scientific advancement and the improvement of transport by land, sea and air, vast quantities of raw material, food and manufactured goods are daily transported across the surface of the earth in satisfaction of demand.

Improvements in communications have helped to create a world market. Radio, telephone, teleprinter, television and satellite communications have linked countries closely together and made trade possible between buyers and sellers in distant lands. The development of radio and radar has had great effects on both the shipping and aircraft transport industries. It is now possible to control their movements so that the maximum benefit can be obtained from their use.

Despite the growth of external trade the complexities of international trade have increased during the twentieth century and particularly during recent years. From Britain's point of view, many of the former customers now manufacture their own products, and countries like Australia, Canada and India have become, or are becoming, more industrialised.

Britain is, therefore, no longer in a position to rely to such a great extent on her investment interest from abroad as previously. In addition the pattern of Britain's world trade has been changing. As the developing countries of the Commonwealth assert their independence, Britain's share in this sphere has been diminishing. Whilst the Commonwealth trade is still a very important item in Britain's economy, other outlets have had to be found for British products. Hence in 1973 Britain became a member of the European Economic Community in order to create closer economic ties with the member and associate nations.

Common Market Headquarters in Brussels.

3. THE EUROPEAN ECONOMIC COMMUNITY

The European Economic Community, or Common Market as it is frequently called, is a fully economic and partly political union of nine countries having a combined population of over 250 millions. It is one of the most important trading areas in the world with headquarters in Brussels having an interest in all sectors of world trade.

The Community was formed in 1958 by the Treaty of Rome, signed by the six founder member countries—Belgium, France, Italy, Luxembourg, Netherlands and West Germany—agreeing to closely co-operate in the three important fields of trade, Coal and Steel, and Atomic Energy. These countries in 1973 were joined by three further countries—Britain, Denmark and Eire —to form the group of nine that comprises the present community.

(a) Control

Within the Community there are four principal areas of control:

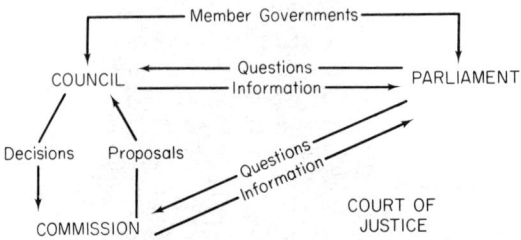

(1) The Council of Ministers. Consists of at least one Minister from each member State who assumes the Presidency of the Council by vote for a period of six months. The Foreign Minister of each government is frequently one of the members appointed especially as important policy decisions are often made affecting the respective members. Provision is made for specialist members to present their case when necessary on questions of agriculture and finance etc.

On matters of major importance affecting vital national interests, the Council can only act on a *unanimous* vote. On all other matters the treaty provides for a system of weighted voting in order to obtain a *qualified majority*—a minimum of 41 votes from not less than six members is required. The allocation of votes to members is Belgium 5, Britain 10, Denmark 3, Eire 3, France 10, Italy 10, Luxembourg 2, Netherlands 5, West Germany 10, making a total of 58.

(2) The Commission. Is made up by 13 Commissioners appointed by member states for a period of four years. Britain, France, Italy and West Germany each have two members, the remainder appoint one each. Every Commissioner is assisted by a full time staff and allocated responsibility over a department connected with the day to day administration of the Community. In numerical terms, the Commission is the largest of the four main institutions and is the 'civil service' of the Community. It has executive powers found in the Treaty of Rome and in the decision of the Council. Members act independently of their national interests and are responsible for formulating proposals for consideration by the Council. The Commission also ensures that the Community acts in a consistent manner and ensures that the decisions of the various institutions are implemented.

(3) The Court of Justice. Situated in Luxembourg and consists of 11 eminent judges who would be eligible to sit in the highest court of their respective countries, and who act independently of all other institutions. The judges are appointed for six year terms of office to settle disputes in accordance with the terms of the Treaty and to interpret rules and regulations made by both the Council and the Commission. Procedure is broadly similar to the courts of member states and the Court is able to award damages, impose sanctions etc. on cases brought before it by the Community institutions, member states, companies or individuals.

(4) The European Parliament. Is situated in Strasbourg where its 198 members meet annually, the allocation of seats to members being, Belgium 14, Britain 36, Denmark 10, Eire 10, France 36, Italy 36, Luxembourg 6, Netherlands 14, and West Germany 36.

Its role is to some extent largely consultative although it is able to influence the Commission in aspects of control over administrative expenditure. The Parliament debates all major aspects of policy and members are able to put questions on policy and administration to both the Council and the Commission. It has also the power by a two-thirds majority vote to compel the resignation of the entire Commission.

(b) Other Institutions. Under the control of the Community there are a number of institutions and organisations. The principal ones being:

(1) The European Coal and Steel Community. Established by the Paris Treaty 1952 and absorbed into the larger Community in 1958. It ensures a common market in coal and steel throughout the community in terms of investment, production, labour etc. Producers are free to fix their own published prices which may vary according to transport costs. The Commission however reserve the right to fix upper and lower limits if necessary.

Investment projects require the examination of the Commission who may grant loans or guarantees in approved cases.

The Coal and Steel Community obtains its funds from levies charged to the producers which cover administration costs, loans, grants and research projects. It may also borrow from outside private sources for investment in the Community.

(2) The European Atomic Energy Community (Euratom). The Commission is concerned with the peaceful use and development of all nuclear industries in member countries and it acts as the co-ordinator of national programmes. It is responsible for the publication of technical information, the supply of material and all research projects throughout the Community.

(3) The European Investment Bank. Controlled by a Board of Governors made up from the Ministers of Finance from member states, a Management Committee and a Board of Directors. The bank's capital is from money subscribed by its members and from the issue of bonds on the capital markets of the world. Its principal aim is to act as banker to the Community and also to give assistance to the less developed regions in member states in order that programmes of industrial modernisation may be undertaken.

(4) The European Development Fund. Provides grants out of contributions by member states to overseas countries who because of their previous dominion or colonial status need assistance in the development of their industries.

(5) The European Social Fund. Is administered by the Commission and financed by member states and community revenues. It provides aid to regions, industries or companies that have suffered as a direct result of Community policy or decisions. The fund also finances many occupational retraining schemes for redundant workers throughout the Community.

(6) The European Monetary Co-operation Fund. Administered by the Committee of Governors of the nine Central Banks in order to regulate (a) a monetary pool for supporting members experiencing short-term deficiencies; (b) a European monetary unit of account used as a basis for the calculation of indebtedness amongst members. (c) Unilateral action for the purpose of reducing margins between the exchange rates of member countries.

(7) The European Agricultural Fund. Accounts for the major proportion of Community budget expenditure and is divided into two sections:

(a) The *Guidance Section* which is concerned with the development of long term projects on farm land, equipment, buildings, etc. as well as the consolidation of farm holdings into larger units.

(b) The *Guarantee Section* dealing with the principal community expenditure. Through this section, community farmers are able to recoup any difference between the prevailing market price and the agreed guaranteed price for their products. There is therefore a common agricultural policy throughout the community and this applies equally to all farmers and horticulturalists.

The Common Agricultural Policy

One of the basic aims of the Treaty of Rome was to establish a common agricultural policy among member states. As both productivity and efficiency in European farming generally was below average compared with world producers, the common agricultural policy has been a means of positive improvement to the more backward areas. From the many fragmented small-holdings that were common on the Continent the policy has been one of rationalisation into larger units to increase productivity. It provides the consumer with adequate supplies at reasonable cost and also ensures a reasonable standard of living for all agricultural workers.

The Common Agricultural Policy is concerned with maintaining 'common' prices throughout the community for most agricultural products grown within the regions. These are fixed annually by the Council and are divided into three groups:

(a) The target price that is to be the objective for all producers.

(b) A threshold price being the base price for the assessment of levies on produce grown *outside* the community. The market is therefore not used as a dumping ground for surplus products by outside producers.

(c) An intervention price at which national agencies will purchase all produce offered to them should market prices fall below this level.

The community farmers and horticulturalists are therefore offered a guaranteed price for most of their products including cereals, vegetables, dairy products, fruit, meat and sugar.

Customs Union

One of the principal objects of Community policy has been to create a trading area free of *internal* customs duties on industrial goods and the establishment of a common *external* tariff applying to all non-members. Arrangements are also incorporated to prohibit the dumping of surplus products within the area to the detriment of any branch of community industry.

Community Budget

Member countries are required to contribute towards Community funds each year out of revenue. The amounts paid by each member differ as does the amount of benefit received out of community funds.

Associate Members

Full membership to the Community is restricted to the nine

principal countries forming the union. The Treaty allows the addition of associate members to receive preferential treatment or special provisions in view of their position with full members. In addition to protectorate or colonial territories, associate membership is extended to Greece, Spain and Turkey.

Other commercial interests dealt with in the Community include decisions regarding the movement of labour, regional policy, taxation, transport and capital movements. All of these therefore are designed to promote harmonious development and closer relations between member States.

4. THE ADVANTAGES OF EXTERNAL TRADE

From the economic point of view, international trade has many advantages:

(1) The gifts of nature are distributed over a greater area, and therefore when they are exchanged a greater number of wants are satisfied. Britain has abundant supplies of a few raw materials, but the range of agricultural products is limited on account of climate. Countries such as Canada, the United States, France, Nigeria, the West Indies etc., have natural conditions which favour agriculture, and are able to grow produce which cannot be grown or produced in this country for climatic reasons. The exchange of goods between the countries of the world leads to a higher standard of life for the inhabitants of all participants.

(2) Countries differ in climate and geological formation, and various zones of the earth have their own distinctive products. Foreign trade enables each country to specialise in the production of that commodity for which it is most fitted by natural conditions, and to avail itself of the advantages of the division of labour. Taking the countries quoted above as an example, one can associate products such as wheat, wines, cocoa, sugar and so on that are grown or produced in large quantities. This specialisation leads to a greater output and a superior product.

(3) The peoples of the world differ in natural ability just as much as material commodities differ in other respects. The differences may be in the skills acquired by tradition, or those taught through having the opportunity of proper education and

training. Foreign trade enables the world to make the best use of these differences that exist amongst the peoples of the world.

(4) Foreign trade makes the countries of the world inter-dependent, and the well-being of each country is to the benefit of all. The industry of the world is like one huge machine, where there are a thousand parts and each depends on the smooth and efficient working of the others. Self-sufficiency, which is the opposite of foreign trade, involves a lower standard of living, since each nation, under such a system, must live on its own resources.

The above advantages of foreign trade are considered solely from the economic point of view. Unfortunately, political and other motives often prevent many countries of the world from obtaining the full advantages or rewards of this trade.

5. BRITAIN AND FREE TRADE

Britain's prosperity depends on the prosperity of those who buy her exports, and theirs will depend upon how they sell their exports in the markets of the world including Britain.

Being an island, having few natural resources and needing to support a large population Britain is therefore dependent more than any other country upon her exports. Thus Britain is a strong advocate for the removal of artificial barriers to trade and plays a leading part in supporting the following organisations.

(a) *The International Monetary Fund* (I.M.F.). Most of the countries in the Western world are members of this organisation. The principal aim is to create a fund of currencies out of which members may draw certain amounts when trading difficulties are experienced. A loan is therefore given to a member that has to be repaid (with interest) when the appropriate measures have been taken.

(b) *General Agreement on Tariffs and Trade* (G.A.T.T.) seeks to increase the volume of world trade by the gradual reduction of tariffs and other barriers to trade such as import licences, quotas, etc., on both industrial and agricultural goods. There are over 70 members throughout the world. Tariff reductions and agreements for future reductions are applicable to all members.

6. BRITISH IMPORTS AND EXPORTS

In the Department of Trade and Industry returns, imports and exports are classified under five headings:

(1) Food, Drink and Tobacco.   (4) Manufactured Goods.
(2) Basic Materials.   (5) Postal Packages.
(3) Minerals, Fuels and
    Lubricants.

The above are broad classifications and include all visible exports and imports amounting to many millions of pounds. For the purpose of trade statistics, IMPORTS are taken at their c.i.f. value, which includes the cost of the goods with the charges for insurance and freight. EXPORTS however are taken at their f.o.b. value, including only the cost of the goods delivered to the ship or aircraft at the British port.

The following tables show (a) Britain's chief imports and exports, (b) her best customers in monetary terms and (c) the commodity composition of foreign trade between this country and the rest of the world.

(a) IMPORTS AND EXPORTS

Imports	*Exports*
Food, Drink and Tobacco	Engineering products
Semi-manufactured goods	Road Vehicles
Basic raw materials	Aircraft
Finished goods	Chemicals
Fuels and Lubricants	Electrical goods
	Scotch whisky
	Glassware

(b) BRITAIN'S BEST CUSTOMERS

Britain imports from	*Britain exports to*
United States	United States
Canada	West Germany
West Germany	Eire
Netherlands	Netherlands
Sweden	Sweden
France	Canada
Eire	France

(c) COMMODITY COMPOSITION OF BRITAIN'S EXTERNAL TRADE

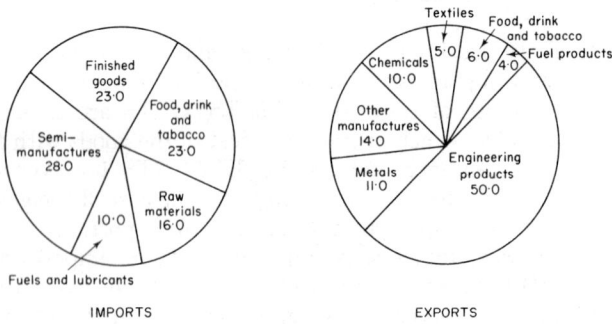

IMPORTS   EXPORTS

(Percentage of Total Values)

The above tables relate only to the 'visible' or tangible goods that are bought or sold by this country. On the imports side the most notable change over recent years has been the increase in the proportion of finished goods in the form of capital equipment and industrial components. Semi-manufactured goods have likewise increased and now represent the highest percentage of total imports. This is partly because the developing countries that previously supplied only the raw materials are today devoting a greater interest in the subsequent stages of manufacture.

By far the greatest volume of exports is of manufactured goods. This figure includes the products of very many factories, engineering works, mines, mills and quarries throughout the country. It also includes re-exports that form an important sector of the distribution network seen at the principal British ports.

7. THE BALANCE OF PAYMENTS

International trade relates to the import of goods *and services* into Britain in comparison with the export of goods and services from Britain to the rest of the world.

An individual *in the long run* must be able to pay his debts out of his income. If, for example, his yearly income is £2,000, then if he did not borrow, receive credit, or use up any savings, he would not spend more than this amount on himself or his family. If he did borrow or secure credit then ultimately he would have to repay this plus interest out of his then current income.

Likewise in international trade, a country *over a period of time* must live within its income, so that it sells in the form of exports in order that it can import from others goods and services that it is unable to supply itself.

The importance of this concept can be seen by the fact that Britain accounts for less than 2 per cent of the world population, yet it is the third largest trading nation. International trade has been of vital importance to this country for over a century, particularly for the supply of raw materials for industry and food for a large population.

In order to pay for the imports Britain must export both goods and services that are required by her customers overseas. Britain is therefore a major world supplier of machinery, vehicles, aircraft, electrical goods, etc. It should be noted however that all of these items require varying amounts of imported raw material in their construction that perpetuates the import cost. Nevertheless whilst the engineering industry have dominated export earnings over recent years particularly in the new and expanding industries such as electronic equipment, office machinery and plastics, attention should also be given to many of the old established industries, including iron and steel, chemicals, paper, pottery, glass etc.

International trade may be subdivided into two trading branches:

(*a*) *Visible Trade.* This refers to the *exchange of commodities* mentioned above and it is to this branch of British trade with foreign countries that the Department of Trade and Industry returns of Imports and Exports refer.

(b) *Invisible Trade*. Refers to *the services* that one country performs for another. Britain, for example, performs a great many financial and shipping services to other countries: these and other services are known as *Invisible Exports*. Similarly, services performed by other nations for this country are known as *Invisible Imports*.

Official returns are kept on Britain's trade with the rest of the world. These cover periods of one year ending 31st December. It should be realised however that these are only 'snapshots' of what is in reality a continuing process. The returns are divided into the following sections:

(a) Current Account

(1) The Balance of Trade (Visible Trade). As the term suggests, this amounts to the difference between the *visible* imports and exports for a given year. In the following table three years are given for comparative purposes, expressed in £ millions:

				1962	1968	1971
Imports	.	.	.	4,095	6,916	8,585
Exports	.	.	.	3,993	6,273	8,882
Deficit	.	.	.	−102	−643	+297

With the exception of only a very few years (including 1971) Britain has imported in monetary terms more visible items than have been exported. This deficit on trade however is usually more than made up by a surplus on the invisible account.

(2) Balance of Payments (Invisible Trade). This takes into account both the visible and invisible trade. It therefore clearly shows the position of a country on a year's trading after allowance has been made for services rendered by one nation to another. Britain's Invisible Trade consists of the following Imports and Exports:

| INVISIBLE EXPORTS | | | | INVISIBLE IMPORTS | | |
| *Receipts £m.* | | | | *Expenditure £m.* | | |

	1962	1968	1971		1962	1968	1971
Government	39	44	55	Government	399	510	576
Shipping	647	1048	1588	Shipping	668	1025	1657
Interest, Profits and				Interest, Profits and			
Dividends	754	1115	1441	Dividends	420	774	920
Travel	183	282	469	Travel	210	271	443
Civil Aviation	119	235	354	Civil Aviation	97	206	310
Others	633	1070	1441	Others	357	656	787
				Surplus	224	352	655
	2375	3794	5348		2375	3794	5348

A closer look at the individual items shows the importance of each to the economy.

(a) *Government:* represents the expenditure of the British Government outside the country on items including the upkeep of bases, embassies, consulates, subscriptions and contributions to international organisations, etc., together with the receipt of money from foreign governments in this country.

(b) *Shipping:* the receipts are the earnings of all foreign going British ships carrying cargo on the trade routes of the world, compared with the expenditure by Britain on foreign vessels.

(c) *Interest, profits and dividends* relate to the money received from the considerable investments held abroad by the Government and private enterprise. Likewise the expenditure includes the profit, and transfers, of foreign firms in this country paid to the parent company abroad.

(d) *Travel:* represents the money spent by visitors *to* Britain as distinct from the money spent abroad *by* British businessmen and holidaymakers.

(e) *Civil Aviation:* includes receipts from British and foreign airlines, landing fees, etc., and is of growing importance to the British economy.

(f) *Other receipts* and expenditure include much of the

financial and allied services of the City of London, private and foreign government money transfers, including legacies, gifts, pensions, migrants assets, royalties, film and television transactions and other miscellaneous services.

The Balance of Payments for a particular year (always ending on 31st December) is calculated by combining the Visible and Invisible Imports and Exports in the following manner:

	1962	1968	1971
Surplus on Invisible Account	224	352	655
Deficit on Visible Account	−102	−643	+297
Net Surplus or Deficit on Trade	+122	−291	+952

(b) Long Term Capital Account

Is in reality a form of investment account for both the public and private sector. Income includes the investments of foreign governments into Britain together with the investments of foreign companies (and individuals) attracted by high interest rates or profit potential. This is offset by similar investments in foreign countries by the British Government, companies and individuals on *long term* capital projects.

(c) Monetary Movements

This account is solely concerned with the adjustment of bank and currency balances taking the above into consideration. Receipts may include inflows of currency, additions to balances held in the City of London or Government borrowing from institutions such as the International Monetary Fund. Likewise expenditure may include outflows of currency, reduction in balances held in the City or repayment of Government loans abroad.

Taking the visible and invisible *trading items* together with the 'investment' or long-term *capital* items as a whole the net result is either a cash inflow to London from foreign centres or a loss of gold and foreign currency out of London. Over the long term of course it is necessary for countries to equate surplus and deficits in order to reap the advantages of stable exchange rates.

Nevertheless whilst one should appreciate the particular importance of this trade to Britain as a whole the manner in which it is carried out should be considered. The Government by various means and incentives gives every encouragement to further international trade. Associations and Chambers of Commerce likewise add weight to the situation. The Press and Television report on the imports and and exports in terms of money values. Yet in fact the whole business of the import and export trade is undertaken by many thousands of different people, organisations and companies throughout Britain, completely independent of each other and without knowledge of the others activities. It is these units that in total enable us to acquire the surplus of other lands and maintain the standard of living we have come to expect.

QUESTIONS

1. In what way does the External Trade differ from Home Trade?

2. From what sources are statistics compiled to show the imports and exports of this country?

3. Explain the following terms in connection with Foreign Trade: (a) entrepôt trade, (b) tariffs, (c) quotas, (d) customs draw-back, (e) invisible trade.

4. What are the factors which make the work of a businessman engaged in foreign trade more onerous than that of one trading only in the home market? (London G.C.E.)

5. 'The items which go into the measurement of our balance of payments are visible trade, invisibles and long-term capital.' Explain what is meant by this quotation. (R.S.A.)

6. (a) Why is foreign trade important to (1) the exportnig country (2) the importing country?

(b) In what respects is foreign trade more complicated than home trade? (Cambridge G.C.E.)

7. Either (a) what is the Exports Credits Guarantee Department? Describe its work.

Or (b) Briefly describe the organisation and work of the Corporation of Lloyd's. How is a marine insurance effected there? (Cambridge G.C.E.)

Chapter 5

The Export Trade

I. IMPORTANCE OF THE EXPORT TRADE

The visible export trade of Britain mainly consists of the export of manufactures made in this country of imported raw materials. These products are mostly high quality goods and are distributed to all parts of the world, so that today Britain ranks as one of the leading trading nations accounting for about 7 per cent of world trade. The chief reasons why Britain has attained this position are:

(*a*) The industrial development has been continuous and uninterrupted since the early days. British people attained their freedom before those of other countries, and her history has been comparatively free from internal strife and disorders.

(*b*) The Industrial Revolution occurred in Britain from about 1760 to 1860 much earlier than in other countries when the factory system of manufacture took the place of the Domestic System. During this period, important engineering inventions were made and Britain became the 'workshop of the world'.

(*c*) Britain was one of the first in acquiring colonies which supplied raw materials for her factories and offered markets for her manufactured goods.

(*d*) This country was the first to apply the power of steam to manufacture, and later, to transport. Railways and steamships enabled Britain to influence the future pattern of world trade at a very early stage.

(*e*) The geographical position of these islands makes Britain an important distributing centre for Northern Europe, and also helps to facilitate trade with North America. Specialist markets were developed in London for the sale of raw materials and these were renowned for their correctness and fair dealing.

(*f*) Britain developed a system of banking which has enabled her to become an important financial centre of the world.

The above reasons could be expanded at great length, but they are sufficient to indicate why Britain plays an important part in developing the trade of the world.

2. MEANS OF PROCURING ORDERS

Methods of export trading vary considerably, according to the firm, the industry, the product and the market. A considerable amount of the export business, especially of the smaller firms, is conducted through specialist export merchants. Many firms, however, conduct their trade with foreign importers and consumers through agents, branch offices, resident representatives, or subsidiary companies established abroad.

The competition between British firms has been reduced by the formation of associations and combines, but foreign manufacturers have often an initial advantage in their nearness to the market. The British exporter therefore has to pay particular attention to market conditions. These include the design of the goods, climatic conditions, foreign regulations and so on.

Orders for British exports may be obtained in the following ways:

(**1**) **Advertisements and Circulars.** Many firms obtain orders by advertising their goods in trade journals which circulate in other countries. Circulars and catalogues are therefore sent to firms likely to be interested in a particular line of goods. Considerable care is needed however in the drafting of the circular, catalogues or even name of the product. There have been numerous examples of notable home produced products failing on the foreign markets simply because of the different meaning or association of ideas attached to certain words or phrases when translated into another language. Perhaps the major drawback to this method is that it is very expensive and it lacks the personal element which is an important factor in obtaining orders.

Advertising is more useful in *maintaining* the sales of an existing market, whilst circulars and catalogues are likely to arouse interest if distributed to prospective customers by properly trained representatives who are aware of market conditions.

(2) Representatives. Many firms encourage a personal relationship with their customers, and obtain new customers by sending a representative abroad. He should have a commercial or technical knowledge of the language of the country which he visits, and should be a man of quick perception and good judgment to enable him to send to his principals accurate reports regarding the state of the market. Once again this is an expensive method of procuring orders unless large contracts are obtained. Some of the larger organisations with diverse interests therefore give their representatives wide discretionary powers to achieve a lucrative export contract.

(3) Visits of Foreign Buyers. Representatives of foreign firms or trade missions visit this country periodically to make purchases on behalf of their governments or firms. The leading financial papers and trade journals give particulars regarding such visits, and British firms are able to contact the foreign buyers. This method of obtaining orders has many advantages particularly as the personal relationship often leads to further orders.

(4) Foreign Depot. If sales abroad are likely to be large a firm may open a foreign depot or warehouse where stocks may be kept and inspected by likely customers. An after-sales service may also be maintained to cater for guarantee renewals, repairs, etc. Direct sales may also be established from the point of contact with the overseas consumers or tradesmen. Alternatively, the depot may be used as a showroom, and delivery made from this country.

(5) Trade Fairs and Exhibitions. British exporters take advantage of fairs that are regularly held every year in many countries. including those at Leipzig, Milan, Hanover and at numerous other places throughout the world. Buyers and sellers are attracted from almost every country, whilst firms exhibit their goods and distribute catalogues which often lead to firm orders being received.

In Britain, specialised fairs such as the Motor Show, the Boat Show and the Royal Highland Show attract large numbers of trade buyers from home and overseas as well as members of the public. The fairs also provide a useful means of advertising through the medium of reports on television, in the daily papers and trade journals, etc.

Participation in 'British Weeks' and store promotions abroad is also an important form of obtaining export orders for which the Government through the Foreign and Commonwealth Office and the Department of Trade and Industry, etc., often provide information, facilities and advice.

Nowadays there is less distinction between exhibitions and fairs as they both have the same objects—the promotion of

An assembly line for an export order.

sales, introduction of new ideas and efficient methods, and the display of new lines. Many exhibitions are held annually and at a certain time of the year, especially during the autumn and spring months. The results of international exhibitions are difficult to measure: increased sales are not the only test of the success, for if the exhibits make a good impression, other orders may follow.

3. THE RECEIPT OF AN ORDER

A foreign buyer may place his orders for British goods in several ways:

(*a*) Direct from the manufacturer where the latter produces high quality goods such as machinery, or where the products are specialised or renowned throughout the world.

(*b*) From an export merchant who undertakes the distribution of goods for the manufacturer.

(*c*) The foreign buyer may place his order through a Commission Agent, who would have a knowledge of the goods to be purchased and also the requirements of the market to which they are to be sent.

4. EXECUTION OF AN ORDER

The execution of an order in general terms would be as follows:

(1) Receipt of Order. A foreign order is called an *Indent*, and is made out in as much detail as possible in order to prevent mistakes and misunderstandings. If an agent is employed the indent will state (1) exact details of the goods required, (2) the approximate price, (3) the date of delivery, (4) instructions regarding packing and shipment, (5) the date of shipment, (6) the amount of commission payable to the agent.

There are two types of indent:

(*a*) *An Open Indent* instructs an agent to order certain goods and to attend to their shipment, but does not instruct the agent to order them from any particular firm.

(*b*) *A Closed Indent* instructs an agent to order goods from a certain firm and gives the same instructions as the open indent referred to above. The reader may wonder why the order contained in a closed indent is not sent direct to the firm named. This is because the manufacturer usually specialises in industrial processes, and leaves the formalities connected with the export of goods to agents and export merchants who are specialists in this branch of distribution.

(2) Placing the Order. If the Commission Agent receives a *Closed* Indent, he contacts the named firm giving instructions regarding his foreign principal's requirements. These will be quoted from the indent, together with any additional details which have been left to the discretion of the agent.

If the agent has received an *Open* Indent, he will obtain quotations from several firms. According to the instructions, he will either place the order, or communicate with the foreign buyer for confirmation of the price which he recommends. When agreement has been reached, the agent will place the order with the selected firm, and await delivery.

(3) Packing. This may be done by the manufacturer or wholesale merchant, or by firms which specialise in packing goods for delivery abroad. The following points must be borne in mind:

(a) Customs regulations abroad: in some countries duty is charged on the gross weight, and therefore, light but strong cases or containers are desirable.

(b) The weights and measures of the foreign country.

(c) All cases should be marked in accordance with instructions given in the indent. The marks often consist of a geometrical figure enclosing the initials of a firm or person, and are used for purposes of identification. Each package is also numbered, and the corresponding number is given on the invoice, so that the contents of each package are easily recognised.

(d) The size of any packet or packing-case should be suitable for acceptance into containers with the minimum loss of space.

(4) Forwarding to the Ship. For the purpose of illustration the procedure dealing with the transport of goods by sea is described but in many cases a similar procedure is used with air transport. Also the movement of goods by road particularly to many parts of Europe is commonplace today. Similar documents and procedures are involved with the addition of the T.I.R. system now widely accepted by many countries.

If the manufacturer has packed the goods, he will send them by road or rail to the port of embarkation. On arrival at the port, the carrier notifies the shipping company, which sends a *Shipping Advice Note* to a dock company, instructing it to collect the goods from the carrier, and to place them on board a certain ship. In the latter case if no Bill of Lading is available, a *Mate's Receipt* is issued: it is signed by an authorised officer of the ship, and states that the goods have been received in good condition. If any of the wrappers are torn, or if the packages are damaged in any way, a note is made on the Mate's Receipt.

(5) Shipment of the Goods. The packing and forwarding agents also attend to the preparation of the Bill of Lading and to the insurance of the goods.

- (a) *The Bill of Lading* is made out in sets of three, each being a document of title, and signed by the captain of the ship or his authorised deputy, who retains an additional copy of the bill for reference (see page 91).

- (b) *Freight Note.* Is sent by the shipping company to the exporter, stating the amount that has been paid to the company for the carriage of cargo. The leading shipping companies (through the shipping conferences) draw up tariffs from time to time, and thus protect themselves against unfair competition. The tariff arranges goods into classes, and freight is charged according to (a) the weight (b) the cubic capacity, or (c) the value of the goods. As heavy cargoes do not occupy a great deal of space in proportion to their weight, they are charged at so much a tonne weight. On the other hand, light bulky goods are charged according to measurement, 1,000 kilogrammes being taken as 1 cubic metre. Valuable goods, such as bullion, jewels, etc., are usually charged a percentage according to the declared value.

(6) Insurance. The agent insures the goods against sea-risks through an insurance broker, who quotes a premium depending on the nature of the risks to be insured. (The subject of Marine Insurance is dealt with in Chapter 3.)

(7) Customs Specification. This requirement must be completed before the clearance of the ship and details have to be given to the Customs officials at the port of embarkation. These include full particulars regarding the goods exported, including the f.o.b. value that enables the Customs to compile statistics regarding exports.

5. PREPARATION OF EXPORT INVOICE

When the Agent has attended to the various formalities connected with the shipment of the goods, he prepares a financial statement, showing all the charges incurred.

(a) The Invoice. In the export trade this is very detailed giving full particulars of the goods sent to the foreign buyer together with f.o.b. cost and other charges.

(b) Consular Invoices. A number of countries insist that all imports are accompanied by an invoice signed by the Consul of the country to which the goods are being sent. If an exporter in London, for example, is sending goods to the United States, he must present a detailed invoice to the American Consul for his signature. The invoice is made out in triplicate: one is given to the shipper, another to the Customs abroad at the port of unloading, whilst the third is retained by the Consul.

(c) Certificate of Origin. The European Economic Community and a number of other countries charge a lower rate of duty on goods manufactured in Britain. The Certificate of Origin is therefore a guarantee that the goods named are of British manufacture. It is signed by the Secretary of the Chamber of Commerce or Customs official in whose district the goods have been manufactured.

Assistance in the above may be obtained from the numerous privately-owned **Export Finance Houses** whose main role is to provide both medium- and long-term credit to British exporters. These institutions may also act as principals to manufacturers and arrange for the collection of trade debts from overseas buyers.

6. GOVERNMENT ASSISTANCE TO EXPORTERS

The Department of Trade and Industry is a government department under a Secretary of State having general responsibility for the United Kingdom's Commerce, Industry and Overseas Trade. The department's principal concern is to assist British Industry and Commerce in all aspects of trade. It is therefore concerned with the development of policy and in particular the application of measures affecting government, public industry, private industry and commerce. Responsibility is also taken for overseas commercial relations and all matters affecting the export trade. In addition statistics are published giving particulars of Britain's imports and exports, etc., which are of considerable use and interest to the businessman.

Sources of Information. The Department relies on the Customs authorities to furnish it with details regarding all goods entering and leaving the country. In order to obtain uniformity of description, two Official Lists are published—the Customs Import List and the Customs Export List.

When goods are exported, the exporter is required to complete a Customs Specification, within a few days of the sailing of the ship. This gives full particulars of the goods, stating the quantity, value and destination of the consignment. The shipping company is also required to inform the Customs authorities of a ship's cargo shortly after the ship's departure.

The Customs have therefore a complete record of all goods leaving or arriving in this country by sea. Customs officials are also stationed at airports, where similar records of imports and exports are kept. From this information the Department's Returns are compiled and are printed as follows:

(a) *An Annual Statement* of the Trade of the United Kingdom with the European Economic Community, the Commonwealth and the rest of the world.

(b) *A Monthly Statement*, giving particulars of trade with the above sectors during the preceding month.

The Annual Statement of foreign trade gives particulars of Britain's trade with other countries up to the previous 31st

December. It is issued in two volumes—in the first, the commodities are the basis of classification, whilst in the second volume it is the countries concerned. The following particulars are listed:

(1) *The Values of Imports and Exports* for the year. The values of the imports are those on arrival in this country and therefore include insurance and freight charges. The values of the exports however are their values when they are placed on board ship and include no such charges. Imports are divided into (*a*) articles free of duty, (*b*) articles subject to duty, whilst re-exports are tabulated separately.

(2) *Alphabetical Classification of Imports and Exports*. These are arranged in alphabetical order, giving the respective weights, lengths or numbers in tabular form.

(3) *Alphabetical Classification of Countries*. The countries trading with Britain are listed alphabetically and a detailed statement of the trade with this country is given.

(4) *The Trade of each port in Britain*. An analysis of the trade of each customs port in Britain is listed, showing the chief goods imported or exported together with their weights and values.

Monthly Statement. This return is issued in the middle of each month and gives a summary of the imports and exports for the preceding month. Comparative figures are also given for the corresponding months of preceding years.

Detailed statistics of these figures follow: commodities are arranged in alphabetical order, with particulars of their weights and values. The countries of origin or the destination of the goods are shown in tabular form.

The above description of the work of the Department applies to foreign trade. It is equally concerned with home trade, and publishes valuable statistics relating to Britain's internal trade.

The Commercial Relations and Exports Division. Exporters requiring assistance and advice are able to consult the Department in London or its branches in this country, or the commercial attachés of H.M. Diplomatic service overseas.

A close liaison is maintained between London and the overseas officers on information concerning trade between Britain and the foreign centre, which is readily available to the businessman.

Overseas representatives regularly report on the local economic and commercial conditions. Additional information on the state of the markets and potential contracts in which businessmen may be interested are also available. From these details the Department is able to provide the businessman with the following information on *any* country in the world.

  (a) the prospects for British exports and details of particular markets.
  (b) regulations imposed by foreign governments that affect trade including tariffs, quotas, customs duties, etc.
  (c) local tastes and preferences in design, size, weight, etc., together with the usual method of trading.
  (d) the commercial standing of firms with whom the British exporter contemplates business.

The sources of information may be classified as follows:

(a) *The British Commonwealth.* Trade Commissioners are appointed to various parts of the British Commonwealth in order to develop trade between Britain and the Commonwealth.

(b) *The European Economic Community.* In addition to Commercial attachés, Legations and Consuls throughout the area, Britain is represented in the European Parliament, the Council of Ministers and the Commission, etc. Britain also makes monetary contributions to a number of community trade development organisations.

(c) *Foreign Countries.* In countries outside the above, two services are organised:

  (1) *The Commercial Diplomatic Service.* Numerous representatives are attached to British Legations in the principal foreign countries.
  (2) *The Consular Service.* Consuls are appointed to reside in a foreign country to watch over British commercial interests, and to protect British subjects residing in that country.

The principal object of the Commercial Relations and Exports Division is to extend British trade abroad and to provide assistance without interference. In addition to the above its activities include the following services to exporters:

(1) *Trade Information* of general or specialist nature including:

   (a) Reports on contracts open to tender, such as the construction of say a new railway, an electrification scheme, a new hotel, etc.

   (b) The names of foreign firms who prefer to buy British goods.

   (c) The names of suitable agents for the sale of British goods.

   (d) Market conditions abroad, including the nature of the competition, methods of payment, imports from other countries, strikes.

   (e) Customs, tariff and exchange control regulations.

   (f) Availability, quality and price of raw materials.

   (g) Transport regulations and methods available.

   (h) The protection of British trademarks.

(2) *Exhibitions and Fairs.*

   (a) The Division collects information about exhibitions and trade fairs both at home and overseas, organises official participation in them when necessary, and advises on commercial and industrial publicity destined for overseas.

   (b) *British Weeks.* As opportunity occurs, British weeks are organised abroad to advertise this country's goods.

(3) *Reports.* The Division places its information at the disposal of British importers and exporters by the following means:

   (a) The issue of Annual Reports.

   (b) The publication of pamphlets on the trade of particular countries.

   (c) Personal contact with British manufacturers. Officials regularly visit the industrial centres of Britain, and become acquainted with the latest methods of manufacture and new products. They also address Chambers of Commerce and trade associations from time to time in order to inform exporters of the requirements of the markets which they represent.

The Exports Credit Guarantee Department (E.C.G.D.), is a commercial undertaking of the Department of Trade and Industry providing insurance for exporters against the main risks of selling overseas. Covering over one third of Britain's export trade it is required to conduct its business on a self supporting basis. The principal risks against which the British exporter may insure are:

(a) insolvency or protracted default of the buyer.

(b) the action of a foreign government prohibiting the transfer of money to the British exporter.

(c) the outbreak of hostilities between the buyer's country and Britain, or revolution in the buyer's country.

(d) the imposition of import restrictions by the foreign government.

(e) any other cause of loss occurring *outside* Britain, not within the control of exporter or importer and not normally insurable with insurance companies.

In addition the department provides financial guarantees for British banks and finance houses who lend money to British firms engaged in the export trade. Loans may also be made to overseas purchasers of large capital items made in Britain.

The British Overseas Trade Board is comprised of representatives from government, industry and commerce. In general terms its day to day work is controlled by the Department of Trade and Industry. This includes export intelligence, promotion of export activities, assistance and advice to British firms engaged in the export market, arranging inward commercial visits by foreign buyers and businessmen, etc.

Whilst most of the export business is ultimately in the hands of the private sector of industry and commerce, the government endeavours to create favourable conditions by its efforts both at home and overseas. In addition to the above Boards and Divisions, government economic policy includes the use of fiscal, statutory, credit restriction and other methods to curb or reduce home demand. Action is also undertaken through international organisations to reduce or remove the barriers to international trade.

QUESTIONS

1. What principal methods are used by British merchants and manufacturers to obtain orders abroad? (U.L.C.I.)

2. 'Export trade is no longer dependent on salesmanship. It is now a matter for negotiation by diplomatists.' How far is this assertion true? (R.S.A.)

3. What are the essential features of a Bill of Lading, regarded from the point of view of a merchant exporter? What other documents are required in connection with the export of goods? (R.S.A.)

4. Explain the economic importance of (a) Trade Fairs, (b) Exhibitions, (c) British weeks.

5. Distinguish between the 'Balance of Trade' and the 'Balance of Payments'. Describe the probable effect of an unfavourable Balance of Payments on the industry and commerce of a nation. (R.S.A.)

6. What facilities should be provided at docks and harbours for dealing with imports and exports? Why is it essential for ships to be loaded and unloaded without delay? (R.S.A.)

7. Give in outline the main sources of commercial information available to an exporter seeking new markets. (U.L.C.I.)

8. Describe the various ways in which exporters obtain orders. Give three reasons why trading abroad is more difficult than trading at home. (J.M.B.)

9. What factors tend to discourage the British manufacturer from exporting? How does the government help in overcoming these difficulties? (A.E.B.)

10. A company, making and selling a branded and well-advertised product in Britain, wishes to sell it in Commonwealth markets. Describe the information you think the company should have to enable it to extend its market, and say how the information could be obtained. (R.S.A.)

11. What is a c.i.f. contract in the export trade? Describe briefly the functions of the main documents which would be needed for consignments of goods being exported by sea under the terms of such a contract. (Oxford G.C.E.)

Chapter 6

The Import Trade

I. NATURE OF IMPORTS

The imports of Britain consist of four classes of commodities:

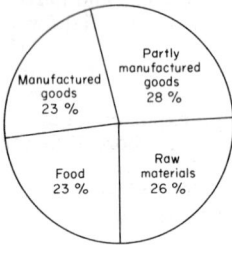

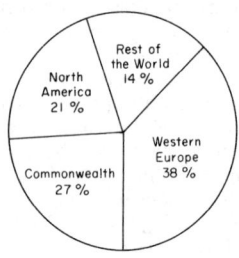

PRINCIPAL COMMODITY IMPORTS   SOURCES OF SUPPLY

(a) **Food, Drink and Tobacco.** The population of Britain increased considerably during the nineteenth century, and today is about 56 millions. With a fully developed pattern of agriculture, this country is capable of maintaining perhaps 20 million people, and even under such conditions many articles of everyday use, such as tea, coffee, cocoa, rice, etc., would be lacking. Foodstuffs must therefore be imported in order to supplement home supplies, and to enable the population to enjoy the use of commodities that cannot be grown for climatic reasons.

(b) **Raw Materials.** During the nineteenth century, Britain developed as a manufacturing country, and until comparatively recent years was looked upon as the principal 'workshop' of the world. The development of manufactures has made it necessary to import supplies of raw materials, since Britain's home produced supplies are quite inadequate for modern needs. Britain relies entirely on foreign lands for supplies of raw cotton, rubber, and most metal ores in order to keep industries in production.

(c) **Partly Manufactured Goods.** Materials from abroad may be partly manufactured before being sent to this country. They may be refined to remove impurities or, as in the case of iron ore smelted where it is mined or quarried. Such preliminary processes of manufacture reduce the cost of transport and enable specialist markets to be set up in London and elsewhere. Because of this, a foreign country may have special facilities for completing the early stages of manufacture before sending its products abroad. These partly manufactured goods therefore also become the raw materials of Britain's industries.

(d) **Manufactured Goods.** Although the import of manufactured goods is in some cases discouraged by means of quotas, tariffs, etc., many countries have natural or acquired facilities for the manufacture of their raw materials. The cost of production in many foreign lands may be low because of geographical advantages or of a lower standard of living. They have consequently specialised on the production of certain lines of goods. Such countries are able to compete with British manufacturers despite the tariff which is placed on manufactured goods on their arrival in this country. Japan for example is renowned for its micro-electrical industry, Hong Kong for its textiles, and so on. Goods from these and other countries are imported to compete with the products of British and E.E.C. manufacturers at competitive prices.

2. METHODS OF IMPORTING

Britain is a member of the European Economic Community which in itself aims at a tariff free area with the free movement of goods between member states. A few goods however such as drugs, arms and ammunition are of necessity restricted by import licence or quota because they present special difficulties and in many cases can only be imported through certain ports.

The following are the most usual methods by which goods are imported into this country:

(a) Direct Orders. A manufacturing firm in Britain may order supplies of raw materials from producers abroad: this procedure would be adopted where no organised market exists for the marketing of the raw material required, or where the manufacturer requires raw materials in such large quantities that he can deal direct with the foreign producer or wholesaler. An importer of say French wines may deal direct with the foreign exporter, whilst an importer of copper for example would place his order through an agent or dealer on the London Metal Exchange.

(b) Subsidiary Companies or Branch Offices. Many of the larger British firms have subsidiaries or branch offices abroad, and instruct their representatives to make purchases for them. Similarly, a foreign firm often has its subsidiaries or branch offices in this country and sends its products to its representatives here in order to find a market.

(c) Consignments. This is the usual method for the import of raw materials and foodstuffs, which are consigned to an agent or broker in this country. The foreign producer may place a reserve price on the goods, or he may leave all such problems to the judgment of the agent. Alternatively the goods may be effectively graded, sold by description or specification, in which case the agent will make use of one of the highly organised commodity markets or exchanges found principally in London. The agent in this country attends to the landing of the goods, and to all Customs requirements. He warehouses the goods, and arranges for their sale on one of the great produce exchanges or by private treaty. When the consignment has been sold, the agent sends an *Account Sales* to his principal. This shows the amount realised, the expenses in connection with the transaction (e.g. insurance, dock dues, commission, etc.) and the net proceeds which are due to the exporter. Payment is made by the agent usually through the international banking system.

3. THE BILL OF LADING

The large shipping companies have specially printed bills, stating the conditions on which they will carry the goods. These are made out in sets by the shipping agents giving the following details:

(a) The quantity, quality (if known) weight and approximate value of the goods taken on board, and the number of packages and the distinguishing marks on each.

(b) The name of the ship carrying the goods, the port of loading and destination.

(c) A statement that the shipowner is only responsible for loss or damage due to his employees. Other losses must be covered by Marine Insurance (usually through Lloyds). Such losses include fire, tempests, war-risks, and generally, all risks that cannot be reasonably foreseen.

When the goods are loaded at the docks they are checked against the Bill and any deficiencies or damage are noted. (A Bill without any note of deficiency or damage is known as *a clean bill.*)

The ship's master or his agent certifies that the goods have been loaded by signing the copies of the bill which now act as valid receipts and are used in the following ways:

(1) One is retained by the shipping company.

(2) Two are sent to the importer in this country by different mails or routes: this is done to avoid the risk of delay or loss, since it is necessary for the importer to receive a copy of the Bill of Lading before can obtain delivery of the goods on board ship. The copies are usually forwarded by air mail, to ensure that the importer receives at least one of them before the arrival of the slower cargo ship.

On receipt of the Bill of Lading, the importer watches for the arrival of the ship carrying the goods. This can be done by reference to *Lloyd's List and Shipping Gazette* which lists a considerable number of shipping movements daily or by *Lloyd's Shipping Index* which is also a daily paper giving the latest position of most ocean-going vessels in alphabetical order.

When the ship arrives in port, the importer claims delivery from the shipping company by presenting one copy of the Bill of Lading. It should be remembered however that the goods which he is importing may be (*a*) dutiable or (*b*) non-dutiable, as a different procedure in landing the goods is necessary in each case.

The importance of the Bill of Lading is therefore as follows:

(1) It serves as an acknowledgment of the receipt of goods by the shipping company.

(2) It is an agreement to carry the goods: the master of the ship is legally the agent of the owner of the goods and is bound to deliver the goods to the consignee or his nominees.

(3) It is a negotiable instrument and is transferable by endorsement. Since the Bill of Lading usually arrives before the goods, the consignment whilst still at sea can be sold by the importer by endorsing the Bill of Lading.

4. ENTRY OF NON-DUTIABLE GOODS

Whether goods are liable to duty or not, certain Customs forms must be filled in by the importer and handed to Customs officials. These forms give full particulars regarding marks, numbers, description of the goods, quantity and c.i.f. value. Penalties are imposed if inaccurate returns are made. The particulars on these Customs Forms are the basis for the returns of Imports and Exports which are published periodically by the Department of Trade and Industry.

If no duty is payable, the Customs officials issue a form entitled '*Entry for Free Goods*' which is to be completed and signed by the importer. This gives full particulars regarding the importer's goods on board the ship. The goods are classified according to the Official Import List together with the quantity, value and place where they are to be consigned. The Customs Officer compares the particulars with the ship's report, and releases the goods if all the statements are correct.

5. CUSTOMS DUTIES AND EXCISE DUTIES

The purpose of placing a *Customs duty* or tariff on certain imports is twofold.

(*a*) It protects the home producer or manufacturer by raising the price of the imported article and

(*b*) the increase in price restricts the home demand and therefore reduces the amount of imports thus assisting the Balance of Payments.

Agreements between countries, however, have in recent years tended to gradually reduce or abolish duties on many articles. This is seen clearly amongst the British Commonwealth and European Economic Community countries (who give preferential rates to each other) and also the countries who are signatories to the General Agreement on Tariffs and Trade (G.A.T.T.).

On the other hand *Excise duties* are charged on goods which are produced *within the home country* for the following reasons:

(*a*) to raise revenue for the State as a form of indirect taxation and

(*b*) to restrict consumption on the home market in order to release more goods for the export market.

Excise duties include the value added taxes paid by the home consumer on motor vehicles, television sets, washing machines, etc., or the duty paid on petrol, tobacco, wines and spirits, etc. There are thus two types:

(*a*) *Specific duties* which relate to the quantity of the commodity purchased, e.g. a litre of petrol, and

(*b*) *ad valorem* duties which are additional charges based on a percentage of the price, e.g. value added tax or certain stamp duties.

Both Customs and Excise duties are determined by the Government who publish lists setting out the duties payable on certain commodities. Amendments are announced from time to time and are printed in the monthly journal published by the Department of Trade and Industry. These duties together amount to many millions of pounds each year and are an important source of revenue for the Government.

6. ENTRY OF DUTIABLE GOODS

The procedure in entering *dutiable* goods depends on whether they are required for immediate use or whether they are to be placed in a bonded warehouse.

(a) Entry for Home Use. A form known as an 'Entry for Home Use' is filled in by the importer when dutiable goods are required for immediate use. This document gives full particulars of the goods, and states the final destination of the goods in Britain. This form is given in duplicate to the Customs officials; the importer pays the duty at the Customs House and the goods are released by the Customs officer on board the ship. The exact amount of the duty may not be ascertainable before examination; an estimate of the duty is made, and the difference is paid later if too little has been paid, and similarly the excess is refunded if too much has been paid.

(b) Entry for Warehousing. This is a document given by the importer to Customs House officials, stating that it is the intention of the importer to store dutiable goods in a Bonded Warehouse. This document gives full particulars of the goods, and states where they are to be warehoused.

Bonded Warehouses exist in the principal ports of this country, and goods subject to duty are allowed to remain in these warehouses until the duty is paid or the goods are re-exported.

Bonded warehouses are under the control of the Customs, but are the property of a private firm or a joint-stock company. The owners of these warehouses enter into a bond with the Customs or Excise Authorities by undertaking to allow no goods to be removed until the duty is paid. The goods are removed from the ship, under special regulations, by the wharfinger or dock company owning the warehouse, and there they are stored until the duty is paid.

The bonded warehouse is only opened in the presence of the Customs officer; whilst the goods are in bond, the importer is allowed to prepare them for sale. Wines and spirits for example may be taken out of the warehouse, blended, bottled, packed and later returned. Alternatively he may invite prospective buyers to inspect the goods before auction on one of the commodity exchanges.

Release from Bond. Whilst the goods are in bond, they may be sold by the broker or importer. The owner of the goods must present a 'Home Consumption Entry' to the Customs House, and pay the required amount of duty. A Duty Receipt is issued, and this authorises the warehouse-keeper to release the goods. If goods on which duty has been paid are re-exported to foreign countries, the money is refunded by the Customs: this repayment is known as a *Customs Drawback*.

QUESTIONS

1. Describe the passage of either tea or coffee from the plantation to the British consumer, paying special attention to the documents involved at each stage of the journey.   (R.S.A.)

2. How do foreign manufactured goods reach the British consumer? Illustrate your answer by reference to some such commodity in common use.   (R.S.A.)

3. Examine the purposes served by bonded warehouses (a) from the point of view of the Government, (b) from the point of view of a merchant importing dutiable goods.   (R.S.A.)

4. What is the difference between Customs Duty and Excise Duty? How are they levied and how do they affect the trade of the country?

5. 'A Port Authority and H.M. Customs co-operate, but the work of one is distinct from that of the other.' Explain this statement.   (Cambridge G.C.E.)

6. (a) 'Customs duties may be either specific or according to value, but H.M. Customs do not levy duties.' Explain.

(b) Why is it necessary for H.M. Customs to make statistical records of exports and imports? How do they obtain the information for such records?   (Cambridge G.C.E.)

7. Describe how the Department of Trade collects statistics of Foreign Trade and how the information is published.   (R.S.A.)

8. What gives rise to international trade? Why is business with foreign countries more difficult than the home trade?   (R.S.A.)

9. One country's exports are clearly another country's imports. Yet in most countries the importance of exports is stressed and, at times, imports are regarded almost with disfavour. Why is this?
      (R.S.A.)

Chapter 7

Markets

I. DEVELOPMENT OF MARKETS

The term 'market' used to refer to a building or place where buyers and sellers met to make their purchases or sales. It is still used in this sense today, for many towns have their market halls or market squares, where buyers and sellers meet for the same purpose.

The meeting of people at agreed places for the purpose of exchange is one of the oldest practices of civilisation. People gathered together at a convenient place, such as a port, cross-roads or near a castle, at a certain time of the year, or on a certain day of the week, in order to interchange foodstuffs and other necessities. Such assemblies gave greater variety and greater security, since in early markets all transactions were backed by the authority of the local courts.

The student of law will be familiar with the dealings of the early merchants from the Mediterranean and Europe who brought their customs and usages of trade to this country. These were gradually applied throughout the land by becoming accepted as the standard method of dealing in the markets. Where there was dispute, the courts, with the authority of a strong Government, ensured that fair dealings in accordance with the established practice of the trade were imposed.

Thus trade with Britain developed, there was greater political freedom than in other parts of Europe so that Britain, and in particular London, became a place where trade was truly international in character.

The London markets administered by the Corporation of the

City of London are of outstanding importance in the distribution of foodstuffs and raw materials, particularly imported supplies. Some of the markets are known to have existed for a thousand years. The principal ones are:

Billingsgate	— renowned for the sale of fish before the Norman Conquest.
Smithfield	— meat provisions and poultry—known to have existed since 1253.
Covent Garden	— fruit, vegetables and flowers—established under a Charter in 1661.
Leadenhall	— meat and poultry.
Spitalfields	— fruit and vegetables.

In addition there are numerous exchanges and markets which specialise in commodities other than food. A complete list of London markets would serve no useful purpose, but a few examples may be given:

The Baltic Exchange	The Stock Exchange
London Diamond Market	London Metal Exchange
London Tea Auctions	London Money Market

Markets may therefore be classified in the following ways:

(a) Chartered Markets. From the twelfth century it was customary for the Crown to grant a charter to the Lord of the manor or an ecclesiastical body such as a monastery or a municipal corporation. The charter empowered the person or body named to hold a market and to charge tolls. Many of these markets exist at the present day and can be found in most of the county towns or principal places of government.

(b) Markets established by Act of Parliament. Many special local Acts of Parliament have been passed to authorise the establishment of a market in a particular place, perhaps at a particular time.

Examples of this can be seen all over the country. Not only do some towns hold regular market days throughout the year, they sometimes hold a seasonal fair in addition which attracts buyers from a much wider area.

The term 'market' can also be used in another sense, and

often refers, not to a particular place, but to a set of conditions which are world-wide.

We may refer to the London Money Market, which relates to an area in the City of London, where there are a number of finance houses, specialising in international monetary exchange. In a broader context, a market may refer to a part of the world with whom a country has strong commercial ties. The United States, for example, is a good market for high-class manufactured goods. Britain is a ready market for the raw materials of many European and Commonwealth countries, etc.

The usual *type of dealing* on any market will depend upon the accustomed usages of trade, but will include one of the following:

(a) Dealing by Description. A great deal of trading is undertaken by this method especially where it is not possible to show the article because of its size, etc. A description according to strict rules of the market are accepted and shown in previously printed catalogues, brochures or leaflets.

(b) Dealing by Sample. Commodities have increased in both number and variety over recent years, which has added to the difficulty of display. Sometimes it is impracticable to exhibit the goods because of their volume and therefore a sample of the consignment is displayed in the market. This is an advantage to the seller as he has fewer goods to handle, and to the buyer as he has a greater variety of choice.

The buyer is protected when purchasing in this manner in that the seller by custom agrees to the sample corresponding to the whole consignment. Selling by sample is particularly suitable for the sale of bulky commodities such as tea, rubber, wool, etc.

(c) Selling by Grade. Developed from selling by sample: where commodities can be accurately graded or classified, fewer samples are necessary, and therefore the scope of the market is widened. Raw materials in particular can be classified according to quality, and in buying from description, the buyer knows exactly what goods to expect when delivery takes place. In produce markets for example the raw material is graded by independent authorities according to agreed standards, and the quality of any commodity is known from description alone.

Grading may be undertaken by either:

(a) An association of merchants who agree to the establishing of certain grades. The Liverpool Cotton Association for example, divides the cotton into numerous grades on its arrival at Liverpool prior to its sale on the Liverpool Cotton Exchange.

(b) The State. Both the American and Canadian Governments grade the principal commodities exported from those countries. These are usually accepted by the markets and associations in Britain.

In addition to the advantages of grading given above, the following points should also be considered:

(a) Commodities can be graded irrespective of the time and place at which they are produced.

(b) Grading makes possible dealings for future delivery, since the quality can be definitely specified in any contract that is made.

(c) Banks are more willing to grant loans against the security of goods whose quality is known.

(d) Specialisation of Market. The modern market has become specialised, and is world-wide in its operations This is due to the increase in the number of commodities, and to the standardisation which grading has made possible. Improvements in communications have linked up markets which were formerly distinct from each other, and nowadays prices only differ slightly. This can mostly be accounted for by the cost of transport. These world-wide markets are operated by specialists, who make a study of the methods of dealing in one commodity or group of commodities. Examples of such markets are the London Diamond Market, the London Metal Exchange the London Money Market, etc. In addition London is the world's most important philatelic market and also the leading international centre for the sale of works of art.

2. THE GROWTH IN SIZE OF THE MARKET

Many reasons may be given for the increase in the extent of the market:

(a) Man has obtained greater control over the gifts of nature throughout the centuries: the progress of agriculture, for example, has increased the supplies of raw materials and has made possible the development of manufacture during the present century. Each country of the world, therefore has specialised in the production of that commodity for which it is best suited by natural conditions, and a world-wide system of exchange has developed.

(b) Improvements in transport have made it possible to trade over a wider area, united local markets and created national markets. The improvements have created international markets to an extent hitherto unknown. It is now possible to move bulky articles over any distance at high speed and relatively low cost.

(c) The growth of world population together with the general increase in the accepted standards of living has resulted in a greater demand for all types of commodities.

(d) Improvements in communications by the use of satellites, teleprinters, television, telephones, etc., have linked up the various markets of the world, so that the conditions of buying and selling a commodity are similar in the world market.

(e) The advance of scientific knowledge has rendered the system of grading possible. Consequently the extent of the market has become greater, since goods can be bought by description, which can be easily communicated by modern methods.

(f) Banks have developed an international system of banking and monetary exchange since the principal banks have their agents all over the world. Banks are therefore able to direct the flow of capital, and to arrange for the payment of debts between the merchants in different countries without the use of notes and coin.

3. CLASSIFICATION OF MARKETS

Markets may be classified in the following ways:

(a) **Markets for Raw Materials.** These are known as *Produce Markets*, where importers sell raw materials to wholesale dealers. Well-known examples are those for cotton, wheat, copper and rubber. Produce markets are localised in some important city, but their transactions are world-wide. Dealers usually meet on an Exchange, where the method of dealing is by sample, or by grade. The Exchange issues periodical Market Reports, which are summarised in the press and on radio, and regulates all transactions by its rules. A fuller account of the organisation of Produce Exchanges is given later in this chapter.

(b) Markets for Semi-manufactured Goods. Many raw materials go through several processes during the course of manufacture. Raw wool, for example, requires a lot of treatment before the final article is available to the consumer. Similarly paper, leather, wood, oil, etc., all require specialist attention before they are in acceptable form. Each of these require the services of specialists and middlemen to pass the commodity on to its next stage of production.

(c) Markets for Manufactured Goods. When the processes of manufacture are completed, the manufacturer may distribute the goods to the retailer himself. Alternatively he may sell them to the wholesaler, who warehouses the products of many manufacturers and distributes them to the retailers or to other wholesale dealers at home or abroad. The wholesale market extends, therefore, over a wide area. The orders received from the retailers are passed on to the manufacturers, and in this way the course of production is determined.

(d) Retail Markets. These markets are usually local in character. They exist in many forms: the most usual being the retail shops, which are classified as department stores, multiple traders, retail co-operative societies and independent retail businesses. In addition a large volume of trade is undertaken by mail order firms, mobile shops, tied and leased businesses, automatic vending machines, etc.

The retail market forms the last stage in the course of production, since it is in this market that the finished product is passed on to the consumer.

(e) Financial Markets. London is the financial centre of Britain and for a large proportion of world trade. A great deal of settlement through Documentary Credits, Bills of Exchange, etc., is arranged through the London Money Market.

Capital is also required by British industry for the production of goods for both home and foreign markets. Thus vast sums of money are necessary and London is the centre at which both lender and borrower meet.

The term 'market' in this context therefore refers to the following places and institutions which deal with finance:

(a) *The Capital Market* refers to such institutions as the Finance Houses, or the Stock Exchange, which provide a market for the raising of new capital.

(b) *The Money Market* refers to places where money is borrowed and lent: the 'price' of money is the rate of interest that borrowers pay to lenders. The chief lenders on the Money Market are the Joint Stock and Merchant Banks, and the Insurance Companies, whilst the chief borrowers are the Government, Discount Houses, Accepting Houses, Bill brokers, and members of the Stock Exchange.

(c) *The London Gold Market* is under the general supervision of the Bank of England. It is one of the world's principal centres for the sale of gold. Dealings are concentrated in the hands of a few specialist member firms who meet twice daily to fix a price for the official London quotation.

(d) *The Foreign Exchange Market* refers to authorised persons and financial institutions which deal in the buying and selling of foreign currencies. It consists of over two hundred authorised banks and firms of exchange brokers in the City of London. It is subject to the exchange control regulations of the United Kingdom which regulates the buying and selling of foreign exchange. The market is under the control of the Bank of England which allows only the authorised dealers to participate. The market itself is not located in any particular building in the City. Most of the dealings are completed on the telephone between members, and overseas centres.

Financial markets are world-wide in their extent, on account of the improvements in communications which have occurred during the last century. A fuller account of these markets is given later.

4. METHODS OF DEALING

The method of dealing between buyer and seller is determined very largely by the nature of the commodity. Those which can be graded or sold by description are dealt with on an Exchange: but those commodities which vary in quality are sold by auction, opportunity being given to wholesale buyers to inspect samples before the sale takes place. Many goods are also sold by direct dealing between buyer and seller, without resorting to the more formal methods of the Exchange or Auction Sale.

(a) Exchanges. The organisation of most Exchanges is uniform. An Exchange provides a meeting-place for members, who agree to conduct their business according to a set of rules drawn up by a Committee elected by the members. Membership of an Exchange is in many cases limited and is regarded as a valuable privilege by most traders.

An Exchange often consists of a large hall, round which are the offices of some of the members. The floor of the Exchange is the meeting-place for members, who may be dealers acting on their own account, or brokers acting for other traders. Very little formality is observed in buying and selling; when a transaction takes place, the details are jotted down in a note-book and later a *Contract Note* is made out by the clerks of the parties concerned. If any points of difference arise, a discussion between buyer and seller usually results in an agreement being reached. If no agreement is reached, the points at issue are submitted to the Arbitration Committee of the Exchange, whose decision must be accepted as a condition of membership of the exchange.

Transactions are either for immediate (spot) or future delivery. Dealings for the former are completed from existing stocks, whilst the growth of the latter is due to the system of grading, which has made it possible for buyers to state the grade of a commodity required.

(b) Auction Sales. This is the usual method of marketing goods which cannot be graded into well-defined classes; commodities such as wool, tea and tobacco vary in quality so much that they cannot be bought before inspection. Dealings on an exchange for these commodities is therefore impossible, and the auction sale has been instituted to enable prospective buyers to examine and sample the goods before making any purchases.

When a consignment arrives, it is stored in a warehouse until the auction takes place. In the meantime, it is examined by the brokers who have been instructed to conduct the sale, and from samples the brokers are able to form an opinion of the quality of the goods.

The goods are divided into lots, and the broker circulates catalogues among possible buyers, who may inspect the goods before the sale and thus form an opinion of their value and suitability.

(c) Direct Dealing. Many goods are sold by private bargaining between buyer and seller. An importer, for example, may have a large number of customers who make regular purchases from him, or he may have a reputation for expert knowledge in a particular line of goods. In such cases, the importer may dispose of his stocks by dealing direct with the purchaser, instead of selling them on an Exchange or at an Auction Sale.

Direct Dealing is also the usual method of exchange in retail markets, where the retailer comes in contact with the consumer.

5. AGENTS

Agents play an important part in the markets of the world. An agent is a person who is employed to do anything in the place of another: the person who employs him is called the principal.

The duties of an agent are:
(1) to perform the work in person;
(2) to carry out his work according to the terms of the agency;
(3) to keep his principal informed on all matters;
(4) to keep proper accounts on behalf of his principal. The majority of agencies in business are created verbally, but they may be made in writing or implied by the conduct of the parties concerned.

Types of Agents. The most important types are:

(1) **Factors.** A factor is an agent employed to sell goods which have been delivered to him by his principal; he is frequently known as a Commission Agent. The characteristics of a factor are as follows:
(*a*) He has possession of the goods which he has to sell.
(*b*) Sells in his own name.

(c) Receives payment and gives valid receipts.

(d) He may give credit to a reasonable extent.

(e) Has an insurable interest in the goods.

(f) He may pledge the goods.

(g) Can sue on contracts made by him.

(h) Has a legal claim for the balance of his charges on any of his principal's goods.

(2) Brokers. A broker is an agent employed to make bargains and contracts between other parties for a commission or brokerage. The main characteristics therefore are:

(a) He has not possession of the goods.

(b) He does not sell in his own name.

(c) Generally speaking, the broker has none of the powers of the factor; his function is to bring together two parties for the purpose of trade. He is able to do this on account of his expert knowledge of markets.

(d) A broker often acts as the agent of a foreign producer. He sees to the clearing of the goods through the customs, and makes arrangements for warehousing the goods until they are sold. He prepares samples, if necessary, for prospective buyers, and attends to all the formalities of selling the goods.

(e) A broker often buys goods on behalf of his principal: he frequently specialises in a particular line of goods, and is thus able to take advantage of the best market conditions.

(3) Commission Agent. This term is rather loosely used to indicate any agent who works on commission, but should not be confused with the Factor above.

(4) Partner. In a partnership, an ordinary partner is an agent of the other partners, and can bind them in any business transaction within the scope of the partnership.

(5) Del Credere Agents. An agent often guarantees payment in any transaction which he arranges: such an agent is known as a Del Credere Agent, and receives an additional commission for this service. He is therefore responsible for any bad debts that may arise.

6. TRADE ASSOCIATIONS

Over the past hundred years the private sectors of industry and commerce have increasingly entered into voluntary associations. The chief reasons being:

(a) to exchange information and create uniformity in methods of dealing, etc, within the framework of a particular trade.

(b) to negotiate on a broader and more national front with trade unions on rates of pay, and conditions of work.

(c) to establish a link between the government and the trade so that the members interests are protected.

The principal aims of such associations are to organise the marketing of the world's produce and to protect the interests of their members. Some of the better known ones include:

Association of British Travel Agents.

British Textile Employers Association.

Electrical and Allied Manufacturers Association.

Jute Spinners and Manufacturers Association.

Tea Brokers' Association of London.

The Motor Agents Association.

The Road Haulage Association.

The Timber Trade Federation.

Trade Associations control the trade of the commodities in which they deal by making rules which the members of the association undertake to follow as a condition of membership. The activities of each association vary according to the nature and requirements of the commodity; an association which deals with the marketing of raw material has different functions from one which organises the marketing of manufactured goods or provides a service to the public. Two common features of most associations, however, are the drawing up of a standardised form of contract, and the making of arrangements for the settlement of disputes.

A trade association which embraces a number of manufacturing firms may perform the following services for its members:

(1) It places at their disposal certain 'non-secret' information regarding the latest methods of production.

(2) It promotes research which individual members could not afford.

(3) It collects statistics which are published for members.

(4) It often introduces standard grades and products which it encourages its members to adopt.

(5) Credit references on other firms and organisations are supplied to members; this is important to exporters who desire to know such particulars regarding their foreign customers.

(6) Information is given to members regarding foreign customs, regulations, foreign legal procedure, etc.

(7) A publicity campaign may be undertaken either at home or abroad on behalf of the members of the association.

7. CHAMBERS OF COMMERCE

A Chamber of Commerce is an association of the principal business concerns of a town or area: there are over 100 Chambers of Commerce in Britain, representing more than 60,000 business firms. The Association of British Chambers of Commerce unites the British Chambers of Commerce into one organisation; the Federation of Chambers of Commerce of the British Commonwealth consists of all the principal Chambers of Commerce in the Commonwealth, whilst the International Chamber of Commerce is representative of Commerce in all the principal countries of the world.

Objects. The primary objects of a Chamber of Commerce in this country may be summarised as follows:

(1) To promote both the home and foreign trade, and in particular, the trade of the district in which the Chamber is established.

(2) To consider legislation affecting all types of trade, and to support or oppose legislative measures as necessary.

(3) To co-operate with both home and foreign Chambers of Commerce in effecting common objects.

(4) To watch the administration of Acts of Parliament by various authorities, and to organise combined action, if necessary, to prevent injury to commercial interests.

(5) To review the legislation of foreign and commonwealth countries, and to consider their Customs regulations and tariffs

in the light of British interests. When necessary, representations are made to the Department of Trade and Industry or other Government Departments.

Commercial Intelligence. Chambers of Commerce in large cities collect statistical and other information concerning the trade of particular areas, and are able to give advice to their members on such subjects as the following:

(1) Customs tariffs and exchange control regulations of every country of the world.

(2) Appointment of agents abroad.

(3) Recovery of debts in foreign and commonwealth countries.

(4) Certificates of origin.

(5) The law of Patents and Trade Marks in the United Kingdom and abroad.

(6) Confidential information from trade correspondents at home and abroad.

(7) Regulations affecting overseas travel.

(8) The Shipment of Goods.

(9) Acts of Parliament and administrative regulations concerning particular trades.

(10) Facilities for translations.

There are other functions performed by Chambers of Commerce, such as the advancement of commercial education, and the settlement by arbitration of disputes arising out of trade, commerce and manufacture. The above particulars will, however, be a sufficient indication of the scope of their operations.

8. CHAMBERS OF TRADE

Chambers of Trade are more local in character and are found in many of the smaller towns. They are composed of retailers and tradesmen of the immediate district who meet periodically to discuss any topic which affects trade, e.g. parking restrictions, organising an advertising campaign in the local press, hours of business, etc.

Shopkeepers also form associations in order to exert pressure on the local authority. A strong pressure group can exert its influence on decisions taken by District Councils etc, especially in matters directly relating to trade. These include demolition orders, compulsory purchase orders, parking restrictions, road schemes etc, all of which have an effect on business activity.

9. THE CONFEDERATION OF BRITISH INDUSTRY

The C.B.I. founded by Royal Charter in 1965 is financed by the subscriptions of its members and is a completely independent body free from political affiliation. Membership embraces over 13,000 companies engaged in industry and commerce together with numerous trade associations and employers' organisations. It has a regional organisation in Britain and has a considerable number of correspondents throughout the world.

Its objects are:

(1) To act as an advisory and consultative body to its members, the public and the Government, providing them with information and statistics on matters affecting British industry.

(2) To develop the contribution of British industry and commerce to the national economy.

(3) To encourage the efficiency and competitive power of its members.

C.B.I. representatives sit on a number of Government advisory committees, on other statutory bodies and on many voluntary committees concerned with questions affecting trade. In matters of common concern, the C.B.I. often acts jointly in this country with the Chamber of Commerce, or internationally with the Council of European Industrial Federation.

QUESTIONS

1. What do you understand by the term 'highly developed market?' Mention the chief features of such a market.   (U.L.C.I.)

2. What is the difference between a merchant, a *del credere* agent and a broker? What useful function does each of these persons serve in commerce?   (U.L.C.I.)

3. Why are some important commodities usually sold by reference to standard or grade, while others are usually sold by sample? Give *one* example of each type of commodity to illustrate your answer.   (R.S.A.)

4. What do you understand by a 'market' and by 'market

analysis'? Show how transport difficulties may limit a market. Account for the rise, in the case of some commodities, of very important international markets.   (R.S.A.)

5. Chambers of Commerce, Trade Associations and the Confederation of British Industry are all concerned with the promotion of trade. Discuss the work of any two of them.   (R.S.L.).

6. Describe the work of two wholesale produce markets or exchanges. Explain how they perform a useful function in commerce.   (London G.C.E.)

7. Describe the special features of (a) sale by sample, and (b) a tender. For what kinds of transactions is each used?

(A.E.B.)

Chapter 8

The Marketing of Commodities

I. BUSINESS RISKS

The marketing of commodities involves many risks, particularly where raw materials and foodstuffs are concerned. The dealer is interested not only with present supplies of a commodity, but he must estimate the future likely demand and supply. If a reduced supply or an increased demand is anticipated at some future date, the prices of a commodity will be affected. A manufacturer may make a contract to deliver goods in say six months, and he may want to protect himself against changes in the prices of raw materials during the period of manufacture. and quote a slightly higher (or lower) price, depending on his anticipation of the market.

Dealers in these specialised markets are highly qualified experts. They study market conditions, and their forecasts of demand and supply depend on their skill and knowledge. Dealers in certain agricultural commodities from North America are able to use the reports issued by the United States and Canadian Governments where the Departments of Agriculture collect information regarding the area of land under cultivation, weather conditions, etc., and issue monthly reports which show the prospects of the various crops. By a careful study of these and the market reports which appear in the press, the dealers are able to forecast the size of the new crop with a considerable degree of accuracy, and are able therefore to anticipate price movements.

2. SPECULATION

The term speculation has many meanings, but in Economics it is used to cover business operations undertaken in the expectation of making a profit from movements in price. Two examples of speculation in commodities are given:

(*a*) A dealer may have good reason to anticipate an excellent crop of a certain commodity. He may not possess any stocks and will therefore make contracts *to sell* for future delivery at present-day prices. If his anticipations are fulfilled, he will be able, in due course, to take advantage of the fall in price due to the size of the crop, and make his profit on the difference between the present-day and future prices. The following diagram illustrates the contract between the dealer and the manufacturer. The former sells to the latter at the higher price (dotted line) and purchases at the lower price taking the difference in the prices as his profit.

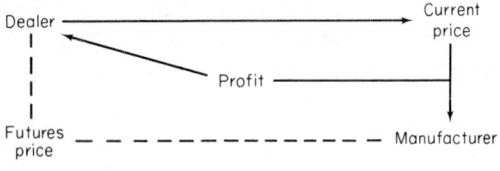

THE FUTURES MARKET

In other words suppose on *January 1st* the dealer agreed to sell *stock he has not yet got* at say £20 a tonne to a manufacturer on *July 1st*. Now suppose that on July 1st the current price on the market is £18 a tonne the dealer will purchase the required amount at this price and sell to the manufacturer at the previously agreed price thus making a profit of £2 a tonne on the whole transaction.

In addition to commodities, similar deals take place on other highly specialised markets such as the Stock Exchange and the London Money Market where they are known as *'Bear transactions.'* or conversely *'Bull transactions'* (see page 326).

From the buyer's point of view, he has been guaranteed a

certain price and has been able to make contracts based on this figure. The risks of last-minute alterations in the size of the crop, due perhaps to weather, political or other conditions, have been taken by the dealer, who may be called a 'specialist in risks'.

(b) A dealer may, however, anticipate a poor crop. In such a case, he will *buy now* at existing prices, and make his profit by *selling later* at higher prices which the reduced supply will cause (assuming that the demand remains unaltered).

From the above examples, the economic effects of speculation may be seen:

(1) Price changes are made more gradual. If a good crop is anticipated, the dealer sells for future delivery at present-day prices. The fall of prices, due to the good crop, is more gradual than it would be if the commodity were placed on the market at the time of its harvest. Similarly, the rise of prices, due to a bad crop, is spread over a longer period. Dealers begin to buy supplies now, and the increased demand causes a rise in the price. The increased price has the following effects:

(a) It checks the rate of consumption, since, on account of the higher price, the demand will be reduced. The shortage due to the poor crop will therefore not be felt so acutely, since part of the existing stocks may be carried over to the new period.

(b) The increase in price, due to the purchases of dealers, will be gradual, and thus the increase due to the poor crop will appear less than it otherwise would.

(2) Speculation relieves the manufacturer of many market risks. The speculator guarantees a certain price in the future, and thus enables the manufacturer to make contracts with the knowledge of what his raw material will cost him in perhaps six months time.

The above benefits of speculation assume that the market operator bases his forecast on expert knowledge of the commodity in which he deals. Speculation by outsiders who have not made a study of market conditions is to be condemned, since their object is not to forecast price movements, but to cause them, in the hope of making large profits.

3. THE FUTURES MARKET

Many businesses are dependent for their success on the provision of some raw material, the supply of which is variable. The woollen, rubber, sugar and chocolate industries, for example, are entirely dependent upon supplies of raw materials which vary from year to year according to the size of the harvests. The markets are in the hands of brokers who study the harvest prospects long before they are gathered in. They will make contracts for the delivery of these commodities at some future date, and base their price upon their estimate of the harvest or available stocks at the date of the completion of the contract.

The broker therefore guarantees to the buyer to provide him with a given quantity of goods in the future at a certain price, and thus relieves the buyer of the risk of market fluctuations. The chocolate manufacturer, for example, knows how much future supplies of raw material will cost him, and is therefore able to fix his selling prices and enter into contracts for the supply of his products.

Dealings. Dealings in cocoa, coffee, copra, hides and skins, etc., take place daily on the London Commodity Exchange. Here dealers spread their risks by making fresh contracts with other dealers, and therefore losses and gains are spread evenly over the market. This has all been made possible by the system of grading of raw materials that can be accurately classified into well-defined classes or grades. It is therefore possible for buyers and sellers to make contracts at what the price will be when delivery is due in say three, six, nine, twelve or even eighteen months time.

Hedging. The Futures Market is used as an insurance against risks due to changes in price. A manufacturer may accept an order to deliver a commodity at a certain price at some future date: he may not wish to buy the raw material now, and so he protects himself against a rise in price by buying futures—i.e. the seller of the futures guarantees to deliver to the buyer a certain quantity at a fixed price decided now, at a future date. The price paid represents the collective opinion of expert dealers regarding the available supply at a future date.

If the price rises beyond the price of the futures contract, the manufacturer *either* accepts delivery, *or* receives the difference between the price on the Spot Market (current price) and the price of his futures contract. In this case,

the *gain* on the futures ⎱   ⎰ the *loss* on the raw material, contract   ⎰ = ⎱ due to its rise in price.

If, however, the price has fallen, the manufacturer buys on the Spot Market and pays the difference to the dealer in futures. In such a case,

the *loss* on the futures ⎱   ⎰ the *gain* on the raw material, contract, due to not ⎰ = ⎱   due to its fall in price. accepting delivery

This method enables a manufacturer to know the price of his raw materials many months ahead. It is the dealer who buys or sells futures *without intention of accepting delivery* who bears the risk of changes in price.

Hedging takes place on numerous markets. A miller may buy wheat, but before it was marketed, the price might fall. In order to protect himself against this, he sells futures—i.e. makes a contract to sell flour at a certain price. If the price falls, the miller does not receive his anticipated return by selling at a lower price, but he is recompensed by receiving the difference on his futures contract from the dealer or speculator.

Hedging is therefore a protection against price fluctuations, and has three important results:

(1) It enables a manufacturer to quote prices for goods to be delivered some time ahead.

(2) It economises the use of capital, for by buying futures the manufacturer need not buy his raw material until a convenient time.

(3) It enables stocks of the commodity such as wool, wheat, barley, maize, coffee, etc., to be warehoused. Many such commodities are financed by banks whilst they are being stored, and in order to protect themselves against a fall in price, the banks usually insist that the commodity should be hedged.

4. THE MARKETING OF RAW MATERIALS

Britain is one of the leading manufacturing countries of the world, and it is necessary to import a large proportion of the raw materials which the industries require during the process of manufacture. This country possesses abundant supplies of most fuels, but the home supplies of raw materials are either inadequate or non-existent, and Britain is dependent upon other lands for many products. Cotton, rubber or copper ore, for example, cannot be produced or mined in Britain for climatic or geographical reasons, whilst the home supplies of wool and timber are inadequate to meet the demand. Various organisations have therefore developed to facilitate the marketing of raw materials.

(a) Cotton

Origin. The principal source of supply of raw cotton is the United States, supplying about 40 per cent of our requirements. Cotton is also imported from Turkey, Sudan, East Africa and South America.

Most of the cotton manufacturing industry in Britain is located in Lancashire, the north-east of the county concentrating on weaving whilst the south-east concentrates on spinning. Liverpool is the principal port for the import of the raw cotton, whilst Manchester is the commercial centre of the industry. Increasing foreign competition together with greater use of man-made fibres have severely curtailed the industry in recent years which has been re-organised on a more economic basis.

Uses. The demand for cotton is nevertheless world-wide: it is extensively used for clothing throughout the world, and has many other uses, including furnishing and decorative fabrics, whilst various oils and fats are obtained from the seeds.

The Liverpool Cotton Association was founded in 1882 and has about 140 members. The Association undertakes the *grading* of raw cotton by the publishing of standard rules accepted by both members and growers. Trading today is largely between one member's office and another using the telephone, telex, etc., and based on description between buyer and seller. Liverpool firms by virtue of their world-wide connections also frequently arrange for the sale of cotton between other countries. The Association has established acceptable and uniform methods of trading used throughout the world and has set up a scale of charges for services, etc.

The Arbitration Services for all growths of cotton are universal; a large number of foreign contracts are made, *'subject to Liverpool Rules'*. Thus many importers and exporters whose cotton may never reach these shores make their contracts subject to Liverpool terms and arrange to have disputes resolved by arbitration in Liverpool.

(b) Wool

Origin. The wool textile industry in Britain is the largest in the world. Of the home-produced supplies, West Yorkshire is the most important centre whilst Scotland and the west of England specialise in the production of high-quality cloth. In addition to the home supplies, wool is imported into this country from Australia, New Zealand and South Africa: coarser grades of wool, suitable for the manufacture of carpets and blankets are sent to this country from India, and the Middle East. The wool is consigned by the growers to their representatives or agents in London who, on receipt of the Invoice and the Bill of Lading, claim the consignment from the shipping company. It is then stored in wool warehouses and insured against fire until arrangements are made for its sale.

Arrangements for Sale. The product is inspected by the broker who has been entrusted with its sale. He takes a sample from each bale, and values the wool, taking into consideration the quality, the closing prices at the last sale, and the prospects at the forthcoming sale.

The broker issues a catalogue, which is sent to prospective buyers stating the name of the ship in which the wool has been brought to this country, the address of the warehouse where the wool is on view, the type of wool, the number of bales in each lot, and the identification marks and numbers of the bales. Buying brokers visit the warehouse to inspect the consignment in order to ascertain the quality and estimate a price.

The London Wool Exchange. Is the chief European centre for the sale of imported wool. In the early part of the nineteenth century, wool sales took place in London Coffee-Houses, but now take place in a separate building in the City of London. Wool is *sold by auction*, as grading is impossible on account of the fact that it is an animal product, and therefore the wool from the same country varies from year to year. On the London Wool Exchange, auctions take place six times per year, each auction lasting about three weeks, buyers coming from the wool-manufacturing districts of Britain and the Continent. The prices are on the basis of pence to the kilo, and the prevailing rates are cabled to all parts of the world.

In addition to the auction sales of fine wool, as described above, there are four or five auction sales per year of the coarser variety. As much of this is brought in whole fleeces and arrives at irregular intervals, the dates of the sales of coarse wool depend on the number of fleeces available.

Some wool is sold by private treaty: the manufacturer informs the broker of his requirements, and a price is agreed upon between the two of them. A manufacturer usually employs the same broker in making his purchases, and as a result the broker knows the requirements of his regular customers. Dealings in futures are also undertaken on the Exchange, allowing the manufacturer to know the buying price of his raw material up to eighteen months in advance.

(c) *Jute*

Origin. Jute is a vegetable fibre that is grown under conditions of a moist hot climate. About 90 per cent of the total world supply is grown in Bangladesh and Northern India with Brazil, Burma and Nepal making up the rest. Unlike cotton, rubber or tea it is not grown in large plantations, but by over a million farmers known as 'ryots' who farm the product with other products on their small farms. At harvest-time the stems are cut and after processing the farmers sell the raw fibre to dealers who visit the numerous villages. Eventually all the fibre is collected, baled and later transported to the mills for further processing.

Uses. Dundee and district in Scotland is the centre for the

British jute industry. It was established there for a variety of reasons, the chief one being that the city had for many years been concerned with the making of coarse materials before the importing of jute from India in the early nineteenth century.

Except for cotton, more jute is used in the world than any other textile fibre. The product has a wide variety of uses, including the making of sacks as well as forming the base for the carpet, linoleum, shoe, and furniture industries.

(d) Metals

London is an important market for metals of all kinds. The market for the raw material may be divided into two parts, which are closely connected.

(a) The London Metal Exchange, founded in 1881 as a place where dealers from this country and abroad could meet to transact business. It is the premier metal market in the world in so far as the price quotations for each metal dealt in are regarded as being authoritative. Membership is by election through an elected committee after furnishing evidence of financial stability.

Stocks of imported metals are stored in the warehouses of the Port of London Authority and at other ports in Britain, Europe and elsewhere. The Exchange issues official contracts for each metal, and publishes official lists of buying and selling prices for both spot and future dealings.

Dealings take place in copper, lead, tin and zinc—i.e. the non-ferrous metals together with silver. Business is conducted by private negotiation between members, and five-minute periods are devoted to each metal in both the morning and afternoon markets. A considerable amount of speculative business is carried out in the market for approved metals which have been registered with the committee. These include Copper Wire bars, Copper Cathodes, Tin of certain purity and weight, etc. A manufacturer, for example, may contract to deliver a large quantity of tin plate at a certain date in the future: he therefore instructs a broker to buy for him, say, Standard Tin for forward delivery and so covers himself by obtaining raw material at the price he may quote in the contract.

In addition, dealings for large amounts of metals for *bulk*

The British Steel Corporation works at Port Talbot.

delivery are undertaken in dealers' offices outside but within the jurisdiction of the Exchange.

(b) The British Steel Corporation. The steel industry has for many years been subject to some form of public supervision. The Iron and Steel Act 1967 brought many of the steel-producing companies under public ownership, controlled by the British Steel Corporation. The main producing districts are South Wales (sheet steel and tinplate), the North East and Scotland (heavy steels), Sheffield (special alloy and high grade steel), Lincolnshire, Lancashire and Flintshire. Supplies of raw materials are obtained from foreign markets including Norway and Spain, using special purpose built ore-carrying vessels owned by the Corporation in addition to supplies quarried in this country.

The Corporation's duties are to promote the efficient and economic supply of iron and steel products throughout Britain, to assist in the expansion of exports and research and development necessary for the future of the industry. In addition the Corporation is responsible to Parliament for its finances in the same way as other nationalised industries.

Many other examples could be given of the way in which raw materials are marketed: Britain has to import large quantities of chemicals, timber, rubber and metal ores, etc., so that specialist markets or trade organisations have been developed over many years in London and elsewhere that are renowned throughout the world for fair dealing and whose rules are often accepted as basis for contracts between buyer and seller.

5. THE MARKETING OF FOODSTUFFS

Today Britain imports about half of the food required to feed her population of 56 million people whereas at the beginning of the nineteenth century, when her population was about 12 millions, this country was almost self-sufficing.

The advent of the industrial revolution and the increased use of machinery enabled Britain to *specialise* at an early stage in the production of manufactured articles. This has continued to the present day in very much larger quantities and these are exchanged for the products of many lands. Improvements in transport, refrigeration and marketing enable Britain to import products which because of climatic conditions cannot be grown in this country.

The following examples show how foodstuffs are marketed on their arrival in Britain.

(a) Wheat

Origin. A large wheat market is essential to Britain in order to feed her population. The product is imported chiefly from the United States, Canada, and Australia and is used to supplement the British harvest. As the product does not deteriorate quickly it can be stored until required in the large warehouses to be seen at the principal ports in this country and abroad.

Expert dealers forecast the crop year by year, taking into consideration the area under cultivation, the weather conditions and reports concerning injury to the crop by insects. The leading London firms have their agents abroad in the great producing countries, who buy from the growers and tranship the wheat to London, Liverpool or to some continental port.

Grading. Like most other agricultural products, wheat can be classified into well-defined grades. The wheat from North America, for example, is graded by the United States and Canadian Governments whilst Australian wheat is graded by the Australian Government; the grades frequently indicate the province where the product has been grown such as Canadian Manitoba No. 1, or alternatively a grade such as U.S. Red Winter No. 2 or Australian Prime Hard, etc. The dealers in, say, London have no need to inspect the product beforehand and may rely on the description in order to assess a price for both spot (present) and future shipments. Wheat from other countries is graded by Corn Trade Associations which exist at London, Liverpool and other ports where cargoes arrive, whilst home-grown wheat is sold by sample on the London or Liverpool Corn Exchanges. Disputes regarding quality, etc., are settled later by the Corn Trade Association to which all dealers belong.

Marketing. Supplies of wheat are sold on two important Exchanges in London:

(1) *The Baltic Mercantile and Shipping Exchange,* which is the principal European market for grain. This exchange also deals in the chartering of ships and aircraft as well as cargo space in them. In addition dealings in grain, vegetable oils (coconut, sunflower, soyabean, etc.) and seeds of all kinds take place. Its members consist of shipowners, shipbrokers, shipping agents, grain dealers, merchants and brokers, totalling about 2,500 members in all.

The importers sell their wheat on the Exchange to the grain dealers in large quantities and the former then sell in smaller quantities to dealers on the London Corn Exchange in Mark Lane. No samples are allowed on the floor of the Baltic Exchange as all dealings are of imported grains sold by description: transactions are based on documents—bills of lading, warehouse warrants, dock warrants, etc., whilst dealings in futures is a regular feature of the market particularly in wheat and maize.

(2) *The London Corn Exchange.* This exchange is in Mark Lane near the Baltic Exchange, and brokers are usually members of both exchanges. In addition to selling foreign wheat, bought on the Baltic in smaller quantities, the supplies of home-grown wheat are sold by sample on the Corn Exchange. Here, firms from every part of Britain are represented and dealers sell the wheat purchased to millers, who convert it into flour and sell to bakers.

London Corn Trade Association. This Association consists of members of the leading businesses connected with the grain trade, together with members from all countries from which Britain imports grain.

The work of the Association is:

(1) the standardisation of all contracts for the sale of grain. The contracts of this Association are recognised all over the world.

(2) arbitration on all disputes regarding quality.

(3) it lays down conditions concerning the sampling of grain. Samples are taken from each shipment, and delivered to the Association to be available in disputes regarding quality.

The members of the Corn Exchange study the present and prospective supplies of all countries which export grain, and are able to forecast price movements with their expert knowledge. Dealings in futures are an important aspect of the market which is advantageous to the miller. He is able to make contracts for the sale of flour based on a price he has negotiated say three months previously.

(b) Tea

Origin. Tea was introduced into this country by the Dutch in 1650, but the first importation on any large commercial scale did not begin until 1669 by the East India Company.

The most important tea-growing countries in the world in order of yearly output are India, Sri Lanka, China (who consume most of the tea they grow), Japan and East Africa.

Britain imports large quantities of the product principally from Sri Lanka and East Africa.

Arrangements for Sale. On arrival at the warehouse, the tea chests are weighed and stacked in groups of the same grade from the same estate. The broker is permitted to inspect the product at any time and to take samples from each chest. Tea cannot be graded accurately, but names are given to the differing types which signify the areas of origin—Pekoe, Darjeeling, etc.—the value of a quantity of tea is a question of individual judgment.

The broker prepares a catalogue of the chests of tea which are to be sold, and circulates it with samples amongst prospective buyers both at home and overseas, who are given an opportunity of tasting the product before making any purchases.

Tea vividly illustrates the extent of the *entrepôt trade* passing through London for Western Europe. The cargo is transported in bulk from the growing areas of the world to London where it is stored in warehouses and later auctioned on the London Commodity Exchange. In addition to providing the supplies necessary for home consumption, London is an important centre for the whole of Western Europe. Supplies are purchased by foreign buyers and the product is distributed in smaller quantities to the European outlets.

The London Commodity Exchange in Mincing Lane, provides a market for many products—tea, coffee cocoa, sugar, vegetable oils, spices, etc. The Tea Brokers' Association hires the largest sales room, and tea is sold by auction every week of the year.

The auction is attended by two sets of brokers—those who represent the estate owners wishing to sell the product and those who represent the tea merchants wanting to buy.

The selling brokers draw lots each week for the order in which they will sell. Bids are called from the floor of the Exchange and as much as 300,000 kilogrammes of tea can be sold in an hour. The price of course varies according to the time of the year as well as the demand for and supply of a particular grade.

Terms of Sale. The selling broker retains the Warehouse

Warrant until the buyer pays the amount due: a maximum of three months' credit is allowed, after which period the broker can sell the tea again. When he receives the payment for the tea purchased, he remits the proceeds, less commission, to the grower.

The buyer of the tea receives the Warehouse Warrant when he settles his account. This is a document of title, enabling him to remove the tea from the warehouses. The product is then prepared for sale by blending and packing. It is later distributed to the numerous retail outlets throughout Britain and the Continent.

(c) Sugar

Origin. The refined product was first introduced into this country by the merchants of Venice during the fifteenth century. It was then a luxury product and it is recorded that one shipload arriving in London was valued at one million pounds sterling. The commodity was often referred to in those days as 'white gold.'

Marketing. British commercial interests in the product came later with the development of the Commonwealth. Large estates for the production of raw cane sugar were established in the West Indies and other parts of the world, including Australia, Fiji, Mauritius, Nigeria and East Africa. Today Britain imports large amounts of the product from these areas which is refined for both home consumption and export. The largest refineries in the country are owned by the Tate and Lyle group of companies at London, Liverpool, Greenock and elsewhere.

Sugar beet is also an important source of supply, which, after processing, accounts for about one third of total home requirements. The crop is grown principally in East Anglia and Lincolnshire where most of the sugar beet refineries are situated. The *British Sugar Corporation* makes contracts each year with the growers, to purchase the whole of the sugar beet crop: the price paid is guaranteed beforehand and is largely dependent upon the crop's sugar content, after which the product is refined for domestic, commercial or agricultural use.

The Sugar Board. Because of the relatively small size of world production, coupled with an increasing world demand, shortages and surpluses are heavily reflected in price changes with each new crop. In order to overcome wide variations in price, the government established the Sugar Board in 1957. Its aim is to act only as an accounting agency to smooth out the fluctuations in prices charged to the refineries thus ensuring a steady price charged to the consumer.

The London Sugar Market. London is the centre of the world sugar market where daily spot and future sales are held. Prices are quoted in £ per tonne c.i.f. and attract dealers from this country and abroad. Manufacturers and dealers make agreements with the sugar brokers for present delivery or forward delivery up to eighteen months hence at guaranteed prices. Manufacturers therefore are assured of a steady supply of raw material and are able to quote firm prices to their customers.

(d) Perishables

Markets for the sale of perishable goods exist in every large town, and are visited by retailers regularly in order to obtain fresh supplies. Separate markets are usually found for meat, fish and agricultural produce: three well-known examples of London markets are:

(1) **Covent Garden Market,** situated at Nine Elms in south London from 1973, specialises in fruit, vegetables and flowers. In this market, supplies totalling well over 1 million tonnes, from Britain and overseas are bought and sold each year. Home-grown supplies of fruit, flowers and vegetables arrive daily: supplies from overseas arrive at regular intervals and the increased use of cold storage, both at home and abroad as well as during transport, has made it possible to market most fruits all the year round.

The busiest period of the day is early in the morning, when retailers arrive to make their purchases and to take the goods away with them in their own transport. Wholesale merchants and commission salesmen also make large purchases, and distribute the products to all parts of Britain.

(2) **Smithfield Market** is one of the oldest markets in

London and is owned by the Corporation of London. It is managed by a committee made up by members of both the Corporation and market traders. They are responsible for the day to day management together with the safeguarding of trade interests, cleanliness, etc. The turnover of the market amounts to approximately 400,000 tonnes per annum, supplying London, the Midlands, and the South with meat and poultry. The market is never closed for the arrival of supplies, which come from both home and abroad.

Farmers abroad sell their cattle to firms which slaughter the animals, and freeze or chill the meat. The carcasses are sent to this country, and on arrival sent to Smithfield Market. Supplies often arrive during the night in order to catch the market when it is busiest in the early morning in order to obtain the best price.

In addition to home produce, the market receives regular supplies of meat and poultry from such countries as Eire, Denmark, Holland, New Zealand and the Argentine. The produce is stored in large refrigerated warehouses until required ensuring a steady supply to the consumer.

(3) Billingsgate Market. The principal wholesale distributing centre for fish in Britain is Billingsgate Market in London which handles over 300 tonnes a day.

The method of distribution is usually through wholesalers located at the ports such as Hull, Grimsby, Fleetwood, Aberdeen, etc., where daily fish auctions are held. The product is then distributed to Billingsgate and other markets throughout Britain. In addition, large amounts are purchased by private firms catering for the quick-frozen ready-packed market through numerous retail outlets.

Speedy marketing is necessary because of the perishable nature of the product. In addition to road transport, special fish trains are run to enable the fish to be in London and other centres ready for sale early in the morning.

The stall-holders obtain their supplies in one of three ways:
(a) they are forwarded to the market by a merchant on the coast to be sold on commission.
(b) they are ordered by themselves from merchants at the ports.

(c) representatives of the stall-holders buy the fish at the ports and send it to London.

The stall-holders display samples on their stalls, and as retailers make their purchases, they receive tickets which authorise porters to transfer the fish required from the stall-holders' lorries to the vans of the retailers.

6. MARKETING BOARDS

Most home-grown agricultural products are marketed through private channels such as producers co-operative organisations, livestock auctions or corn merchants. Large amounts are also sold by contract farming methods whereby farmers and growers sell their fruit and vegetable crops under contract direct to the freezing and processing industries.

For certain commodities, however, Marketing Boards have been set up under government control to safeguard the interests of both the producers and the consumers. These fall into two broad categories:

(a) those which have the powers to act as the selling agency for the product as a whole throughout the country, or alternatively control the contracts entered into between producer and first buyer.

(b) those which maintain a control over marketing conditions, leaving producers free to dispose of their produce.

Before a Board is established, therefore, a scheme of marketing is agreed upon with the producers which will form the basis for all future dealings with the consumer.

A marketing scheme is a form of statutory co-operation which comes into existence only if desired by *a majority of the producers* who will be affected by it, but once in existence, it is binding on *all of them*. A marketing scheme may be applied to any agricultural or horticultural product, any article of food or drink, fleeces or animal skins.

The Marketing Boards are producers' organisations with powers to regulate the marketing of products in which they have an interest. Producers are able to promote schemes with the board for particular commodities conferring wide powers on them. The Boards have power to buy and sell the whole of the home-produced commodity, and to prescribe terms of sale, as well as the quantities and description of the product that might be sold by its registered producers.

Apart from certain specified exemptions, it is compulsory for all producers wishing to sell a commodity covered by a marketing scheme to register with the Marketing Board concerned and to abide by its directions and regulations. As a safeguard, however, these schemes must be approved by Parliament in order to protect not only the producers but the consumers and the public in general.

Marketing schemes are in operation for Milk, Potatoes, British Wool and Hops. The Ministry of Agriculture, Fisheries and Food is generally responsible for the first three schemes operated through producers' marketing boards.

Marketing Schemes. Synopses of the Milk, Potato, Wool and Hop schemes are as follows:

(a) *Milk Marketing Scheme.* The Milk Marketing Board has full trading rights. All milk produced on a wholesale basis must be sold to the Board, and retail sales by producers are subject to Board licence. The Board arranges for the collection of milk from farms, and is responsible for finding a market for it. The Board fixes *maximum* retail prices for milk sold for liquid consumption: it also fixes the prices of milk for manufacture after consultation with the buyers.

(b) *Potato Marketing Scheme.* The Potato Marketing Board has powers to buy, but not to be the sole buyer. It has extensive powers, and prescribes the description and terms of sale for potatoes sold by producers for human consumption, and licenses merchants to whom alone sales may be made. The Board may also prescribe *minimum* prices.

(c) *British Wool Marketing Board.* This Board has full trading powers and is the sole buyer of home-produced fleece wool. It employs agents to collect, grade, and value the product in accordance with the *maximum* prices published by the Board in advance of each season. The wool is sold by auction by the Board in competition with imported wool.

(d) *Hops Marketing Scheme*. The Hops Marketing Board has full trading powers and is the sole buyer of home-produced hops. It regulates supplies by means of a quota system by which each producer is allotted annually a share of the estimated total market demand.

7. LOCAL RETAIL MARKETS

The right of holding a market is the oldest form of municipal enterprise, and two-thirds of the boroughs of England and Wales possess this right, which was granted by the charter of the town, or by a separate grant from the Crown. Markets are usually held weekly at some convenient place for transport: in many parts of the country, they are held at the county town,

A local Provision Market, Norwich (Norfolk)

but where the county is populous, several market towns exist in the same county.

The market is under the control of the local authority, which charges a rent for the stalls that it provides. In many cases, a Market Hall is provided also, and traders find it profitable to rent a stall for the whole week inside the hall. On market days, farmers from the surrounding countryside bring to the market agricultural and dairy produce which they sell direct to the consumer. Many local shopkeepers display their goods in the market on market days, and itinerant traders travel from market to market, visiting a different town every working day of the week.

In these local markets, all transactions are retail and for cash. Prices are usually lower than at retail shops, since the buyer is dealing, in many cases, with the producer of the goods, and the rent of a stall is less than that of a retail shop. The seller of goods makes his profit by virtue of a large turnover. Statutory powers are given to the local authority to control cleanliness, etc., and in addition the councils are required to enforce the established grading and labelling of both fresh home-grown and imported supplies. These powers relate specifically to apples, pears, tomatoes, cucumbers and cauliflowers.

QUESTIONS

1. Describe the organisation of a produce exchange as a market, making special reference to the classes of dealers engaged, and the methods by which the business is transacted in the market.
(U.L.C.I.)

2. Write down three imported foodstuffs or raw materials which are usually sold by auction when they reach this country. Trace the subsequent course of one of them on its way to the ultimate consumer.
(R.S.A.)

3. What is meant by dealing in 'Futures'? Briefly describe the method of dealing and show how it benefits the marketing of certain commodities.

4. Consider, in some detail, the work of trade associations in the grading of qualities and the standardising of contract forms in the import trade in raw materials and foodstuffs.
(R.S.A.)

5. Compare the marketing of imported raw materials and foodstuffs in Britain with the marketing of home-manufactured consumers' goods.
(London G.C.E).

6. (*a*) Briefly describe a local retail market.

(*b*) It is sometimes said that since local retail markets compete with shopkeepers, such markets should be abolished. What is your opinion on this?   (Cambridge G.C.E.)

7. What is the Milk Marketing Board? Why was it established and how does it affect your family and yourself?

(Cambridge G.C.E.)

8. 'By means of "futures" a manufacturer may protect himself against losses caused by fluctuations in the price of the commodity in which he is dealing.' Explain the meaning of the quotation and state in which commodities future contracts are commonly made.

(R.S.A.)

9. Few people would buy a car merely on description yet most manufacturers buy a high proportion of their raw materials almost entirely by description. How has this become possible? Give examples.   (R.S.A.)

Chapter 9

The Marketing of Manufactured Goods

I. COSTING

When businesses were on a small scale, cost accounts were relatively simple, and the cost of production could be ascertained with sufficient accuracy by rule-of-thumb methods. But with the growth of large-scale production, more exact methods of costing have become necessary. A good system shows how much the manufacturer's products cost to produce, and enable the manufacturer to fix prices and make estimates for future deliveries. Profits therefore depend to a large extent on the accuracy of the costing; during recent years, this has become a specialised study which aims at reducing the cost of production by eliminating wasteful methods.

Costs may be analysed into the following categories:

(a) Manufacturing Costs that may be further divided as the diagram shows:

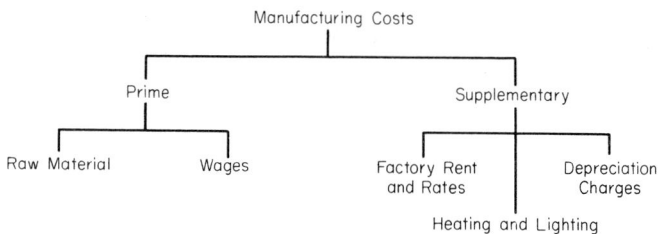

The distinction between the prime and supplementary costs is important in assessing the factory cost of production:

(1) *Prime Costs* consist of the materials used in the manufacture of an article, together with the wages of labour. Accurate records are kept of the purchase of raw materials, stock, and charges that make up the cost of materials used in the production of any article.

(2) *Supplementary Costs* consist of the expenses that are necessary in running a factory: they include such items as factory rent, rates and taxes, heating and lighting, depreciation, etc. These expenses are spread over the total output during a given period, therefore the greater the output, the less is the supplementary cost for each article. These costs vary little whether the factory is on full time or short time, whereas the prime costs stop when the factory ceases production. No exact figures are available for the allocation of supplementary costs to each unit of production and a percentage is usually added to the prime costs of the various categories of unit produced. The percentage is found by experience, and varies with the output, and from firm to firm.

(b) Selling Costs. When the goods are ready to leave the factory, the manufacturer may dispose of them in several ways: he may establish his own selling department, and deal direct with the consumer, or he may sell to the wholesaler or to the retailer. He must therefore add the costs of distribution to the manufacturing costs; these vary with the method of selling the goods, and may include such items as representatives and salesmen's commissions, transport charges, and advertising.

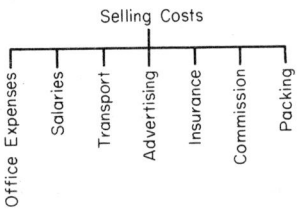

Selling Costs — Office Expenses, Salaries, Transport, Advertising, Insurance, Commission, Packing

Over a long period, the manufacturer must receive the total cost of production, together with the normal rate of profit to reward him for his enterprise. In the short run, however, he may sell below the total cost of production. In times of depressed trade, for example, when prices are low, the manufacturer may produce sufficient to cover the prime costs rather than discharge men and allow the machinery to depreciate. The prime cost therefore represents the minimum level of prices at which the manufacturer can sell his products. It must be remembered, however, that the supplementary costs continue irrespective of the amount of the output.

2. MANUFACTURER AND WHOLESALER

The usual channel of distribution for manufactured goods is through the wholesaler who organises the market. He performs the following services for the manufacturer:

(a) He buys in large quantities allowing the manufacturer to reap the advantages of large-scale production.

(b) The wholesaler collects orders from retailers, and passes them on in bulk to the manufacturer, who is thus saved the expense of dealing with small orders.

(c) The wholesaler enables the manufacturer to run his business on a smaller amount of capital than would be possible if the manufacturer undertook the distribution of his own products. The manufacturer does not carry large stocks. The wholesaler receives only a short period of credit from the manufacturer, and consequently the capital of the manufacturer is released for further production.

(d) The orders of the wholesaler determine to a large extent the course of production: he is in touch with the market, and his orders show the manufacturer the changes in demand.

(e) The wholesaler sometimes undertakes the responsibility for the finishing processes. He buys semi-manufactured goods from the manufacturer and undertakes the later processes, such as the bleaching, dyeing or finishing of textile materials. Alternatively as in the case of tea he may blend and packet the products of various sources in order to produce a grade required by the retailer and ultimately the consumer.

The wholesaler in most cases is essential to both manufacturer and the retailer. He undertakes the risks of the market which traders are unwilling to bear. Large retail stores are, however, strong enough financially to bear these risks and therefore often dispense with the services of the wholesaler.

Generally the pattern of trade is as the following diagram illustrates:

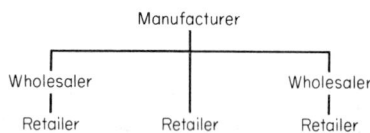

3. MANUFACTURER AND RETAILER

The manufacturer may deal direct with the retailer where the turnover is slow, as in the case of furniture, electric cookers, television sets, etc.: in addition, there is a growing tendency to deal direct with the retailer in the grocery trade, where there is a regular demand for prepared foods, which have been popularised by successful advertising.

In order to deal direct with the retailer, the manufacturer must establish a Selling Department, which does the work of the wholesaler: the profits due to the elimination of the wholesaler are taken by the manufacturer or passed on in part to the retailer and the consumer.

The manufacturer may approach the retailer by several methods:

(a) **Representatives** who are employed in given areas covering the sales territory is the usual method of keeping in touch with the retailers. They call on retailers to obtain orders, and at the same time keep the manufacturer informed of the state of the market. The representative seeks to extend the market by obtaining orders from new customers, and by developing districts where the demand is small. They are usually paid a fixed salary, and receive a commission on sales.

(b) **Agents** may act for the manufacturer and dispose of the whole of his output. Alternatively, the manufacturer may appoint retail agents in each district with the sole right of selling his products. They are frequently employed where the demand is not large enough to justify the wholesaler stocking the goods, as in the case of motor vehicles, electrical goods, etc. By the employment of agents, the manufacturer is able to control sales without establishing a separate selling department: but on the other hand, agents are difficult to control, since they may through carelessness give the product a bad name, or their energy may be determined by the rate of commission.

(c) **Selling Agency.** A separate company may be formed to take over the selling activities of a manufacturing firm or a group of firms. The Selling Agency may, subject to the Resale Price Maintenance Act, fix the price of goods to the retailer who has no fear of others under-selling him and the price to the consumer is stable.

(d) **Advertisements.** Large sums of money are frequently spent by manufacturers in order to create a demand for their goods. By constantly displaying the name of a line of goods, a demand is created for them: the demand produces orders from consumers and therefore compels retailers to buy from the wholesaler or manufacturer. The retailer benefits from the publicity campaign organised by the manufacturer, since more customers visit his shop to ask for the goods which they have seen advertised.

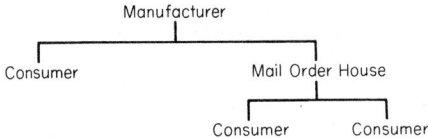

4. MANUFACTURER AND CONSUMER

The manufacturer occasionally may sell direct to the consumer in order to retain for himself the profits usually made by the wholesaler and the retailer: he may, of course, pass on part of the profit to the consumer by means of a reduction in price in order to stimulate demand.

Direct Sales by the manufacturer to the consumer have many advantages:

(a) when the volume of trade justifies it, the manufacturer may establish a selling department of his own, and thus increase his profit.

(b) time is saved in the distribution of perishable goods.

(c) the producer comes in direct contact with the consumer, and so is able to deal with complaints promptly.

(d) the manufacturer can follow changes in demand, and is able to adapt his products to meet the changes.

(e) where the manufacturer makes a varied range of goods, he meets the demand of a wider circle of customers. He is therefore more likely to benefit from direct selling than a manufacturer who produces only one line of goods.

(f) products such as computers, etc., requiring technical knowledge on the part of salesmen are particularly suitable for direct selling, since the merits of an article can be explained by experts; in addition, an after-sales service is frequently provided.

On the other hand, direct selling is not profitable in seasonal goods, since the sales organisation will be idle in slack periods unless another line of goods can be introduced.

Branded Goods. These are sold under a distinctive trademark or trade name which has been registered by the manufacturer. They are usually made up in packets, which are easily recognised from their distinctive appearance and which guarantee uniformity of weight and size. They are widely advertised in order to familiarise the public with their appearance and to maintain or increase demand.

Branded goods have the following advantages:

(a) no other manufacturer can use his trade name, and the extent of his sales depends upon how far he can convince prospective buyers that his brand of goods is the best. Examples that readily spring to mind include Heinz Beans, Fairy Snow, Beechams Powders, Chanel, etc.

(b) maximum recommended prices of branded goods can be fixed by the manufacturer. The retailer however is often able to sell the product more cheaply than the recommended price, especially if his turnover (sales) are large.

(c) the branding of goods is usually a guarantee of quality and demand will decline if it is not maintained. As the consumer knows the source of supply, a fall in quality of one product may seriously affect sales of other products supplied by that manufacturer.

(d) The manufacturer is anxious to promote a good image to the consumer and is usually willing to replace faulty goods.

(e) successful advertising reduces the cost of selling since the supplementary costs are spread over a larger number of articles. The retailer orders without inspection in response to the increased demand, and has less trouble in buying his stock, since the goods are made up in standard sizes and qualities.

Methods of distribution. When the manufacturer deals direct with the consumer, he may distribute his products in several ways:

(a) *Direct Orders.* Some goods are not made in standardised sizes, and therefore special orders must be sent by the consumer direct to the makers. A spare part, for example, may be required for a machine, or some replacement may be necessary for an article of domestic use. Where an article or part of an article has to be *specially* made, the consumer usually deals direct with the manufacturer.

Direct orders are received by the manufacturer for articles which are expensive and only in occasional demand. He sometimes has showrooms in large centres of population where displays include such articles as accounting machines, furniture, etc. There are in addition numerous articles in everyday use such as bricks, gas, water, etc. which the consumer accepts direct from the manufacturer.

(b) *Mail Order Business.* This form of dealing direct with the consumer is an extension of the method described above: by using the facilities provided by the Post Office, the manufacturer can deal with direct orders from consumers in different parts of the country. Large sums of money are spent in advertising the products of the manufacturer, and catalogues are issued to show the range of the goods. Sales have increased over recent years as this has become a popular method of trading in the comfort of the home. To save the manufacturer expense he often appoints local agents (perhaps a housewife) who collect the orders of a district and also the money on a commission basis. Costs can be cut by the manufacturer sending one order to the agent who will distribute the goods in that area.

Many household articles are sold by this method as well as gardening equipment, sports accessories, watches, clothing and electrical goods: for more expensive items, manufacturers frequently adopt the hire-purchase or deferred terms system of payment, and this also can be incorporated in the framework of the mail order business, the instalments being collected and banked by the agent.

(c) *Retail Shops*. Where the demand is regular and extensive, manufacturers frequently open their own shops in different parts of the country and sell the products of their factory. This method of distribution is characteristic of the shoe industry, and of men's clothing. Where this method of distribution is adopted, the demand should not be seasonal, for the shops have to be maintained all the year round. The goods must have a wide range, and where different types exist, as in the case of shoes, the factory must be able to turn out a variety of styles, colours and sizes. In addition to advertising, the manufacturer frequently adopts a trade name by which his goods can be instantly recognised by the consumer.

QUESTIONS

1. How far is it possible for the home manufacturer to eliminate the middleman in the distribution and sale of his product?
(R.S.A.)

2. Enumerate the constituents of (a) prime cost, (b) factory cost, (c) final cost in the case of manufactured articles. (R.S.A.)

3. Assuming that you are a manufacturer exporting your own manufactured products, explain clearly the arrangements that you could make for (a) securing payment from your customer, (b) obtaining advances on your shipments. (R.S.A.)

4. Enumerate the conditions which encourage manufacturers to sell direct (a) to the retailer, (b) to the consumer. (R.S.A.)

5. (a) '*Self service* became possible only after *packaging* and *branding* had become common.' Explain the meaning of the terms

in italics and indicate how far you think the statement as a whole is true.

(*b*) Indicate what you consider to be **three** main advantages of self-service shops. (Cambridge G.C.E.)

6. **Either** (*a*) Suppose you are a wholesale merchant. You find you are losing business as some of your customers tend to buy direct from manufacturers. What might you do to stem this tendency?

Or (*b*) Suppose you are a prosperous retailer. To expand the business you need more capital. How might you obtain it?
(Cambridge G.C.E.)

7. What is a mail-order business? Describe its methods of (*a*) contacting customers, (*b*) delivering goods and accepting payment. Give reasons for the recent growth in this form of retailing.
(A.E.B.)

8. Do you consider the modern tendency of manufacturers selling their products direct to the public to be as effective as the older methods of distribution? Give reasons for your views.
(R.S.A.)

9. Manufacturers use different channels of distribution for their products. Discuss the chief methods used nowadays. (R.S.A.)

10. What services can a wholesale organisation render to small retail grocers? What steps can wholesale organisations take to meet the risk that they will be by-passed by large-scale retail firms which deal direct with producers, or by manufacturers who deal direct with retailers? (Oxford G.C.E.)

Chapter 10

The Retail Trade

Retail business in Britain for purpose of comparison of the number of establishments and total amount of yearly sales is classified by the Department of Trade and Industry under the following headings.

  (a) *Independent retail businesses* which includes the small multiple stores with few branches.
  (b) *Multiple stores* other than the retail co-operative societies and those included above.
  (c) *Retail co-operative societies.*
  (d) *Department Stores.*

There are in addition other retail outlets including Electricity and Gas showrooms together with the Mail Order business houses which add to the main groups in retailing to make up the Census of Retail Distribution conducted periodically by the Department.

The retail trade provides a service that accounts for a high proportion of *consumer* expenditure in Britain that at current prices amounts to over £40,000 million per annum. This covers a wide range of goods and services including food, drink and tobacco, housing, clothing, durable goods, running costs of private vehicles, etc. Consumers purchase these out of their net current income, or from savings, or by borrowing. The Department of Employment traces the trends of consumers' expenditure each year, presenting tables and graphs that show the changes in pattern of spending which are important for the planning of future investment in both the public and private sectors. Taking an extreme example we see that the expenditure today on coal and coke is considerably less than say twenty years ago whilst expenditure on cars, electricity and gas is considerably more. Using 1963 as a base year and adjusting all prices to 1963 equivalents, the Department publishes the following table:

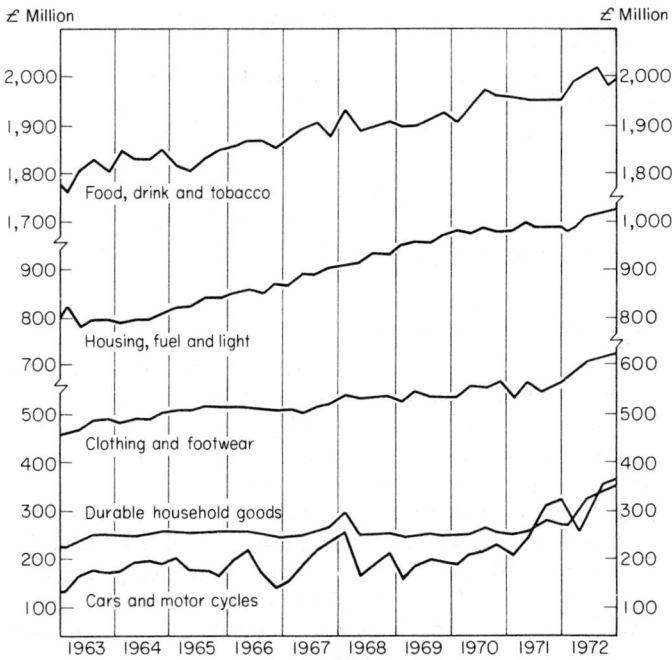

Trend of consumer expenditure in Britain.

The following are the principal retail outlets through which most of the expenditure is directed:

I. INDEPENDENT RETAILERS

The majority of retail establishments are privately owned (private company, partnership or sole trader) although over recent years their numbers and share of total trade has been declining. The small independent shopkeeper in particular finds increasing competition from the larger retail units in the field of prices, type of goods sold and use of specialised staff to perform different functions.

The factors which have helped to keep the small shops in existence include:

(*a*) their attention to detail in relation to the personal service given to the customer.

(*b*) their willingness to extend credit facilities with little formality to the consumer for short periods.

(*c*) their ability to provide a livelihood to a family who help in the shop at busy times and who often have other sources of income such as wages or pension.

(*d*) the 'corner shop' in a residential district which is open for long hours and stocks a wide variety of requirements for the local community.

2. MULTIPLE STORES

The term 'multiple store' is applied to that form of retail organisation which has a number of branches within the same town or country. Often the establishments are easily recognised by shoppers as they have a standardised form of shop front or display material. There are two types:

(*a*) *Single trade shops*, dealing in one group of articles and found in most large towns. Examples of multiple shops specialising in one trade include W. H. Smith and Son, J. Lyons & Co., Curry's, Boots Chemists, and most of the shoe shops.

(*b*) *Self-service Shops*. This development in the retail trade has contributed more than anything else to the expansion of sales especially through the multiple outlets. The service is based upon an attractive display of a wide variety of goods in congenial surroundings. Supermarkets would be included in this category since they are self-service shops with a minimum sales area of over 200 square metres and having at least three check-out points. The principal product is food and household articles and again the shopper sees familiar names in many towns throughout the country including Sainsbury's, Tesco, Fine Fare, etc.

Organisation of Multiple Stores. The above forms of business enterprise have one common feature—central buying. Large orders are distributed amongst many manufacturers according to their customers requirements. Because of these orders, the multiples are able to demand good quality and special brand names from well known manufacturers. In addition they are able to set up their own research and inspection departments to maintain high standards for the customers benefit.

Apart from the hypermarkets, the multiples are supplied from a central warehouse from which the goods are delivered to the branches throughout the country. Occasionally firms manufacture their own goods, distributing them through their own warehouses to retail outlets. The hypermarket being similar to a warehouse, usually receives the goods direct from the manufacturer in bulk and stores them in the market itself.

In the multiple trade, the retail shops are usually uniform in design, such uniformity having an advertising value. The stock is adapted to the needs of the neighbourhood and displayed in a manner that is pleasing to the eye. Inspectors visit the different branches from time to time, not only to maintain efficiency, but also to improve the organisation of the branch.

Advantages of Multiple Stores.

(1) Central buying enables a firm to deal direct with the manufacturer, and therefore to obtain favourable terms.

(2) Improvements in transport have facilitated the distribution of goods to the various branches from a central warehouse. In populous areas, branch warehouses can be opened to reduce the cost of transport, and to enable branches to renew their stock at short notice.

(3) Multiple stores are usually run on a cash basis, and costs are reduced.

(4) The different branches can be graded, and the stock adapted to the district which the branch serves.

(5) Customers are able to purchase the same type of article as in their home town when away on holiday, etc.

A similar type of enterprise can be seen in the *Variety Chain Stores.* These also have many branches throughout the country and are well known to most consumers. Examples include Marks and Spencer, Woolworths, Littlewoods, etc., that sell their goods on the open display principle. Their premises can be seen in the chief shopping areas of most towns and cities.

3. RETAIL CO-OPERATIVE SOCIETIES

These are voluntary non-profit-making organisations engaged in retail trade and controlled by their members, who are also their customers. At the present time, there are about 170 retail co-operative societies in Britain, each one being self-governing and serving its members in a well-defined area. The largest is the London Co-operative Society, with over 1 million members. They vary greatly in size and a third of the total membership of the movement is in the hands of about 20 large societies. There are of course a number of small societies with 1500 or fewer members but these are gradually being absorbed in the larger units which are expanding. The movement is no longer a working-class movement: the professional classes are frequently members and the total membership of all the societies in Britain is more than 12 million. Their total annual sales in Britain amounts to over £1,100 million whilst the average amount of dividend 'distributed' to members is about 4p per £ of purchases.

The range of goods sold by co-operative societies has also increased; foodstuffs, as in the early days, still form the greater part of the sales, but many societies have established departments for the sale of coal, furniture, clothing, electrical and luxury goods, etc. Societies have also organised direct services for their members, by establishing garages, laundries, health services and cafés, as well as providing facilities for social and educational matters.

Organisation of a Society. The principal features of the organisation may be summarised as follows:
(1) *Membership*
   (a) Is open to all on payment of an entrance fee, usually about 5p. Unlike a company, the share list is never closed.

(b) Each member is only allowed one vote irrespective of shareholding at any meeting of members and must be present at the meeting in order to record that vote.

(c) No member is allowed to invest in a society more than £1,000.

(d) Persons over 16 and under 18 can subject to the rules of the local society, be members but cannot be elected to the committee of management.

(2) *Shares*

(a) Shares are usually of the value of £1, which may be purchased immediately, or paid by instalments, or by the accumulation of dividends.

(b) The share capital of any amount may be withdrawn at short notice.

(c) As long as a member has at least one share he is entitled to a proportion of the operating surplus which is returned periodically to members in the form of dividend. The amount distributed to the members is proportionate to the value of individual member's purchases.

(3) *Management*

(a) A society is managed by a Committee of Management elected by the members. They retire in rotation at regular intervals, but are in most societies eligible for re-election.

(b) Since the Co-operative Societies are bound by the Industrial and Provident Societies Act, a return of the accounts must be forwarded annually to the Registrar for Friendly Societies.

(c) Persons under 18 are ineligible to be elected to the Committee of Management as are members of neighbouring societies, trade competitors, contractors to the society and, in some societies, employees.

(4) *Internal Organisation*

The Committee of Management usually consists of twelve members elected by the members themselves. The members also elect a President, who presides at Committee meetings, and at the half-yearly meetings of the members.

The Committee of Management (who are unpaid) decide all

questions of policy: its decisions are carried out by paid officials over whom is the General Secretary or Manager of the society. In the large societies with several departments the functions of top management are divided between two separate full-time officers. A secretary is responsible for committee work, accounts and office work and a manager is in charge of the trading side assisted by departmental heads.

The Committee sets aside funds for educational and social purposes and elects sub-committees to undertake control of finance, education, buildings, etc.

Advantages. The advantages of retail co-operation are as follows:

(1) Stability of trade is assured through the 'dividend' on purchases. A member realises that it is to his interest to buy from the society. The most regular demand is, of course, for foodstuffs, accounting for about 70 per cent of the total sales of all co-operative societies.

(2) A co-operative society can gauge the demand better than a private firm, since it has a private market consisting of its own members, whereas a private firm has many occasional customers.

(3) The loyalty of the members to the society is assured, not only for reasons of self-interest, but also because many of them believe in the movement for social or perhaps political reasons.

(4) The co-operative society is an important agency for thrift: many members allow their dividends to accumulate and gain interest.

(5) Members have an equal voice in the management of the society, since each member can have only one vote at a meeting irrespective of the amount of share capital invested. In this way, democratic ideas are applied in the management of the society.

(6) Co-operative societies have modernised their methods during the last twenty years, especially in the large cities. More up-to-date premises and methods of self-service have been adopted in order to compete with other large-scale retail organisations.

Criticisms.

(1) A high proportion of the goods sold by co-operative

societies is from non-co-operative sources; the larger the society, the greater is the volume of such goods. Co-operative societies are therefore acting as distributing agents for rival firms.

(2) In large metropolitan areas, rival co-operative societies may compete with each other; attempts at definition of areas or amalgamation have sometimes proved unsuccessful.

(3) The qualifications of the Committee of Management to run a large business have often been questioned. Many of the members of the Committee may lack the necessary experience and ability, and in addition the method of election can be haphazard.

(4) Many members judge the success of the society by the amount of dividend, and the majority of the members do not trouble to attend the meetings.

(5) Co-operative societies do not confine their sales to members only; they tender for public contracts and are inclined to extend their activities into much wider fields.

4. THE DEPARTMENT STORE

Development. There are about 750 department stores in Britain today many of which developed from a drapery business by the gradual addition of new departments. These are defined as a store having twenty-five or more persons concerned with selling a wide range of commodities notably clothing and household goods.

There are two main reasons why the department stores have developed:

(1) Improvements in transport have made it profitable to establish large-scale retail establishments in populous areas, where they are able to attract customers from a radius of twenty miles or more.

(2) Many manufactured goods have become standardised, and department stores are able to obtain their supplies direct from the manufacturer, and thus obtain special terms on account of the size of their orders.

Large-scale retail trading has been further developed by amalgamations of companies providing additional capital which has been used for modernising the premises and central buying at keener prices.

Characteristics. There are three main characteristics of these stores:

(1) They make shopping agreeable and attractive to customers. This is done by building dignified premises in the chief shopping area of a city. They attract customers by their window display, variety of stock and by encouraging them to look round without being pressed to buy. In addition, customers are attracted by the provision of a restaurant, food halls, rest rooms and entertainments of various kinds. Examples include such well known establishments as Harrods and Selfridges in London, Galleries Lafeyette in Paris and so on. Most large cities however have at least one large department store.

(2) They appeal to a wide circle of customers, and not only to those living in the immediate neighbourhood. The store advertises extensively and in this way develops a mail order business, together with delivery services for customers who send their orders by post or telephone.

(3) A department store provides for all shopping requirements by a wide assortment of stock: it may therefore be regarded as a large number of retail shops under one roof. New departments are added from time to time, and each department is run as a separate business. Goods are marked in plain figures, and new lines are usually introduced before the smaller retail establishments adopt them. The customer is able to make all his purchases in the same shop, and at the same time have the greatest possible variety of goods to choose from.

(4) Customers are able in certain circumstances to have a credit account at the store. By this a customer is able to purchase goods up to an agreed value and pay for them monthly over a period of time.

Other forms of retail trade include:

(a) Trade Discount Houses

A recent trend in retail trading has been the trade discount houses offering branded goods at discounts off manufacturers' suggested retail prices. These range between 5 and $33\frac{1}{3}$ per cent and are possible as the firm passes on the benefit of bulk buying to the consumer. Costs are very much reduced as the outlet is situated away from expensive sites in established shopping areas.

(b) Automatic Vending Machines

These can be seen in an increasing number of establishments including factory, office, ships, etc. The range of goods is widening; in addition to the traditional cigarettes, sweets, stamps and platform tickets, there are machines selling hot and cold drinks and food, groceries, paper-back books and other commodities. Most of the machines are situated out of doors to cater for trade after normal trading hours. More machines, however, are being installed indoors as a supplementary service to the existing one.

(c) Shopping Centres

Enclosed shopping centres are of recent origin in Britain and can be seen in numerous redeveloped city centres and new trading areas. The centre usually comprises a large number and variety of shops which are weather protected and often traffic free. Public transport is conveniently close at hand as are extensive parking facilities for customers' cars.

(d) Mobile Shops

These are mainly concerned with food sales, particularly grocery and greengrocery products. Nearly a quarter of the total sales by this method of distribution is concentrated in Scotland due mainly to many widely scattered communities and also the lower density of population in that country.

(e) Hypermarkets

These are in effect very large supermarkets with a larger variety and wider selection of all types of goods. They require a large turnover (sales) in order to be successful in attracting the shopper to buy at greatly reduced prices. Because of this most hypermarkets—especially in France, Germany and the United States—are placed out of town to cater for the car-borne shopper buying his weekly supplies in bulk.

5. VALUE ADDED TAX

In 1973 Britain adopted a new system of taxation in the retail and service trades—the value added tax—being in effect a sales tax on the vast majority of items purchased. There are certain exemptions from the tax including most foods, services given by schools, colleges, hospitals, etc. A person *supplying* goods or services therefore for home consumption is required to account for the tax on his output to the Government by charging his customer an additional percentage of the account. It is administered in the following way:

Suppose the tax is 10 per cent overall and that a manufacturer purchases £1,100 of raw materials, the suppliers will pay £100 to the tax authorities. The material is now made into finished products valued at say £2,000 which are sold to a retailer for £2,200 (ex-factory price £2,000 + £200 tax). As £100 tax has already been paid, the manufacturer pays the remaining £100 to the authorities. Suppose now that the retailer adds 25 per cent profit to his cost price, then the *shop* price is £2,750. To this must be added the 10 per cent tax making the *sale* price £3,025. On selling these goods the retailer is liable to the authorities for £275 tax less the £200 already paid—that is £75.

QUESTIONS

1. What changes in shopping habits are being brought about by self-service? To what extent do you think self-service shopping will develop further? Give reasons.   (London G.C.E.)

2. To what causes do you attribute the success of large department stores? What features in their business organisation do you consider specially commendable?   (U.L.C.I.)

3. The owners of two small chains of shoe shops operating in a busy provincial town decide to amalgamate. What advantages could be expected from the owners' point of view?   (R.S.A.)

4. Explain the difference between the selling and non-selling departments of a department store. Why are department stores so popular with the public?   (J.M.B.)

5. Describe the functions of the independent wholesale merchant. How far is it true to say he is no longer essential?

(Cambridge G.C.E.)

6. Discuss the reasons why department stores hold a sale at particular times of the year.   (A.E.B.)

7. How do you account for the success of the multiple shops, chain stores and supermarkets which are to be found in almost every shopping centre? How much justification do you think there can be for the view that small shopkeepers should be protected from this competition, often referred to as 'unfair'.

(Oxford G.C.E.)

8. Larger shops can usually make high profits because of the rapidity of their turnover. Explain the meaning of the term *rate of turnover* and its significance in relation to profits.

(Oxford G.C.E.)

Chapter 11

Consumer Protection

The increased standard of living afforded to the citizens of Britain have resulted in the creation of demand to satisfy ever-increasing wants. Most people today have more money to spend as they wish, and after satisfying the basic requirements of food, shelter and clothing, find a great range and variety of goods and services available for purchase.

The growth of specialist and often highly sophisticated methods of advertising and retailing may make it difficult for the consumer to be certain of reliability or quality of the product, or there may be a divergence between the consumer's demand through advertising and his real needs. In such cases therefore it is essential for the consumer to be protected by either a recognised code of conduct amongst the traders themselves or by statutory legislation which will enforce acceptable standards.

Legislation designed for consumer protection has existed from early times. It is of interest to note that a national uniform weights and measures system was one of the declared objects of the Magna Carta. Modern thought, however, requires the consumer himself to take a greater interest through the establishment of facilities for the education of the public at large and the creation of 'watch-dog' panels comprised of government, commercial and consumer interests.

Protection can be divided under the following headings:

(a) By the Government

The main role of the Government departments is the

administration of the powers vested in it by legislation. Some departments undertake research work and publish reports which are available to both manufacturer and consumer.

(1) *The Department of Trade and Industry* is responsible for the general policy towards most consumer goods and services. It is concerned with the administration of various Acts of Parliament including the Trade Descriptions Act, Hire Purchase Act, Trade Marks Act, Weights and Measures Act, etc. The Department being divided into numerous regions and divisions that cover the whole of the country has an interest in a very wide field of topics affecting the consumer. In addition to those already mentioned, the Department Inspectors make test purchases at retail establishments, ensure standards of fair trading in markets, shops, stores, etc., and advise on minimum safety standards necessary on both home and foreign produced goods. Extensive campaigns are also undertaken by the Department from time to time to warn the public against particular hazards that may be found in certain products.

(2) *The Ministry of Agriculture, Fisheries and Food* is responsible for the enforcement of proper standards in connection with the Food and Drugs Act, the manufacture and labelling of manufactured foods, slaughterhouses, the quality and cleanliness of milk, etc. It is also concerned with the use of fertilisers and chemicals consumed in agriculture and their possible effect on consumers, domestic animals and wild life.

(3) *The Department of Health and Social Security* is also concerned with the Food and Drugs Act particularly in relation to food hygiene. The Department carries out an extensive advertising campaign informing the public of possible dangers attached to certain practices.

(4) *The Department of the Environment,* (a) The Housing and Local Government Division, exercises responsibility into regulations concerning the construction of buildings. The health and safety of the inhabitants also require minimum standards to be enforced by the Government inspectors. The Division works in close collaboration with Local Authorities on such matters as water supply, sewerage schemes and rent control. (b) The Transport Division exercises control to ensure the

provision of adequate transport services and equipment, minimum standards of safety in both the public and private sectors, together with transport user education campaigns, etc.

(5) *The Home Office* is concerned in the safety requirements of many consumer goods—for example, fireproof garments, in addition to exercising control over dangerous drugs and poisons. The Department also deals with a wide range of other subjects including firearms, liquor licensing, entertainments, public safety in public buildings, fire regulations, etc.

(b) Independent Organisations

A considerable number of organisations exist in the private sector to assist and protect consumers. The principal ones are:

(1) *The Consumers' Association* which is a non-profit-making organisation financed by private subscriptions set up to 'raise and maintain the standard of goods and services'. Tests are made by experts on goods which have been purchased through the normal channels and the results are published in a monthly magazine.

(2) *The Citizens' Advice Bureaux* are financed by grants from local authorities and provide advice and guidance to consumers. The service provided is confidential and covers a very wide field. The bureaux work in close co-operation with many other organisations and publish numerous booklets of practical importance.

(3) *British Standards Institution* is a voluntary non-profit-making body financed by voluntary subscriptions and Government grant. It is incorporated by Royal Charter and concerned with the voluntary setting up of standards acceptable to both manufacturer and consumer. Goods conforming to these standards are given a *kite* mark which is a monogram the shape of a kite and the trademark of the B.S.I. The Institution is controlled by a council representing both sides of industry, government departments and professional organisations.

(4) *The Council of Industrial Design* receives a grant from the Government and is concerned with the improvement of design in both capital and consumer goods. It also encourages industrialists to implement acceptable safety measures demanded by the consumer in the construction of British-

products. The members consist of industrialists, retailers. architects and designers and the Council displays its exhibits at the Design Centre in London and other regional centres.

(5) *Local Consumer Groups* are non-profit-making bodies based on a town or region concerned with the protection of local interests. In addition reports are made to the Consumers' Association on matters affecting the consumer generally.

(6) *Advisory Councils.* The nationalised industries and other government controlled enterprises often have a great deal of freedom in determining their policies. The decisions made at all levels usually have a direct effect on the service given to the public who must pay for what is virtually a state-owned monopoly. Provision is therefore made for Advisory Councils to be set up comprised of representatives of consumer interests. Their function is to voice opinions to the minister having responsibility for the industry on consumer demand and if necessary express satisfaction or dissatisfaction at the way in which that industry is being run.

(c) Legislation

The volume of legislation passing through Parliament requires the businessman to be constantly informed of changes in the law affecting trade. This is usually achieved through trade journals, the press and the local Chambers of Commerce.

A brief summary of the principal acts designed to afford some protection to the consumer would include the following:

(1) *The Trade Descriptions Act 1968* is concerned with the descriptions attached to merchandise by way of quantity, size, composition, method, place and date of manufacture, strength, behaviour, fitness, etc. The Act covers all goods and merchandise sold to the consumer and includes oral statements made by the retailer or his assistants in addition to misleading statements made in booklets, price tickets, advertisements and pamphlets. In addition, local authority weights and measures inspectors have the right of inspection and seizure of goods if necessary. The Department of Trade and Industry may also introduce further safeguards if it is found that the consumer is being put to any disadvantage through the misuse of descriptions.

(2) *The Sale of Goods Act 1893* relates to conditions and

warranties implied in the sale of all goods unless the circumstances indicate a different intention. These include a condition that the seller has a right to sell the goods, that the buyer shall have *quiet possession* and that the quality shall be as the buyer requires them. Customers are sometimes encouraged to sign after-sales agreement forms purporting to introduce or extend guarantees over their purchases. By his signature, the customer often unwittingly signs away his rights against the retailer. By the Sale of Goods Act, however, the retailer is expected to supply goods of merchantable quality unless the customer otherwise agrees. The Act also provides certain safeguards regarding goods sold by description or sample.

(3) *The Misrepresentation Act 1967* is designed principally to protect the consumer from suffering loss through sales literature, advertisements, etc., bearing descriptions which have persuaded him to buy the goods relying on these statements entirely.

(4) *Weights and Measures Act 1963* protects the consumer against shortages in both weight and measure and in many cases requires the seller to inform the buyer the unit of measure he is using. In a few cases the Act requires the seller to sell only in certain specified quantities.

(5) *The Merchandise Marks Act 1953* ensures that trademarks and trade descriptions applied in writing to goods for sale are both honest and accurate. In addition foreign manufactured goods bearing a name or trademark similar to a British name must bear an indication as to their place of manufacture.

(6) *The Consumer Protection Act 1961* empowers the Home Office to make regulations from time to time to ensure that adequate safety precautions are installed by the manufacturer in consumer goods and particulraly those of a potentially dangerous nature. These include fireguards to certain heaters, colour coding requirements for electric wires, and regulations regarding children's toys.

(7) *The Food and Drugs Act 1955* includes the provision of adequate safeguards to ensure that food sold by the retailer shall be fit for human consumption and that it shall where necessary be properly labelled showing its contents. In addition

there are various regulations covering the sale of drugs and the conditions under which they may be sold.

(8) *The Fair Trading Act 1973* endeavours to protect consumers from unfair business practices in all sectors of enterprise. To deal with a particular situation a Director General of Fair Trading may after reference to the *Consumer Protection Advisory Commission* make enforcement orders against offenders. These are enforced by the local weights and measures authorities who in extreme cases may refer continued excesses to the Courts. The Act also gives protection to the public against monopolies and mergers—both local and national—that are likely to be against their interests.

Further legislation enacted which protects the consumer includes the Hire Purchase Act, Advertisement Act, Monopolies and Mergers Act, the Restrictive Trade Practices Act.

2. MARKET RESEARCH

This involves the introduction of various marketing methods in order to find out the extent to which consumers will accept new products, brand names, styles, colour, packing or advertising techniques. The research programme will also test the consumers' reaction to an existing product and invite a critical analysis on how it may be improved.

The following are some of the methods undertaken by most large producing organisations to assess the market potential for their products.

(a) *Consumer Surveys.* Cover a cross section of the public chosen at random throughout the country by numerous sampling methods. The survey usually consists of a questionnaire that the householder or consumer is invited to complete often in the presence of a third party. It has the advantage that a very wide survey may be carried out by the questions asked but has limitations in that it depends upon the goodwill of all parties.

(b) *Area Sampling.* Involves taking samples over a particular part of the country to test the reaction of consumers to existing or new products. The sampling may be coupled with a concentrated but limited advertising campaign after which retail sales are analysed to estimate the possible national sales. The method has severe limitations for certain products in view of the wide differences in consumer demand in various parts of the country.

(c) *Product Sampling.* Is undertaken by a producer of branded goods in order to maintain the high quality demanded by both producer and consumer. Sampling may be by:

(1) External methods such as requesting chosen consumers to make periodic reports on given products purchased locally.

(2) Internal methods carried out by the producer himself at the time of manufacture on a random sample basis.

Thus by all of these methods the consumer is receiving the attention and protection considered necessary having the backing of the law and interest of the community.

QUESTIONS

1. Why do consumers need protection? How are they afforded such protection?   (Cambridge G.C.E.)

2. What are consumer associations? Describe their functions and give an account of any modern developments of these associations.   (U.L.C.I.)

3. Consumer protection has been slow of growth but is now extensive. What are the chief ways in which consumers are protected?   (R.S.A.)

4. What safeguards in regard to the quality of goods are available to the consumer?   (R.S.A.)

5. What is the purpose of consumer protection? In what ways does the government provide protection for the consumer?

(A.E.B.)

6. What do you understand by 'Market Research'? By whom is it carried out and why?   (R.S.A.)

7. An early example of consumer protection was the initiation under Magna Carta of a system of weights and measures, subsequently provided for by Acts of Parliament. Name *three* other Acts designed to protect the consumer, and describe briefly the kind of protection given in *each* case. Give *one* example of how consumers may be protected otherwise than by legislation.

(Oxford G.C.E.)

Chapter 12

Business Organisation

I. TYPES OF BUSINESS ORGANISATION

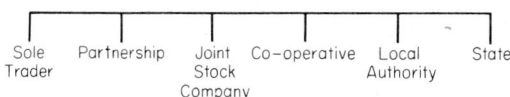

These have developed in order to supply the varying needs of
the community. The *sole trader* was the earliest form of business
organisation, and is still the most usual type particularly in the
retail trade: he requires a relatively small amount of capital,
conducting his own business and supplying the needs of his
customers in a limited area.

The *partnership* and the *joint-stock company* are larger forms
of business organisation, possessing greater amounts of capital,
and usually serving the needs of customers over a wider area.
In recent years the business unit has become larger, for joint-
stock companies have, in many cases, amalgamated to form
even bigger units, combines, trusts or holding companies. In
addition, the *Co-operative* movement has expanded—particularly in the grocery trade, whilst the *State* and *Local Authorities* have received powers from Parliament to conduct various
trading enterprises. We therefore see that the size of the business unit has increased step by step; at one extreme is the sole
trader who runs and finances his own business, whilst at the
other is the State or combine, which is national or international
in its activities, requiring vast amounts of capital to finance its
operations.

2. GROWTH IN SIZE OF THE BUSINESS UNIT

Business Units have increased in size during the present century for the following reasons:

(a) **Improvements in transport** have led to the extension of the market. Up to the end of the eighteenth century, the majority of goods were sold locally, since the producer was usually in direct contact with the consumer, for whom the goods were often made to order. In the same way, food supplies were grown locally and the ideal of self-sufficiency was attained to a considerable degree. Under these conditions, the sole trader or manufacturer was the usual form of business organisation, since only a small amount of capital was required to run a business, when the market was so limited in extent.

With the improvements in industrial techniques and the new inventions which occurred, new and more reliable means of transport were necessary.

The present century has witnessed a revolution in the transport services. Road transport for example has increased to an extent hitherto thought impossible. Fully integrated container services have benefited both manufacturer and consumer. Demand is national in character rather than local and indeed for many commodities the demand is international, making use of modern sea and air services to all parts of the world.

The risks attached to trade today are greater than at any previous time and larger forms of business organisation have evolved in order to meet them. In addition the larger units are able to satisfy the increased demand of a larger area by using greater capital and other resources. They are thus able to take advantage of the opportunities for greater trade which world trade offers.

(b) **Improvements in communications** have also led to an increase in the size of the business unit. In the middle of the nineteenth century, a postal system under State control was inaugurated, whilst later in the century, the telegraph and the telephone were made available for the use of business. The twentieth century has seen the development of radio, teleprinter, television, telex and satellite means of communication. As a result of these improvements, businesses can be controlled over a wider area, world market prices are readily available and the purchase and sale of goods can take place between buyers and sellers separated by great distance.

(c) **The increase in population** which has occurred has led to a greater demand for commodities of all kinds. This has been an outstanding feature of the economic development of all the principal countries of the world during the last hundred years: in 1801, for example, the population of Britain was just below 12 millions; in 1901, it was almost 40 millions and is today about 56 millions. Food supplies and raw materials of all kinds must be brought from all over the world in order to feed and clothe the inhabitants of this country, and thus business units possessing a large amount of capital have become necessary.

The higher standard of living of the population has also contributed to an increase in demand for commodities of every description. Business units have required larger amounts of capital in order that the economies of large-scale production can be made available to the consumer thus producing goods more cheaply on a larger scale.

(d) **The growth of towns and conurbations** is a result of the increase in the population in this country. In 1801 only 20 per cent of the population lived in towns: by 1901 this had increased to over 60 per cent and today partly because of urban spread over 80 per cent of the population live in cities or towns.

The trend nowadays is for the population to be largely urban and sub-urban, spreading away from the centre of large towns and conurbations. This has been possible because of the spread of car ownership, an improved network of distribution and an expansion in public transport serving a wider area encompassing places which were formerly rural.

The concentration of so large a proportion of the population in defined areas has led to the development of large-scale retail trade which has established itself and opened many branches throughout the country. This has necessitated an increase in the size of the business unit in order to finance trade on such a large scale.

(e) **Improvements in machinery** have led to manufacture on a large scale, since, *up to a certain point,* the cost per unit is reduced when more goods are manufactured. Specialisation or the Division of Labour is a characteristic of manufacture, and large amounts of capital are necessary in order to carry the division of labour to an advanced stage. The increased output due to the use of machinery has led to the development of the wholesale trade, which warehouses the products of the manufacturer, and which finances goods whilst they are being marketed by the retailer.

(f) **Limited Liability** has been a feature of joint-stock company organisation since the 1862 Limited Liability Act. Before this date, shareholders of a company were responsible for all the debts of the firm, but the Act made shareholders liable only for the amount invested. As a result, the business unit has become larger, since large amounts of capital can be raised either privately or by appealing to the public to take shares in a company. In both cases the shareholder's liability is limited to the amount of the fully paid shares registered in his name, and he is therefore more willing to invest his money in these ventures.

(g) **The Development of Banking and Insurance** has been made possible by the improvements in transport and communications that have taken place. There is an international system of banking, for every important bank in the world has its agents abroad. Banks direct the flow of capital, and frequently finance trading transactions by making loans out of their accumulated deposits. Large-scale business organisations are therefore possible, since banks and other large financial institutions are able to provide additional amounts of capital when it is required.

Insurance also has developed to provide against the risks of trade which have increased with the extension of the market. Large sums are accumulated by insurance companies who compensate the individual or firm upon whom the loss has fallen. By this means, the risks of world trade are reduced and large-scale operations are possible.

(h) **The growth of foreign competition** is an important factor in increasing the size of the business unit. At one time Britain was the only important manufacturing country of the world. In the twentieth century particularly, other countries, such as the U.S.A., Germany and Japan have developed their manufactures, and compete with British traders in the markets of the world. British firms have therefore sought to reduce the competition between themselves by forming larger units which are able to compete more effectively on the international markets.

3. ADVANTAGES OF LARGE-SCALE BUSINESSES

The large-scale business unit has the following advantages over the smaller organisations:

(a) *Specialisation of management* may be developed to a greater extent in large organisations: the business may be divided into departments, and a specialist placed in charge of each. Consequently more up-to-date and efficient methods are likely to be adopted more readily in a large-scale organisation.

(b) The large-scale organisation has advantages in purchasing its stock. Because of the volume of its purchases, it can deal direct with the manufacturer and may obtain more favourable terms than the owner of a smaller business.

(c) The expenses of running the business, such as rent, advertising and lighting can be spread over a larger amount of sales and the cost is therefore proportionately reduced.

(d) The advantages of large-scale production may be obtained by having large units serving both the home and international markets.

(e) Goods may be stored in a central warehouse, and distributed to the various branches by the firm's own transport, thus saving transport costs.

(f) Computers and other highly expensive equipment may be installed releasing staff for tasks of a less routine nature and providing the customer with an improved service.

Limitations

Certain types of business are more successful on a small scale where success depends on meeting the wishes of each individual customer, as in the case of a tailor or a hairdresser. Generally speaking, those businesses in which the artistic element is necessary are comparatively small, whilst the larger business units deal in standardised products.

A further limitation to the size is the extent of the markets, large-scale businesses catering for a national or international market. Most of the retail trade is carried on by the independent retailers who have neither the capital nor the wish to expand. They serve the suburb of a town and are in direct personal contact with their customers, having a first-hand knowledge of the market which they serve.

Finally, the business unit may become so large that it is unmanageable. Additional management expenses may be incurred which counterbalance the economies due to large-scale production, and the result may be a decrease in efficiency.

4. FACTORS DETERMINING THE SIZE OF BUSINESS UNIT

Many smaller forms of business organisation continue to flourish despite the growth of large-scale businesses. Each form from the smallest to the largest appears to be necessary for the distribution of commodities.

This depends on the following factors:

(a) *The Amount of Capital required.* Different amounts of capital are required for the various forms of business organisations: the retailer may open a shop with a capital of a few hundred pounds, a sum which would be quite inadequate for a larger business unit. Generally speaking, the larger the unit, the greater is the amount of capital required, greater amounts being provided by a group of persons who form a partnership or a company, and sharing the profits or losses between them.

(b) *The Amount of Risk.* The small firm is suitable for those businesses in which the amount of risk is small: these are usually local in character, providing for the needs of customers who live in a limited area. Larger units deal in much wider markets, where the risks are greater. These are shared amongst a large number of shareholders who have provided the capital and accepted the risk.

(c) *The Nature of the Business.* Many businesses are most efficiently run on a small scale; this is so when it is necessary to be in personal contact with the customer, in order to satisfy his particular needs. On the other hand, large-scale organisations are suitable for those firms which supply standardised articles which are in wide and regular demand.

(*d*) *The Extent of the Market.* Small business units are suitable for firms which supply the needs of a small area. Where the market is national or world-wide however, larger business units are more usual since a great deal of attention must be paid to very highly specialised subjects far beyond the capability of the smaller firms. These include research and development projects, forward planning, etc. requiring the services of highly skilled staff at all levels.

(*e*) *Personal Ability.* The size of the business may be determined by the ability of the owner. People differ considerably in their ability to manage a business and in the amount of risk they are willing to take. An enterprising owner will see opportunities for developing his business, and perhaps form a partnership or a company in order to extend the business. On the other hand the owner may not wish to expand beyond a certain point in order to have time for his other interests and more leisure.

Business units of various sizes are necessary in the distribution of goods to the consumer: each form from the largest to the smallest, rendering some service to consumers which could not be given as cheaply or efficiently by any other.

QUESTIONS

1. Give reasons for the great increase during the last fifty years of the joint-stock company form of business organisation.

(U.C.I.)

2. Account for the growth of large-scale enterprise in many industries in recent years. In what circumstances would you expect small-scale enterprise to continue to succeed?   (U.L.C.I.)

3. 'The large multiples (retailers with ten or more branches) have increased their trade at the expense of small independent retailers, but over half of retail trade is still handled by independent businesses, in the main consisting of a single shop or a few shops.' Discuss this quotation and show what measures the independents have adopted to counter-balance the strength of the multiples.   (R.S.A.)

4. Describe briefly the different forms of business unit in this country. Why has no one form driven out all the others?

(London G.C.E.)

5. Outline the factors influencing the location of industry and account for the industrial growth in rural areas in Britain in recent years.   (R.S.A.)

6. What are the principal reasons for the increase in the numbers of *very* large undertakings in modern industry and commerce.

(R.S.A.)

7. Industry is widely dispersed in Britain but it is still possible to distinguish the following as the main concentrations of industry.

London; Yorkshire; Lancashire; South Wales; North East coast of England; Clydeside and the Central Lowlands of Scotland; Northern Ireland.

Describe briefly the main industries in any three of these regions

(R.S.A.)

8. The table shows the cost price and selling price of a number of commodities in a supermarket.

(*a*) Calculate, for each commodity, the profit or loss as a percentage of sales (i.e. the profit or loss margin);

(*b*) calculate the *average* profit as a percentage of sales;

(*c*) give reasons for the differences in the profit or loss margins for the different commodities.

All calculations to be made to the nearest whole number.

Commodity	Cost £	Sales £	Profit or loss margin %
Fruit and Vegetables	250	375	
Butter	170	175	
Cosmetics	50	80	
Sugar	183	180	
Frozen Foods	83	100	
Others	964	1090	
TOTAL			

(A.E.B.)

Chapter 13

The Sole Trader

1. IMPORTANCE OF THE SOLE TRADER

The sole trader is one who runs a business on his own account, and therefore is under no obligation to share his profits with others, as is the case in the larger forms of business organisation. He is usually connected with the retail trade but may be in a service trade such as decorator, electrician, plumber, etc., or in a profession such as business consultant, architect, surveyor, etc.

The sole trader was the earliest and is the simplest type of business organisation: his capital is usually small in amount, is obtained from his own savings, or on loan from a bank or some other financial institution. Under such limitations, the scope of his activities is drastically reduced, but nevertheless, because of the comparative ease with which it is set up, the sole trader is still the most numerous type of business today in spite of growing competition from larger undertakings.

He has great opportunities when dealing in those commodities for which there is a regular demand, such as foodstuffs, newspapers and tobacco, coupled with personal service. His stronghold is in the suburbs of a town and outlying districts, where his shop is conveniently situated to supply the daily needs of his customers. Today there are about 550,000 retail shops in Britain of which some 70 per cent consist of independent retail businesses. Most of the smaller undertakings have working proprietors and unpaid family helpers who assist in the business at peak times. In view of the numerical preponderance of the independent trader, this form of trading is the usual channel of distribution accounting for about 51 per cent of the total retail sales in this country.

2. ADVANTAGES OF THE SOLE TRADER

He has the following advantages over his larger competitors:

(a) He has a *feeling of independence* which is an important factor in accounting for the numerical supremacy of this form of business organisation. A trader realises that there are many advantages in managing his own business instead of working for others for a fixed wage or salary; he is his own master and can run his business in his own way, knowing that the reward for his efforts will come to him in due course. Self-interest is a powerful check on waste, and an incentive to increased efficiency.

(b) His business may provide employment for members of his family: it has been estimated that about 60 per cent of the shops owned by sole traders are family businesses. The shop premises frequently provide living accommodation for the trader's family who act as assistants when necessary. Alternatively the proprietor of the smaller unit may have other means of livelihood and the business is run by another member of the family.

(c) The sole trader is able to manage his business in every detail, on account of its small size. There is no delegation of responsibility, and the centralised control may lead to greater efficiency. Also he is more flexible in his attitude to his customers, no detail being too small for consideration

(d) The sole trader is in personal contact with his customers, whereas the larger forms of business organisation are often impersonal. The sole trader's business is restricted to a small local area, and he is therefore in a position to know the type of goods required by his customers. It is interesting to note that in many instances, differing lines of goods sell more readily in different parts of the country. This may be due to climatic reasons or even local custom, but nevertheless these are points readily understood and acted upon by the sole trader. In addition, he is able to attract custom by his own personality and reputation.

(*e*) A sole trader has often a varied stock though smaller in amount than a larger type of organisation. In view of the smaller size of his business, his customers are not required to go from department to department, since all their requirements can be served over the same counter.

(*f*) A sole trader has an advantage in being local, making journeys to the centre of the town for daily household requirements unnecessary.

(*g*) He often gives credit to his customers, whereas the larger forms of business organisation are conducted on a cash basis except where the customer has made special arrangements through a credit account. The granting of credit by the personal judgment of the sole trader is an advantage that many of the larger organisations cannot match.

(*h*) He is often able to give advice to his customers regarding the goods which he is selling; he may have had experience in the wholesale trade before opening a shop of his own, and may know the processes of manufacture. He is thus in a position to advise his customers regarding the best materials to use for a particular purpose.

(*i*) The growth of towns during the present century has given him new opportunities: the improvements in transport have led to the development of new suburbs, where the sole trader is in a strong position. At the same time improvements in transport and communications have made it easier for him to secure adequate supplies with which to stock his shop.

3. LIMITATIONS OF THE SOLE TRADER

The sole trader's activities are limited in extent for the following reasons:

(*a*) He may lack capital for the development of his business and be compelled to limit his activities to a small area through his inability to obtain any more.

(*b*) He may not have the ability to see opportunities for extending his business or of adopting improved methods. The success of the business depends largely on the personality of one man, whereas in the case of a larger organisation, because of its larger capital etc., there may be greater opportunity to expand.

(c) The sole trader bears all the risks of his business: he is responsible for all the debts, whereas in the larger forms of organisation, the risks are shared by a great many people. In the case of a public company the liability is limited to the amount of the fully paid issued share capital.

(d) The sole trader loses the advantages of specialisation: he has to perform a large variety of tasks which large firms are able to delegate to specialists who have made a study of their particular duties.

(e) He may not be able to buy on equal terms with the larger organisations whose orders, on account of their greater size, frequently obtain more favourable terms from the wholesaler or manufacturer. In the food and grocery trade, wholesaler sponsored *voluntary associations* have been formed in order to centralise the orders of numerous retailers in a given area. By this, purchasing in bulk quantities at a more competitive price is possible. Alternatively 'cash and carry' firms supply many independent retailers with goods at below wholesale prices on certain lines.

(f) The business of the sole trader may lack continuity; in due course, the sole trader will retire from the business, and the extent of his personal influence may then be realised. In contrast to the sole trader, the larger forms of business organisation are less personal, and the loss of one man may not affect the control of the business to the same extent.

4. THE CAPITAL OF THE SOLE TRADER

When a man wants to establish a new business, he must first estimate how much capital he will require. The amount will depend upon the following factors:

(a) The nature of the business: a greengrocer requires a smaller amount of capital than say a chemist, since the former has little expense in the form of fixtures, and turns over his stock rapidly.

(b) The initial expenses on buildings, fixtures and fittings, etc. The premises may be leased, rented or purchased, and in addition, small businesses such as boutiques require expensive furniture and fittings in order to attract customers.

(c) The amount of stock to be carried, and the rapidity of its turnover. The amount of capital required will also depend on the period of credit allowed by the wholesaler or the manufacturer.

(d) The amount of sales that are anticipated and the proportion of cash sales to credit sales.

(e) The amount of capital to be held in reserve, since some allowance must be made for unexpected calls.

When an estimate has been made of the amount required, the prospective trader may obtain it by one or more of the following:

(a) *His Own Savings*. This method of financing a new business may in certain circumstances be the most satisfactory means of providing the initial capital. It makes the trader independent of outside control, and increases his net profits since he has no interest charges to meet. To a large extent, this depends upon prevailing interest rates. It may pay the trader to borrow from another source and keep his own savings intact.

In times of rising prices it may be worth while for the trader to borrow at a certain rate per cent against the deposit of suitable security. This he will do if he is reasonably confident that his return from the business in the form of profit is greater than the amount of interest he will have to pay. His own savings are intact and can be invested elsewhere to bring in additional income, or alternatively used to provide the business with additional capital when necessary.

(b) *The Savings of Relations or Friends*. The trader's success in obtaining such a loan depends upon the confidence which these people have in him, as much as in the nature of the business proposition. The personality and capabilities of the prospective trader will determine the extent to which they will make a loan to him.

(c) *The Bank*. The trader may have been a customer of the bank before opening his business, and in such a case the manager may be willing to make a loan. The amount may depend upon the relationship that exists between him and his bank. The latter may lend money at varying rates for both short and long terms. Should the bank not be willing to lend all of this amount out of its own resources a finance company may be a suitable alternative.

(*d*) *Purchases on Credit.* The sole trader, before opening a new business may have been an employee of a manufacturing or wholesale firm. He may therefore be able to arrange for a period of credit in purchasing his stock. This accommodation on the part of the manufacturer or wholesaler is the equivalent of providing him with additional working capital.

Additional Capital. The sole trader may find it necessary to obtain additional capital for the extension of his existing business, or to purchase additional stock, etc. The need may be either temporary or permanent:

(*a*) *Temporary requirements* may be due to seasonal fluctuations of trade; additional stock is required, particularly at Christmas and during the holiday season. The bank is usually willing to help its regular customers by making a loan or granting an overdraft in this connection.

(*b*) *Permanent requirements* may be due to the extension of the business. In order to provide the additional capital which such developments require, he may be able to use the services of a bank or finance house.

If, however, these methods are insufficient, or if he prefers to share the risks of a developing business with others, he may decide to form a partnership or a private company; these forms of business organisation are dealt with in the chapters that follow.

QUESTIONS

1. Discuss the limitations which a sole trader is likely to meet as his business continues to expand. What advice would you give him to overcome such limitations? (U.L.C.I.)

2. Account for the marked survival of the sole trader in retailing notwithstanding the recent growth of large-scale stores and multiple shop concerns. (R.S.A.)

3. It has been stated that the only function remaining now for the sole trader is to open up in a new district with a growing population and to develop business which he is destined to lose in a short time to multiple shop firms and central department stores.

Discuss this view and set out what you consider to be the proper sphere of the sole retailer in modern trade. (R.S.A.)

4. A retail shop has developed so as practically to exhaust the purchasing power of its immediate neighbourhood. Upon what lines is further development possible? Discuss the relative advantages of the alternatives you suggest. (R.S.A.)

5. State what determines the amount of capital required by a sole trader and show how this capital is obtained. (R.S.A.)

6. What benefits result from specialisation in the retail trade? What limit is there, if any, to the extended growth of this specialisation? (Oxford G.C.E.)

7. Larger shops can usually make high profits because of the rapidity of their turnover. Explain the meaning of the term rate of turnover and its significance in relation to profits.

(Oxford G.C.E.)

Chapter 14

Partnerships

I. TYPES OF PARTNERSHIPS

A partnership may be defined as an association of persons who carry on a business for the purpose of making a profit.

The formation of a partnership is a convenient method of expanding the scope of a business, since by this means the capital may be increased and the management may be specialised. When a number of people decide to form a partnership, a written agreement is usually drawn up, stating the amount of capital to be provided by each partner, and giving particulars of the way in which the firm is to be managed.

There are two types:

(a) Ordinary Partnerships, in which all the partners have equal contractual powers and responsibilities. In an ordinary partnership, each active partner may take part in the management of the business, and each partner is liable for the debts of the firm.

(b) Limited Partnerships, is one where there must be *at least* one ordinary partner, who is responsible for all the debts of the firm, and who therefore has greater powers than the limited partner or partners. The limited partners take no part in the management of the firm, and their liability is limited to the amount of their capital invested. The limited partnership is a compromise between the ordinary partnership and the joint-stock company, since it possesses some of the features of each.

2. ORDINARY PARTNERSHIPS

Ordinary Partnerships are controlled by the Partnership Act 1890 and to a certain extent by the Companies Act 1967. The principal terms of these Acts may be summarised as follows:

(a) Numbers. One of the reasons for forming a partnership is to obtain more capital, the minimum number being two. The above Partnership Act limits the number of partners to twenty. Exception to this is granted by the Companies Act 1967 to accountants, solicitors, stockbrokers and stock-jobbers where larger amounts of capital are required and these professions may have as many partners as are necessary.

(b) Liability. Each ordinary partner is liable for all the debts of the firm. His liability is not limited to his capital invested in the firm, but may include his personal possessions. A creditor may therefore sue the firm as a whole, or any one of the partners for the money due to him.

(c) Powers of Partners. Each *ordinary partner* may act as an agent of the firm, and may bind the partnership in any contract made on behalf of the firm.

(d) Management. Each ordinary partner may take an active part in the management of the firm. Specialisation of management becomes possible and a partner can be responsible for a department or branch of the firm.

(e) Kinds of Ordinary Partners.
   (1) *Active partners* who take a leading part in the management of the firm, sharing profits and losses.
   (2) *Sleeping partners* who invest money in the firm, and share profits and losses but take no part in the management.
   (3) *Nominal partners* who allow their names to be used as partners, but do not take any part in the management, nor do they share in the profits.

(f) Profit-sharing. Partners share profits equally irrespective of the amount of individual capital invested *unless* there is some prior agreement in the Deed of Partnership which will give details of the ratio to be apportioned to each partner.

(g) Dissolution of Partnership. The Partnership Act

states how losses shall be paid, how the assets shall be shared when the partnership is dissolved, and the grounds upon which the partnership can be dissolved.

3. LIMITED PARTNERSHIPS

These are controlled by the Limited Partnership Act 1907. Many of the terms of this Act are the same as those of the Partnership Act 1890. In a limited partnership, however, there are two types of partners—ordinary and limited.

The principal terms of the Limited Partnership Act are:

(a) Numbers. As in an ordinary partnership, a limited partnership usually consists of from two to twenty persons. Exception is given to the professions detailed above who by the Companies Act 1967 are allowed as many partners as are necessary.

(b) Liability. The limited partners have limited liability— that is, they are only responsible for the debts of the firm up to the amount of capital which they have invested in the business. But in a limited partnership, there must be *at least* one ordinary partner who is liable for all the debts of the firm.

(c) Powers of Partners. A limited partner cannot bind the firm in any trading contract; this power is reserved for the ordinary partner or partners.

(d) Management. A limited partner cannot take any part in the management of the firm; it is managed by the ordinary partners.

(e) Registration. A limited partnership and all subsequent changes affecting the partnership must be registered with the Registrar of Joint-Stock Companies; if not registered, it is deemed to be an ordinary partnership.

Details required by the Registrar include:

(1) the firm's name and principal place of business.
(2) full name and address of each partner.
(3) the general nature of the business.
(4) a statement that the partnership is limited.

(f) Withdrawal of Capital. A limited partner may not, during the continuance of the partnership, withdraw any part of his capital without the consent of all the other partners.

This is a common type of business organisation on the Continent of Europe where banks often finance businesses and enter as limited partners. In this country, however, limited partnerships are not numerous, as limited liability for all who contribute the capital may be obtained by forming a private company.

4. THE DEED OF PARTNERSHIP

The Deed of Partnership sets out in writing the terms of the partnership. This document is not essential legally, but it is very desirable, since disputes can be more easily settled by referring to a written agreement.

The Deed varies according to the nature of the business, but such terms as the following may be found:

(a) The names of the partners.

(b) The nature of the business to be carried on.

(c) The amount of the capital and how it is subscribed, for example in cash or assets or both.

(d) The arrangements for the division of the profits.

(e) The amount of interest, if any, to be allowed on the capital.

(f) The amount each partner is allowed to withdraw each year in anticipation of profit and the amount of interest, if any, to be charged on these drawings.

(g) The salaries, if any, to be paid to certain partners for the performance of special duties.

(h) The method of audit.

(i) The amount to be paid to a partner who retires, and how this amount is to be calculated.

(j) Method of determining the goodwill on the retirement of a partner.

(k) Restraint on a retiring partner setting up in opposition.

(l) Method of arbitration in case of dispute, for example by majority vote.

(m) Duration of the partnership if this is known.

5. REGISTRATION OF BUSINESS NAMES

Partnerships can be found in many branches of industry and commerce and the name of the firm often bears no resemblance to the true identity of the partners.

In such cases, the firm's name *must* be registered with the Registrar of Companies in London (or Edinburgh) in accordance with the **Registration of Business Names Act.** The main requirements of the Act call for the registration of the following items:

(1) the firm's business name and principal place of business.

(2) the general nature of the business.

(3) the present Christian names and surnames of each partner together with any previous names.

(4) the nationality of each partner.

(5) any other business occupation of each partner.

Upon registration, the Registrar will issue a certificate authorising the firm to trade under this name, and this must be displayed at the principal place of business.

In addition, by this Act all trade catalogues, circulars, showcards, business letters, etc. on which the firm's name appears must also clearly show the names of all partners in the firm.

6. ADVANTAGES OF PARTNERSHIPS

In considering the advantages, we must bear in mind the distinction between ordinary and limited partnerships, since many of the advantages of an ordinary partnership do not apply to the limited partner or partners, as the latter cannot take any part in the management of the business.

(a) Ordinary Partnerships

(1) The formation of a partnership is a convenient way of introducing new blood into a business. A valued employee may, for example, be made a partner, and in this way his services are secured for the business.

(2) Additional capital may be obtained by forming a partnership, and the activities of the firm may be extended.

(3) In a partnership some degree of specialisation is possible: various sections or branches of the business may be managed

by the different partners, and duties may be allotted according to the ability and qualifications of each.

(4) In a partnership, the amount of the capital can be varied by mutual consent: additional capital may be invested by the existing partners, or by the admission of new members. Similarly, the capital may be reduced by common consent if necessary.

(5) The individuality of each partner is not lost in a partnership as in a company: the partnership retains many of the personal advantages of the sole trader.

(6) There is greater continuity in a partnership than in the case of a sole trader: the retirement or death of one partner may necessitate a reorganisation of the partnership, but the remaining partners have some knowledge which will enable them to carry on the business.

(b) Limited Partnerships

Many of the above advantages apply to limited partnerships, but the following advantages of limited partnerships may be added:

(1) A limited partner has the advantage of limited liability; he is only liable for the debts of the firm up to the amount of capital that he subscribes. In this respect, he resembles the shareholder in a joint-stock company.

(2) He takes a share of the profits even though he has not taken part in the running of the firm.

(3) He may inspect the books of the firm at any time, and may give advice on matters concerning the affairs of the partnership.

7. LIMITATIONS OF PARTNERSHIPS

Partnerships have many limitations compared with the larger forms of business organisation. In considering these, we must again distinguish between the two forms of partnerships.

(a) Ordinary Partnerships

(1) Ordinary partners are liable individually for all the debts of the firm; if necessary, the personal property of each partner may be used to pay the debts of the firm.

(2) Except for firms of accountants, solicitors, stock-brokers

and stock-jobbers the number of partners in a partnership is limited to twenty, and in this way, the risks of the business are more concentrated than in a public company, which may have thousands of shareholders.

(3) One ordinary partner may bind the firm in trading contracts and in this way commit the other partners.

(4) The consent of *all* the partners is necessary for the admission of a new partner. As a result, one partner alone may prevent the admission of a very desirable new member, and thus hinder the development of the firm.

(5) The amount of capital subscribed in most cases is not likely to allow the business to be expanded to its fullest extent.

(6) The success of the business often depends upon the ability of the partners to work harmoniously with each other.

(b) Limited Partnerships

(1) A limited partner has no share in the management of the firm in which he has invested his capital.

(2) He is unable to withdraw part of his capital without the consent of the other partners.

(3) New partners can be admitted without the consent of a limited partner.

(4) A private company is usually preferred to a limited partnership of two or more persons who wish to open or extend a business. A private company may consist of from two to fifty shareholders, each of whom is liable only for the amount of capital invested, whereas in a limited partnership, there must be at least one ordinary partner with full liability.

Whilst many partnerships eventually form themselves into joint-stock companies in order to reap the benefit of limited liability, in some cases this is not possible. This is particularly so in many of the professions such as doctors, dentists, barristers, architects, solicitors, accountants, etc., because the rules relating to these professional bodies prohibit their members forming themselves into limited companies.

QUESTIONS

1. What advantages would be gained by a sole trader by converting his business into a partnership?   (U.L.C.I.)

2. What is the difference between a partnership and a limited partnership? In what circumstances are special advantages claimed for the latter, and what are these advantages? (R.S.A.)

3. Write a letter to a friend who has asked your advice concerning the clauses he ought to have inserted in a partnership deed to which he is a party. Explain carefully to him why you make these recommendations. (R.S.A.)

4. Why is a private trading partnership often converted into a private limited liability company? What advantages and disadvantages would there be for the former partners in such a conversion. (R.S.A.)

5. A garage is owned by two partners, both of whom are skilled motor mechanics. It offers the following services: garage, service, petrol and oil, tyres and accessories, repairs; it employs four other mechanics, a porter and two petrol pump attendants. Each partner tends to feel responsible for all that is done, and as a result there are frequent disagreements when they give conflicting instructions to employees and advice to customers. Discuss this problem in the light of what you know about a partnership, suggesting ways of solving the problems. (R.S.A.)

6. Five grocers in the town of Middleham each run a separate business as a sole trader. Three of them, Mr. Atkins, Mr. Barnes and Mr. Cook, are trying to persuade the other two, Mr. Drake and Mr. East, to join them in attempts to compete more successfully with the grocery chains. Briefly outline the arguments they may use. (R.S.A.)

Chapter 15

Joint-Stock Companies

I. THE DEVELOPMENT OF COMPANIES

Is closely connected with the growth of foreign trade. The discoveries of the fifteenth century opened up new markets in America and India, and the size of the business unit increased in order to provide additional capital and to meet the greater risks of world trade.

The development of company organisation took place in five stages:

(a) Association of Merchants. As early as the fourteenth century, merchants formed associations to protect their common interests in foreign lands. Each merchant traded with his own capital and in his own interest, but by payment of a subscription, he was assured of protective action, if necessary, by his fellow merchants. These associations were later formed into merchant companies known as Merchant Adventurers, and had specific areas in which its members enjoyed trading privileges.

(b) Common Fund. The joint-stock principle appeared during the sixteenth century, when the members of a company contributed to a joint-stock or common fund, in order to undertake trading enterprises beyond the means of an individual merchant. The Muscovy Company (1553) was one of the earliest joint-stock companies with a subscribed capital of £6,000 in shares of £25 each. One of its objects was to open up trade relations with Russia, and the expedition, led by Chancellor and Willoughby, succeeded in establishing an important trading centre at the northern port of Archangel. Perhaps a better known example is the East India Company, granted a charter in 1600, which gave the company a monopoly of trade in the East Indies.

(c) Extension of Joint-Stock Principle to Industry. This occurred during the eighteenth century, and was a result of the Industrial Revolution. Mechanisation and the factory system gradually replaced the domestic system of manufacture. More capital was required, and the general public were invited to purchase shares in these new enterprises. Dealings became commonplace among the wealthy classes and London Stock Exchange was established to provide facilities for the purchase and sale of shares.

(d) Parliamentary Control of Companies. The failure of the South Sea Bubble, 1719, led to the requirement that all new companies were to obtain a charter from the Crown, or a special Act of Parliament. We see here the origin of two important kinds of companies—*Chartered Companies* and *Statutory Companies*. To day a Certificate of Incorporation is issued instead by the Registrar for Joint-Stock Companies, and he sees that the requirements of the various Companies Acts are carried out.

(e) Limited Liability. The principle was introduced by Act of Parliament in 1855 providing the shares were of a nominal value of not less than £10. In 1862, a further Act removed the £10 limit, and since then, small investors can with safety purchase shares in a company, with the knowledge that *when the shares are fully paid up*, no further demands can be made on them. Thus their liability on the debts of the company is limited.

2. TYPES OF COMPANIES

A joint-stock company may be defined as an association of persons formed for the purpose of carrying on a business: these persons contribute money to a common stock, and in return share the profits (if any) in the form of dividend.

It should be noted that a company by law has *a distinct and separate legal existence from its members*, so that it can make valid trading contracts in the same way as an individual.

From the above account of the development of trading companies, *three* kinds may be distinguished:

(a) Chartered Companies. Early companies were formed or incorporated by a charter obtained from the Crown: this bestowed valuable trading privileges on the recipients. The East India Company, the Hudson Bay Company and the Bank of England are well-known examples of such awards.

Nowadays the granting of a charter by the Crown is usually confined to non-commercial corporations such as professional organisations or Local Authorities.

(b) Statutory Companies. Many companies are formed by special Acts of Parliament, which often confer a monopoly on the company concerned. Examples of organisations incorporated by Act of Parliament include:

(1) British Airways.
(2) British Rail.
(3) The Electricity and Gas Authorities.
(4) National Coal Board.
(5) The Post Office.
(6) United Kingdom Atomic Energy Authority.

All of these provide some public service in return for the privileges granted to them. Provisions are made with regard to the amount of capital to be raised, and the responsibility of the controlling authorities. It will be noticed that Statutory Companies, nationalised industries or public corporations as they are sometimes called, provide some public utility in which large amounts of capital are required often far beyond the capabilities of the private sector.

(c) Registered Companies. This class of company is the most usual, and includes all those registered under the various Companies Acts that have been passed since 1862. The most recent Companies Act was passed in 1967, when the law regarding the administration and control of companies was further codified. There are three types of registered companies:

(1) *Unlimited Companies.* Only a few such companies exist in which the liability of each shareholder is unlimited. They are formed usually where the company is intended to be non-trading yet for a specific task such as for educational purposes or the promotion of the arts.

(2) *Companies limited by Guarantee*. These companies again are not numerous and are often set up for non-trading purposes. Each shareholder guarantees to contribute a fixed sum of money to meet the liabilities of the company as long as he remains a member.

(3) *Companies limited by Shares*. Are by far the most numerous, the liability of each shareholder being limited to the *nominal value* of the shares held. Companies limited by shares may be either public or private.

> (*a*) *A public company* must consist of at least seven members, and may invite the public to become shareholders.
>
> (*b*) *A private company* may be formed by any number of persons from two to fifty, but no appeal to the public is permitted.

Every *trading* company must by law be registered with the Registrar of Companies in London (or Edinburgh) under the control of the Department of Trade and Industry. Recent statistics show that there are about 17,000 public companies compared with about 553,000 private companies, and these groups will now be considered in greater detail.

3. PRIVATE COMPANIES

The chief features may be summarised as follows:

(*a*) *Numbers*. A private company may consist of from two to fifty members or shareholders, *exclusive of employees*. As each shareholder has limited liability, it has a great advantage over the partnership form of business enterprise.

(*b*) *Transferability of Shares*. Its shares are not transferable without the consent of the other shareholders.

(*c*) *Appeal to the Public*. A private company is not allowed to offer its shares for sale to the public.

It has many advantages over other forms of business organisations. It makes a strong appeal to a small group of people who wish to run say a small or medium size business requiring only a moderate amount of capital, for the following reasons:

(1) All the shareholders have limited liability—that is, if the company fails, they are only responsible for the debts of the firm up to the amount of the fully paid capital.

(2) The minimum number of members is two; as a result, a private company with limited liability for each shareholder has obvious advantages over a partnership.

(3) In the 'family' type of company the Board of Directors who control the firm may consist of a husband and wife who own most of or all the shares. Others may include members of a family augmented by specialist employees who have given service to the firm over many years.

(4) It is free from many legal restrictions which apply to a public company—for example, no prospectus is necessary.

A private company must send to the Registrar of Companies a copy of its accounts each year, signed by a director or secretary. This must be accompanied by a statement that the company has not issued an invitation to the public to subscribe for shares, and that (if the number of members exceeds fifty) the excess consists of present or past employee members of the company.

4. PUBLIC COMPANIES

The chief features of a public joint-stock company are as follows:

(a) *Numbers*. It must consist of *at least* seven members: the maximum number of shareholders varies from company to company, and depends on:

  (1) the number of parts into which the issued share capital is divided as stated in the Memorandum of Association.

  (2) the number of shares held by various members of the company as they usually hold a number of shares each.

(b) *Limited Liability*. Each shareholder possesses limited liability in the same way as in the private company.

(c) *Transferability of Shares*. In a public company, the shares are freely transferable; shares are bought and sold on the Stock Exchange without any restrictions on the part of the company.

(d) *Appeal to the Public*. When commencing business as a public company or when increasing its issued share capital, a public company issues a Prospectus inviting the public to subscribe for shares.

(e) *Publicity*. It must send a copy of its accounts each year to the Registrar of Companies.

The public joint-stock company is the usual form of business organisation where large amounts of capital are required. Because of limited liability people with small amounts of capital are willing to invest their savings with a minimum of risk.

Advantages of Public Companies.

(1) Large amounts of capital running into many millions of pounds may be raised from a great many people. In this way the risks of the business are distributed amongst a large number of persons who have each contributed only a small portion of the capital.

(2) Each shareholder has limited liability: he is only responsible for the amount of capital he has subscribed or agreed to subscribe should the shares not be fully paid.

(3) The capital may be divided into different types of shares, such as preference shares and ordinary shares, each type having different amounts of risk.

(4) The shares are transferable without restriction. An organised market, centred round the Stock Exchange, exists for the buying and selling of these and other shares.

(5) From the point of view of the company, it is an advantage that the capital cannot be withdrawn: a shareholder who wishes to withdraw from the company by selling his shares must find someone else who is willing to purchase them from him. Hence the use of the Stock Exchange if he is unable to sell them privately.

(6) The company form of business organisation enables people with little or no knowledge of trade to invest their savings more profitably than, say, in a bank deposit account providing that they are willing to take a certain amount of risk.

(7) Greater specialisation of management is possible. The shareholders have the right to attend the annual general meetings of the company, and perhaps to vote in the election of the Directors who decide the general policy of the firm. This policy is carried out through subordinate officials

under the direction of the Managing Director and specialist managers.

(8) A company is continuous; the personnel of the shareholders is constantly changing, but the incorporated association of individuals goes on until it is either terminated voluntarily by the shareholders or on the instructions of a Court of Law.

(9) A public company must submit each year a copy of its accounts to the Registrar of Companies; this publicity is a safeguard against fraud.

Disadvantages. Public companies have been criticised on the following grounds:

(1) They lack the personal element which is a prominent feature of the simpler forms of business organisation. An employee often feels that he is working for a machine, and that his personal well-being is second in importance to large profits.

Many companies recognise this weakness in their organisation, however, and have set up personnel departments to deal with this problem. Others have established social clubs, and, in some cases, model housing estates in order to strengthen the personal relationship between the various interests of the company.

(2) In a large company, ownership and control are often separated; the firm's assets are owned by the shareholders collectively, but the policy of the firm is controlled by the directors. It may be argued that the separation of ownership and control leads to waste unless constant care is taken to detect wasteful methods.

(3) In a company, the shareholders often judge the success of the business by the amount of dividend. They have little interest in the internal organisation of the firm. They may be drawing dividends produced as a result of conditions of which they would disapprove if they had fuller knowledge.

(4) Large companies often tend to become even larger so that they reach a point where it becomes *impossible for one man to control* efficiently or effectively. Rules and regulations become more complex and management becomes further removed from labour.

5. FORMATION OF A COMPANY

Certain legal requirements must be met before a company can commence trading. The principal ones laid down by Parliament are the following:

(a) The Memorandum of Association. Every registered company before incorporation must deposit with the Registrar of Companies a Memorandum of Association. This contains the '*external rules*' of the company giving the following particulars:

(1) the name of the company, with 'limited' as the last word where appropriate.

(2) the situation of the registered office, whether in England, Wales or Scotland in order to make known which law is to apply.

(3) the objects of the company.

(4) a statement that the liability of the shareholders is limited.

(5) the amount of the authorised capital, showing its division into shares.

The memorandum must be signed by at least seven persons if a public company or two in the case of a private company, who must each agree to take one or more shares in the new company.

(b) Articles of Association govern the *internal working* of the company. A public company *must* but a private company *may* draw up articles of association with the Memorandum. A model set of articles is included in the Companies Act, and when a private company does not draw up its own set, it is presumed to have adopted this set of articles known as 'Table A'.

The Articles of Association lay down rules concerning the problems of management and would include amongst many others:

(1) the issue, transfer and forfeiture of shares.

(2) method of dealing with any alterations in the amount of capital.

(3) procedure in calling general meetings and the method of voting.

(4) the qualifications, powers and duties of the directors.

(5) the procedure dealing with the division of profits and the payment of dividends.

(6) the method of audit and other internal or domestic affairs of the company.

(c) Statement of Authorised or Nominal Capital. The Memorandum and Articles of Association are sent to the Registrar of Companies, together with:

(1) a list of persons who have consented to become directors.

(2) a declaration by a solicitor that the provisions of the Companies Act have been complied with.

(3) a statement of the Authorised or Nominal Capital.

The above documents *must* be deposited with the Registrar of Companies, who will inspect them before allowing the company to commence trading by the issue of a Certificate of Incorporation. In addition the promoters of the company will be required to pay the necessary fees and stamp duties which will vary according to the amount of the authorised capital stated in the Memorandum of Association.

After the legal formalities have been completed, these become *public documents* which may be freely inspected at any reasonable time at the Registrar's Office in London or Edinburgh as appropriate.

(d) A Certificate of Incorporation is issued by the Registrar in London (or Edinburgh), recognising the company as a corporate body, and authorising it to commence trading.

This must be displayed at the company's registered office and contains the following information:

(1) the name of the company and its registered number.

(2) a statement that it has been so registered in accordance with the law.

(3) the signature of the Registrar.

(e) The Prospectus applies only to public companies and is an invitation to the public to take shares in the company. It contains detailed information to enable investors to estimate its prospects. It is important that the public should not be misled, and a copy of the prospectus must therefore be filed with the Registrar, and in certain cases approved by the Council of the Stock Exchange.

The prospectus must state the minimum amount of capital that is necessary to enable the company to commence business together with details of the shares offered for sale.

Other information includes:

(1) Names and addresses of directors.
(2) The time of opening of the subscription lists.
(3) The amounts payable on application and allotment of the shares.

6. THE CAPITAL OF A COMPANY

The maximum amount of capital that can be issued is stated in the Memorandum of Association. But it is not necessary to issue all the capital at once: the memorandum may authorise a company to raise say £100,000 capital in the form of 100,000 Ordinary Shares of £1 each. The directors, however, may decide to issue only 75,000 shares in order to commence business. In addition, the directors may decide that each shareholder shall pay only half the face value of his share—the remaining half to be paid at some future date if the directors so decide.

There are, therefore, three kinds of share capital:

(a) The Authorised or Nominal Capital of a company is the amount stated in the Memorandum of Association, and is the maximum amount which the company is authorised to raise. In the above example, the authorised or nominal capital is £100,000.

(b) Issued Capital is the amount that the directors decide to issue to the shareholders. In the above example, the amount of issued capital is £75,000; the remaining £25,000 may be issued later if the directors decide to extend the business.

(c) Called-up Capital is the amount of cash which a company actually receives from the shareholders in exchange for shares ignoring any premiums. If the directors issued £75,000 of capital, and asked each shareholder to pay half the face value of his shares, the called-up capital would be £37,500. The shareholders are liable for the remaining half of the value of the shares when called upon.

Taking the balance sheet of the company as an example, the share capital would be shown thus:

BALANCE SHEET A. GRANT LTD. AS AT DEC. 31ST 19..

Liabilities		Assets
Authorised Share Capital	£	£
100 000 Ordinary Shares £1 each	100,000	
Issued Share Capital		
75, 000 Ordinary Shares £1 each		
50p paid	37,500	Cash at Bank 37,500
	37,500	37,500

7. THE SHARES OF A COMPANY

The capital of a company is divided into shares the face value of which varies from company to company. It may be divided into units of £10 or more, or into units as little as a penny. There is a growing practice however to divide the capital into small units in order to appeal to as wide a public as possible.

Various types of shares may be issued subject to the Memorandum of Association. It may issue both preference *and* ordinary shares or it may issue only one kind of share, say ordinary shares. Investors differ in the amount of risk they are willing to take, and no two companies are exactly alike in this respect. The following classes of shares may be offered; they are arranged in the order in which they share the available profits;

(a) **Cumulative Preference Shares.** The holders of these shares are entitled to a fixed rate of dividend. If there are not sufficient profits to pay this *fixed rate of dividend* in any one year, as they are cumulative the arrears must be paid the following year, or at the first opportunity when there are sufficient profits.

(b) **Preference Shares.** Also have the first claim to the profits available for distribution. A fixed rate of dividend is stated, but if the profits in any one year are insufficient to pay this, no arrears are paid the following year. Preference shares are often regarded as being of the cumulative type unless otherwise stated.

(c) Participating Preference Shares. The holders of these shares are entitled to a fixed rate of dividend, *and in addition* if there is sufficient profit available for distribution they will receive a bonus after the ordinary shareholders have received a certain rate of dividend.

(d) Ordinary Shares. The claims for dividend of the ordinary shareholders come after those of the preference shareholders. Ordinary Shares may be of two kinds:

(1) *Preferred Ordinary Shares*, which have a fixed rate of dividend, which is paid after the claims of the preference shareholders have been met.

(2) *Deferred Ordinary Shares*, are the most usual type issued as they have no fixed rate, but take the remainder of the available profits (if any) after the claims of the other shareholders have been met.

The Ordinary Shares are the 'risk capital' of the company and are the last to be paid a dividend out of the profits available for distribution. In times of plenty they may reap a high dividend whilst at other times they may receive either a very small return or nothing at all. It is factors such as these that often reflect a large rise or fall in the price outsiders are willing to pay for public company shares on the Stock Exchange. These shares are often referred to as *Equities* in the financial press: a high-class equity often being referred to as a *bluechip*.

(e) Deferred or Founders' Shares are shares taken up by the promoters of the company: the holders receive a dividend after the claims of all the other shareholders have been met. These are comparatively rare nowadays as provision is usually made for these shares to be transferred into ordinary shares after the company is incorporated.

It should be noted that a company is not likely to issue all of the above types of shares. The number and kind will depend very much on circumstances and individual preferences.

In all of the above cases the holding of shares in a company would be evidenced by a document known as a *share certificate*. This will contain details such as the name of the company, name of shareholder, type of share and number of shares held.

8 Company Formation in Europe

COUNTRY	TYPE	GENERAL RESTRICTIONS	SYMBOL
Belgium	Private	Share transfers Minimum capital 2–50 shareholders	S.P.R.L.
	Public	Min. 7 shareholders Min. 3 directors	S.A.
Britain and Eire	Private	Share transfers 2–50 shareholders Published accounts	Ltd.
	Public	Min. 7 shareholders Published accounts	Ltd.
Denmark	Private/Public	Minimum capital Residential qualifications Published accounts Trading licences	A/S
France	Private	Share transfers Certain activities e.g. banking	S.A.R.L.
	Public	Min. 7 shareholders Directors to be share- holders Minimum capital	S.A.
Germany (West)	Private	Share transfers Minimum capital Labour representation	GmbH
	Public	Min. 3 directors Min. 2,000 shares Two boards of management	A.G.
Holland	Private	Share transfers No share certificates	B.V.
	Public	Min. 1 shareholder possible Minimum capital Published accounts	N.V.
Italy	Private	Share transfers Minimum capital Published accounts	S.A.R.L.
	Public	Minimum capital Published accounts	SpA
Luxembourg	Private/Public	Government permit Trading licence	S.A.

9. INCREASE OF CAPITAL

It may be necessary for a variety of reasons to increase the capital of a company; if it is expanding, new developments may require additional capital or an expansion of credit trading may call for extra funds. The need for additional capital may therefore be temporary or permanent.

(a) Temporary Increases of Capital are usually provided by one the following means:

(1) *An Overdraft from the Bank*, which will, of course, require security such as freehold property, guarantees, etc. These loans may be short or medium term and in certain circumstances such as the export trade may have the guarantee of the Government.

(2) *Purchases on Credit.* Arrangements may be made with suppliers for a longer period of credit.

(b) Permanent Increases of Capital may be raised by:

(1) Calling up the uncalled capital if any is available.

(2) Issuing the remaining portion of the authorised capital, if any.

(3) Applying to the Registrar of Companies for permission to increase the amount of the authorised capital in the Memorandum of Association where the full amount of capital has already been issued.

(4) The property of the company may be mortgaged: a mortgage deed is drawn up, and the amount of the loan, with interest, is repaid over a period of years.

(5) *Debentures* may be issued by the company. These are loans to the company on the security of its property. A debenture holder is paid his interest *irrespective of any surplus, such as profit.* If the company is unable to pay the interest or repay the loan, the debenture holders could sell the business or take over the management. Thus they are in a very strong position.

(6) *Finance Corporations* are the usual source of *long-term loan* capital. There are numerous financial institutions that have the backing of or are jointly owned by many of the large City institutions such as banks, insurance companies, etc. The more important ones are:

(a) *Finance Corporation for Industry Ltd.* which will lend

amounts *in excess* of £200,000 to companies that require capital in the national interest and are unable to obtain this elsewhere. The share capital is held jointly by the Bank of England, the leading insurance companies and the chief investment trust companies of the City.

(b) *Industrial and Commercial Finance Corporation Ltd.* invests long term capital in British based small and medium-sized industrial and commercial concerns. It also provides both financial and specialist services either directly or through its subsidiaries. The shareholders of the I.C.F.C. are the Bank of England with the English clearing and Scottish joint-stock banks.

(c) *Credit for Industry Ltd.* assist the smaller firms whilst the *Agricultural Mortgage Corporation Ltd.* and the *Ship Mortgage Finance Corporation Ltd.* will lend money to particular industries.

(7) Government assistance can be arranged in the form of loans or grants in certain instances such as the firm's importance to the national economy etc.

QUESTIONS

1. In what important respects does a limited partnership differ from a private limited company? Why is the latter type of business unit much more prevalent in this country? (U.L.C.I.)

2. Give reasons for the increase during the last fifty years of the Joint-Stock Company form of business organisation. (U.L.C.I.)

3. Comment on the advantages of limited liability of Joint-Stock Companies from the point of view of (a) an individual manufacturing firm, (b) the general interests of the community.
(R.S.A.)

4. What commercial activities are usually associated with (a) One-man businesses, (b) Limited Partnerships, (c) Joint-Stock Companies? Can you give any reasons for such association?
(R.S.A.)

5. The Memorandum and Articles of Association of a public limited company prescribe a number of rules regulating the constitution of the company and the conduct of its affairs. Outline the main rules and explain the reasons why the law insists on such strict regulations for limited companies. (Oxford G.C.E.)

6. What are the fundamental differences between a partnership and a private company? Why is it that many professional concerns are partnerships rather than companies? (R.S.A.)

7. In the functioning of a public Joint-Stock Company what part is normally played by (a) the board of directors, (b) the managing director, (c) the debenture holders and (d) the ordinary shareholders? (London G.C.E.)

8. Explain fully the meaning and effects of the expressions 'low geared' and 'high geared' as applied to the capital of a public limited liability company. Enumerate the advantages and disadvantages of each. (R.S.A.)

9. What are the important differences between partnerships and private limited companies? What justification is there for the existence of these two kinds of business organisation? (A.E.B.)

10. 'Voting power, giving ultimate control, is largely in the hands of the Equity shareholders of a company.' Explain this quotation and state who are the other shareholders. (R.S.A.)

11. The owners of two small chains of shoe shops operating in a busy provincial town decide to amalgamate. What advantages could be expected from the owners' point of view? (R.S.A.)

Chapter 16

The Co-operative Movement
State Enterprise, Local Authorities

(A) The Co-operative Movement

I. ORIGIN

Co-operative societies had their origin at the end of the eighteenth century, when great industrial changes were taking place. Until the eighteenth century, most of the manufacture was undertaken in the home, under what is known as the Domestic System: but as a result of the invention of machinery, the Factory System of manufacture developed, and people went to work for wages in a factory instead of being their own masters at home.

The social distress and unemployment which accompanied these great changes in industry were made worse by the fact that during the later period of the Industrial Revolution the Napoleonic Wars were being fought. These produced further industrial changes, and in spite of a limited amount of prosperity during the French Wars, years of distress and nuemployment followed the conclusion of peace in 1815.

The idea of co-operation arose during these years of distress: the aim of the early co-operators was to remedy the distress of the working classes by obtaining some of the benefits of the new machinery and greater production for the workers. Two methods were attempted in order to do this:

(*a*) To set up workshops owned and controlled by the workers themselves: the employees to subscribe the capital, run the factory under the direction of elected foremen, and to share in the profits made from the sale of their products. This idea was borrowed from the French at the time of the French Revolution, and in it we see the origin of what is called today *Productive Co-operation*.

(*b*) To form associations of consumers who would buy their requirements collectively from wholesalers or manufacturers and thus by buying in bulk, would be able to sell to members at a lower price. This principle is the origin of the *Consumers' Co-operative Society*, which is the commonest type today.

Many attempts were made on the above lines to remedy the distress, but usually they failed to accomplish their purpose. The idea of co-operation survived, however, and better-organised movements were more successful from 1820 onwards.

2. THE CO-OPERATIVE MOVEMENT

The modern co-operative movement in Britain dates from the foundation in 1844 of a co-operative store in Toad Lane, Rochdale, Lancashire. Its founders were twenty-eight Lancashire weavers who based the operation of their society on principles which have since been copied throughout the world. These were:

(*a*) open membership
(*b*) democratic control (one man, one vote)
(*c*) the distribution of surplus in proportion to a member's purchases
(*d*) limited interest on capital invested.

The store was started by members investing various small sums of money at low rates of interest and in return a member had the right to vote on policy matters *irrespective* of the amount invested. In addition the net trading profit was distributed as a form of dividend to the members periodically. New members could join on payment of a small sum towards the purchase of a share so becoming eligible to take part in the scheme.

The above principles are still applied today throughout the co-operative movement in Britain which forms one of the largest retail outlets in the country. The *retail consumer co-operative societies* described on page 146 form the basis of the movement particularly in the grocery trade. The following divisions, however, should be considered in relation to the movement as a whole:

(a) *The Co-operative Union*

Is the central organisation of the movement in Britain to which are affiliated the numerous retail societies, the wholesale societies as well as various productive and other societies. It provides advisory services and also co-ordinates the overall planning of the movement.

(b) *Wholesale and Federal Societies*

The co-operative moment in Britain has established its own wholesale societies, the Co-operative Wholesale Society Ltd. (C.W.S.) and the Scottish Co-operative Wholesale Society Ltd. (S.C.W.S.). They serve the retail societies with a high proportion of their merchandise requirements from their own factories using their own transport for this purpose. In addition extensive advertising campaigns are conducted for the movement as a whole. The wholesale societies are also engaged in the administration and control of many tea and cocoa plantations abroad which belong to the co-operative movement. The profits of the wholesale societies are distributed to the retail societies in proportion to their purchases. The respective Wholesale Societies are controlled by Boards of Directors that are the statutory policy-making bodies of the movement. The C.W.S. Board consists of 30 part-time members elected by the regional co-operative societies elected for a period of up to three years. In order to qualify for election, a candidate must be a member of his local Committee of Management or senior official of the retail outlet. The allocation of seats on the Board is subject to periodic review and is based on the trade figures of the local societies with the C.W.S. Voting power is related to the amount of trade undertaken between the members local society and the C.W.S. over the previous twelve months.

The Wholesale Society is divided into two principal divisions:

(a) *Food Division* deals with activities concerned with the bulk supply of groceries, meat, drinks, flour etc. together with centralised buying and packing organisations.

(b) *Non-Food Division* controlling operations in the drapery, textiles, furniture, hardware section of the movement in addition to contract supplies to private and public enterprises.

There are also numerous federal societies usually established and administered by local retail societies which provide goods or services of a specialist nature such as laundry, bakery and dairy services. On a national basis there are also a number of specialist federal societies such as the Co-operative Printing Society, the Co-operative Bank, the Co-operative Insurance Society, etc., through which the consumer may deal.

(c) *Productive Societies*

A small number of productive societies are engaged in production on a co-partnership and profit-sharing basis. The aim of this form of co-operation is to establish productive outlets in which the *employees* provide the capital and take the risks instead of the entrepreneur.

The success of this form of co-operation has been very limited in Britain compared with some other European countries, particularly France. An analysis of the British productive societies shows that they are concentrated mostly in the clothing, footwear and printing trades.

The principal advantages attached to the system of co-operation lies in relation to the payment of a rebate or dividend to the consumer and the fact that he can take part in the control of the business. In addition some of the surplus funds are used for social and educational purposes for the benefit of both members and staff.

The main disadvantages are that the member is often only interested in the dividend and is not concerned with the management of the business or the conditions under which employees are working. Also it is sometimes thought that many of the management committees are composed of persons who are lacking in business experience.

(B) State Authorities

I. THE STATE

The nationalised industries are an important sector of the national economy. They provide many of the basic necessities which are essential to the industrial, commercial and social sectors of the country. In addition the Government often uses the public sector as a means to implement its own economic and social policies. These include measures to curb the level of unemployment, or price restraint of basic commodities, or social welfare measures etc.

Since the middle of this century the State has taken a greater interest and sometimes absolute control of the *basic* industries so that it has been able to invest huge amounts of public money into the undertakings in order to provide a wider and more unified service.

Direct State participation in productive and commercial sectors is usually achieved by the creation of Statutory Authorities through special Acts of Parliament. These industries then become *public corporations* which are placed under the control of a Minister of the Crown responsible to Parliament.

The Act by which the appropriate authority is controlled contains the general outline of the sphere through which it may operate and sets out the delegation of powers to the Minister responsible.

The Minister will appoint a managing board to control the authority and these are persons who are experienced and competent in particular fields. They are not civil servants in the true sense but in addition to the responsibility of management, they are accountable to Parliament through the Minister for their actions.

In order to gain some idea of the role that the State plays in everyday life, the following is a cross-section of Government interests:

Aviation: British Airways
Banking: Bank of England

Power:　　National Coal Board
　　　　　　The Electricity Council
　　　　　　The British Gas Corporation
Transport:　British Rail
　　　　　　National Freight Corporation

The extent to which the Government Minister controls the boards or councils varies from industry to industry. The appointed members, however, usually delegate their authority to area boards and divisions which are responsible for the day-to-day running of the industry. By this method of control, the chain of command remains unbroken in so far as policy decisions are carried out in the most efficient manner.

It is not necessarily essential but it is sometimes desirable that the industry should make a profit *over a period of time.* This can be used either to relieve the Exchequer and reduce taxation or as is more usual, used to improve the efficiency of the undertaking. Any loss that accrues must be borne by the taxpayer who must either accept this as part of a social service, pay more for the service provided, or through the numerous representative consumer councils, advise the board of ways that can overcome the deficiency.

2. LOCAL AUTHORITIES

It is the duty of every local authority to provide and administer certain essential services such as drainage, cleansing, street lighting, recreation facilities, etc.

An authority may, however, provide additional services under powers granted to it by Act of Parliament or other legislation.

Many cities or towns provide their own education services or join with others in forming an education authority for a region. Others invest large sums of money in trading enterprises which cater for the holiday trade. Bournemouth and Blackpool for example provide specialist services to the visitors who in turn bring prosperity to the area.

Control is exercised through a committee of Council representatives who in turn will delegate some of their authority to a paid full-time official. He will be responsible for the day-to-day running of the enterprise and answerable to the Committee for all matters affecting the undertaking.

The initial capital is usually provided by means of loans. Application is made to the Ministry of Housing and Local Government to raise a loan for a particular purpose. If this is approved the authority will borrow by one of the following ways:

(a) Issue bonds repayable in a given number of years and at a fixed rate per cent.

(b) Borrow from the Public Works Loan Board at preferential rates of interest for certain purposes.

(c) Issue stock through the Stock Exchange.

The loans are repaid over a number of years either by further borrowing or by a levy on the rates. Alternatively local authorities may borrow from the banking sector, principally the accepting houses, overseas and private banks of the City of London, on a short term basis of between seven days and three months. In the same manner as the State undertakings, profits of local authorities are used either to relieve the rates or improve the service, whilst losses are borne by the ratepayer. (The student is referred to page 219 for the advantages and disadvantages of State and Local Authority Enterprises.)

QUESTIONS

1. Explain carefully the difference between a distributive co-operative society and a productive co-operative society

(U.L.C.I.)

2. What is the essential difference between the basis of organisation of the co-operative retail store and that of the independent shop? Give some reasons for the growth of the consumers' co-operative movement. (U.L.C.I.)

3. Discuss the relative strength and weakness of co-operative societies and private traders in competition for the retail business of Britain. (R.S.A.)

4. Give an outline of the general organisation of the Co-operative Movement in this country. Comment on its present magnitude and discuss the probable limits to its future growth.

(R.S.A.)

5. In what different ways are publicly-owned undertakings

organised and controlled (*a*) by local authorities and (*b*) by the
Government?   (London G.C.E.)

6. Select one nationalised industry in Britain, describe how it is
organised and controlled, and comment on the problems with
which it has been faced.   (R.S.A.)

7. What do you understand by 'private enterprise'? Compare
the main features of a large-scale enterprise in the private sector
with those of a public utility authority such as British Rail.
                                                          (R.S.A.)

8. What commercial problems arise in nationalised forms of
organisation with reference to (*a*) price, (*b*) capital?

                                                          (A.E.B.)

9. Why is the supply of the essential public services of electricity
and gas undertaken in Britain by regional or area boards? What
authorities are responsible for the supply of water in Britain? How
do they differ from the boards which supply electricity and gas?
                                                          (R.S.A.)

10. (*a*) Name *six* public corporations indicating in each case the
main activity of the corporation.

        (*b*) What are the main characteristics of public corporations?
                                                          (U.E.I.)

Chapter 17

Large-Scale Organisation

I. COMPETITION

During the nineteenth century, the merits of competition were unquestioned, for the economic teachings of that period maintained that the business world would prosper if left to look after itself. The reasons for this belief were:

(a) If the demand for a commodity exceeded the supply, competition between buyers would send up the price.

(b) The increase in price would lead to higher profits.

(c) The increase in profits would attract new capital into the industry: new firms would be established, and as a result, the supply would increase.

(d) The increased supply would bring the price back to normal.

(e) The struggle between sellers would maintain the efficiency of the industry and would lead to the survival of the most efficient firms.

On these assumptions, it was believed that competition was a safeguard against high prices, and that under such a system, demand and supply, wages and profits would adjust themselves.

These views were held at a period when Britain had no serious rivals in manufacture. Competition of course has its merits, since each firm has a direct incentive to improve its methods, eliminating waste and reducing costs. The belief in competition, however, seems to have been well suited to an age when businesses were on a small scale. Even so much of the progress of British Industry during the nineteenth and present century continues to be due to the increase in efficiency which competition produces.

A point is reached, however, when competition no longer leads to greater efficiency and progress: improvements in method are most rapid in the early development of an industry, and under such conditions, competition acts as a stimulus. But as the rate of progress slows down, it leads to waste of effort through lack of co-ordination. Manufacturers, for example, may devote too much of their efforts to under-cutting each other's prices rather than to improving methods and processes.

Competition also prevents the co-ordination of the supply to the demand, and delays the interchange of information and experience upon which industrial progress depends. Under a system of competition, each firm must have its own selling departments and staffs, and must bear its own cost of adver-tising and distribution of goods. As a result of these and many other expenses being borne by individual firms, the cost of a commodity may be greater than under a system of combination, whereby many of the distributing expenses can be pooled.

2. LIMITATION OF COMPETITION

The ideal of perfect competition has never been fully realised, principally due to the presence of restrictions which are imposed from time to time in order to overcome economic difficulties. The following reasons may be suggested for the limitation of such competition.

(a) The Increased Size of Establishments. The number of firms has been reduced on account of large-scale production: smaller and less efficient firms have been absorbed or have closed down. The increased size of establishments has limited competition in two ways:

(1) With *fewer* firms, it is probably easier to make agree-ments regarding accepted standards.

(2) With *larger* firms the competition will probably become fiercer. As a result, 'competition leads to association', and schemes to overcome the effect of, say, foreign competition are put into effect.

(b) The Increased Cost of Equipment. This makes greater amounts of capital necessary, delays the entry of new competitors, and agreements among existing firms become more effective.

(c) Improved Transport. During the nineteenth century, a factory had to be near a coalfield, or near a large consuming centre. With the improvement in transport (especially road transport) during the present century, manufacturers can be nearer together, and their proximity facilitates association for dealing with common problems.

(d) Improvements in Marketing. Developments in transport and communications have led to wider markets, more elaborate methods of marketing have become necessary, forcing firms to combine, in order to reduce costs. This can be achieved by such methods as the reduction of the number of agencies, and the adoption of a common advertising policy.

(e) Scientific Progress. The advance in manufacture has been mainly due to scientific progress. Much of this new knowledge has been in the possession of a few firms who have been able to devote some of their resources towards research. This has been an incentive to combination, in order to reduce costs by pooling knowledge.

(f) Raw Materials. A group of firms acting together may obtain control of the supplies of raw materials, instead of competing amongst themselves for a limited supply.

(g) Import Duties. Tariffs, quotas and import taxes are a protection to the less efficient firm. Inside the country it does not have to compete on equal terms with its foreign competitors.

(h) Foreign Competition. Foreign competition by industrialised countries such as Japan and the United States has shown the value of large combines which compete on world markets. World conditions are therefore making it essential for British and European firms to combine amongst themselves for the purpose of trading on equal terms with firms from other countries.

The extent to which competition has been limited depends upon the nature of the industry or trade: we may, however, distinguish two types of combined effort—voluntary association and amalgamation.

3. VOLUNTARY ASSOCIATIONS

Many kinds of voluntary associations exist, especially in local trade. Such associations are readily terminable, since a member can always resign his membership if he considers that it will be to his advantage to do so.

Voluntary associations may be developed according to the scope of the work undertaken as follows:

(a) **Informal Associations.** The simplest form of association occurs when a number of manufacturers, traders or distributors who would otherwise be competitors meet from time to time in order to discuss ways of increasing trade among the members. The meeting is usually quite informal; there are no documents nor is there any bond except that of good faith. Familiar examples of such associations occur in most large towns, where tradesmen in the same line of business meet periodically to discuss a common policy.

(b) **Trade Associations.** A large proportion of the manufacturers, traders or distributors in a particular line of business form an association for the purpose of regulating the trade. Associations are properly constituted bodies, having rules, officers, entrance fee, etc. The work of an association depends upon the nature of the trade, and a full account of this can be seen on page 106.

The distinguishing feature is that each firm remains an independent unit with full freedom of action in all matters that are not ruled by the association.

(c) **The Cartel.** Consists of a number of firms producing the same articles, and aims at controlling both price *and* output.

The firms in the Cartel form a Selling Agency, which is registered as a separate company: the producing firms hold shares in the Cartel in proportion to their output. Each firm in the Cartel has complete independence, and sells the whole of its output to the Selling Agency at a price just above the cost of production. The Selling Agency, therefore, markets the product of a large number of firms and thus prevents the undercutting of prices by rival manufacturers. The Selling Agency obtains the highest prices possible, and divides the profits amongst the shareholders in proportion to output.

The Cartel controls output by allotting each firm a quota. If the output is exceeded, a fine is paid into the pool: if it is not reached, a bonus is drawn in lieu.

This form of organisation is not common in Britain although it does exist in various forms on the continent. Many of the principles involved relate to forms of restrictive practices which can be damaging to the interest of the consumer.

Weaknesses of Voluntary Associations may be summarised as follows:

(1) Their control is limited because they *are* voluntary. Many traders and firms may refuse to join an association, whilst others may resign their membership if they disagree with the policy of the Association. Under such conditions, complete control is impossible.

(2) Voluntary associations afford the greatest protection to the less efficient traders, who are protected, to some extent, against the competition of more efficient rivals.

(3) Where there is an allocation of output, this may give rise to suspicion amongst members: it is difficult to enforce the allotted output, and mutual jealousy amongst the members delays any adjustments which may be necessary.

Because of the above, experience has proved that the benefits of large-scale production can only be obtained by permanent associations, many of which are found in combines, trusts, or holding companies.

4. PERMANENT ASSOCIATIONS

The weakness of all voluntary associations is that it is often impossible to enforce agreements. In the permanent association, however, there is a strict control as the member firms become amalgamated and fully integrated into the business organisation. Often one firm or directorate will lay down the general policy and the other members will be required to carry out these instructions.

Permanent associations or combines are formed in four ways:

(a) **The Exchange of Shares.** The directors of two or more companies agree upon a scheme of interchange of shares in a given proportion, and recommend the scheme to the shareholders of the individual companies. If the shareholders agree to exchange some of their shares, they become shareholders in a number of companies instead of in one, and a common policy is attained: control of output and prices is made easier, since all the companies have the same body of shareholders.

(b) **Interlocking Directorates.** A group of companies may work together by electing a number of directors to the boards of several companies. These remain under separate control, but some degree of common action is attained by the interchange of directors. Under this arrangement, each director is on the directorate of several companies, and a common system of control can be used throughout the group.

(c) **Amalgamation.** Two or more firms may decide to unite their interests by forming *one* company out of the separate units. The absorbing company may purchase other companies outright, or may obtain a controlling interest by purchasing a majority of the shares. The identity of the separate firms may continue in name, or a new name may be given to the amalgamated companies. In 1968 for example the National Provincial Bank and the Westminster Bank amalgamated to form the National Westminster Group which incorporated the District Bank as well as Coutts and Co.

Generally speaking, where a firm has a reputation for any product, or where the name of the firm is a trade asset, the original name is retained in spite of the amalgamation.

(d) **Holding Company.** Is a prominent feature of the organisation of business today, as it forms an effective means of combining business organisations. As its name suggests, the holding company holds the majority or the whole of the shares in other companies. The other companies are called *subsidiaries* if the holding company is the largest shareholder, and *associated* companies if the holding company is a large shareholder, but has not a majority of the voting power.

A holding company is a financial organisation, which neither manufactures nor buys or sells goods. It makes its profits as the principal or sole shareholder of other companies, whose directors it appoints, and thus secures control of policy. It secures control of other companies in two ways:

(1) When the holding company has been formed, it may use its funds to acquire a controlling interest in other companies by purchasing shares in the companies it wishes to control.

(2) The holding company may persuade the directors of other companies to agree to exchange the shares of those companies for the shares of the holding company. If the shareholders agree to the directors' recommendation, they become shareholders in the holding company instead of in the original firm.

Examples of holding companies would include Imperial Chemical Industries Ltd., which was formed in 1926 to acquire the shares of Brunner, Mond and Co. Ltd., Nobel Industries Ltd., United Alkali Co. Ltd., and British Dye-stuffs Corporation Ltd. Many further additions have been made from time to time so that today I.C.I. is one of the largest companies in Europe employing many millions of capital and thousands of workers.

Other well-known examples include British Leyland Ltd., Vickers Ltd., Sears (Holdings) Ltd., Unilever Ltd., Beechams Ltd., etc.

Holding companies are an important means of obtaining the benefits of large-scale production. By means of one board of directors who control the policy of a group of firms, competition is reduced, production is adjusted to demand, and the products of different firms can be standardised. Redundant factories can be closed, and orders can be distributed amongst the various companies, which may specialise on particular lines of goods.

5. HORIZONTAL AND VERTICAL COMBINES

Horizontal Combines link up firms at the *same stage of production*; for example, a combination of wall-paper manufacturers has gradually secured complete dominance of that trade in Britain. The aims of a horizontal combine are to maintain prices, to obtain lower prices from firms supplying the raw materials, and to check competition by the elimination of overlapping.

Combines of the horizontal type are of great importance in modern industry and examples would include Esso Ltd., Courtaulds Ltd., the Electric and Musical Industries Ltd. and the Debenham Group of Companies. The well-known firm of Courtaulds Ltd., has been built up by means of extensive amalgamations and controls the greater part of the sewing-thread industry of Britain; in the same way, the Imperial Tobacco Company is a combine of a large number of firms engaged in the tobacco industry formed in 1901 to protect the British market from American tobacco interests.

Vertical Combines link up the various stages of production from the raw material to the finished product; the aim of a vertical combine is to reduce costs and so increase profits. Note that with Vertical Combines the attached firms are at *different stages of production.*

A well-known example of such a combine is the firm of Cavenham Foods Ltd., which not only manufactures and markets its products, but also owns cattle ranches in Australia and South America.

A further development is the case of a group of firms which is both a horizontal and vertical combine. The firm of Unilever Ltd., started as a horizontal combine by acquiring a controlling interest in a large number of soap works: later it became a vertical combine also by acquiring control of firms supplying vegetable and animal oils from West Africa.

6. THE ADVANTAGES OF COMBINES

There can be little doubt that combines increase the efficiency of industry, since advantages accrue to a group of firms which are beyond the reach of individual businesses working as separate units. These may be summarised as follows:

(a) Buying

(1) The buying departments of the separate firms may be combined, and purchases can be made in bulk by the estab-

lishment of one central buying department. This results in more favourable terms and larger discounts, and economies in transport charges are made.

(2) Larger orders can be placed direct with the producer, larger trade discounts obtained and the dealings of a number of middlemen are avoided.

(3) A vertical combine can obtain control over the supplies of raw materials by purchasing a majority of the shares in firms which supply its goods. It may go further, and develop large areas in various parts of the world in order to increase and control its supplies of raw materials.

(b) Manufacturing

(1) The cost of production may be lowered by the standardisation of products in the case of articles which are made by machinery and which lend themselves to repetition manufacture. This standardisation of products is an advantage to the distributive trades, since it reduces the amount and variety of stock to be carried.

(2) Factories may specialise on particular processes; each factory may instal specialised equipment, and acquire specialised skill and experience in a particular kind of work. This leads to increased efficiency in production and a greater output.

(3) Redundant factories may be closed, and the work can be distributed amongst those which are best equipped for a particular class of work. All combines have a central Management or Work Study Department, which has an expert knowledge of all problems connected with the layout of a factory; this department deals with the efficiency of all factories, so as to secure the maximum output and lowest cost.

(4) A group of manufacturing firms is in a much better position for dealing with by-products arising during the course of manufacture. These can be collected for treatment at one works, whereas the small quantity of by-product at one would not be worth dealing with.

(5) Work may be more equally distributed when a group of firms is working as one unit, whereas under a system of competition, one firm may be working overtime whilst another may be on short time.

(c) Selling

(1) A combine may arrange that goods shall be delivered from the factory nearest to the customer, and by this means, considerable savings in the cost of transport may be made. In an unorganised industry, it is obviously wasteful for a London firm to send goods to Leeds or Lille, for example, and for those firms to send similar goods to London.

(2) A combine can have its own representatives abroad, whereas an individual firm has to rely on agents who sell on commission. The agent may be acting for a number of firms representing different trades, and may have little knowledge of any of them. A combine, however, can send out specially trained representatives, and obtain a first-hand knowledge of the requirements of a particular market.

(3) A group of firms in a combine can advertise its goods collectively; the advertisements can emphasise the merits of the products rather than the merits of a particular firm.

(4) The combine is able to establish a central selling agency where the products of many firms are identical. Economies are possible by central selling, as separate selling departments for each firm are unnecessary.

(d) Knowledge

(1) In a combine, knowledge of the best methods of manufacture or organisation is placed at the disposal of all the firms.

(2) A uniform and accurate system of costing is necessary for a combine, so that comparisons can be made between one firm and another. Wasteful methods which might pass unnoticed in an individual firm can be detected and eliminated in a combine.

(3) It can afford to encourage scientific research, whereas only the wealthiest individual firms could do so. The knowledge so gained is placed at the disposal of all the firms in the combine.

(4) Statistical information regarding the course and prospects of trade is collected and distributed to all members.

7. DISADVANTAGES OF COMBINES

Combines have become a common feature of industrial organisation, and whilst they have increased the efficiency of production, it is difficult to generalise on any disadvantages in the
short term. The following however may show themselves in
course of time.

(*a*) The decline in importance of the individual firm, with
its personal direction, may be followed by a system of bureau-
cracy and red tape. The separate firms were built up on the
individual initiative and enterprise of the founders, and it is to
be feared that enterprise and initiative may not have the same
scope in a combine as in a smaller firm.

(*b*) The aim of a combine is to obtain control of the market:
when this control has been obtained, it may become stereotyped and resist changes.

(*c*) Many combines in the short run have the benefit of the
experience of men who controlled the separate firms: the
problem of finding capable successors from within may have
to be faced as time goes on.

(*d*) The larger the combine, the more complete is its control
of prices: it is able to charge higher prices and so make greater
profits that are not due to superior efficiency, but to the
possession of what is virtually a monopoly.

(*e*) It can prevent rivals entering the market by its own
financial strength, and by coming to terms with merchants
and traders that they shall only handle the combines goods.
Indeed the large international firms are perhaps today one of
the most important factors that influence economic relations
between countries. A relatively small number control or
influence large sectors of the worlds markets whilst their
individual receipts often exceed the national income of many
poorer nations.

Whilst the advantages and disadvantages in the private
sector have been stated, these may in certain circumstances
apply equally to the public sector of industry and commerce
as in State or Local Authority enterprises.

The State or a Local Authority undertakes, however, to

supply certain services to the community where one or more of the following conditions apply:

(*a*) Where the private sector cannot render an essential service, since its charges would have to be high in order to make even a reasonable profit (e.g. public health services).

(*b*) If competition between private firms is undesirable: consider, for example, the unnecessary expense that would be incurred if there were two postal firms in a country or two electricity undertakings in a town.

(*c*) Where it is necessary to enforce services on a community, in the public interests: the local council, for example, is responsible for sanitation, and compels the inhabitants of an area to accept these services and to pay for them through the rates.

(*d*) When improved services are required for national reasons: for example, in 1910, the National Telephone Company was taken over by the Post Office in order to develop the telephone service in this country.

(*e*) If it is likely that, if left without regulation, private enterprise would choose to serve only remunerative areas: for example, a trading concern might find it profitable to provide electric power in a town, but would be unwilling to extend its services to the countryside.

(*f*) If there is danger that a monopoly owned by a private trading concern may be used to further its own interest.

(*g*) Where vast amounts of capital are required both now and in the future to provide and maintain a national service and which is often beyond the means of private enterprise.

Advantages of Public Undertakings. The advantages of State and Local Authority trading are as follows:

(*a*) The interests of the public are the main consideration; services are provided at prices within the reach of all. A large profit is not a main consideration; a local authority, of course, desires that an undertaking shall pay its way, but it runs many services at a loss for the convenience of the public.

(*b*) Profits are devoted, at least partially, to the relief of the taxpayer or ratepayer, and not to a limited number of shareholders.

(*c*) The financial soundness of these enterprises is secured by State control of all loans to, and borrowings by local authorities.

(*d*) Local Authority enterprises, if successful, lead to a reduction in rates, and low rates attract new industries to a town.

Criticisms of Public Undertakings. The following arguments are sometimes given these enterprises:

(*a*) The absence of the incentive to increase the profits year by year leads to lack of enterprise, since officials are likely to adopt stereotyped methods and to show an unwillingness to adopt new ideas.

(*b*) The ratepayers or taxpayers have not the same opportunities for criticism as have shareholders in a private enterprise.

(*c*) State and Local Authority enterprises often possess a monopoly, and many believe that the absence of competition prevents improvements from being adopted.

(*d*) Control is often far removed in reality so that 'red tape' and impersonal attitudes are sometimes allowed to develop.

QUESTIONS

1. What principal forces are working at present to make large combinations in industry? What are the limits of large-scale industry? (U.L.C.I.)

2. What are the principal effects of amalgamation of businesses on (*a*) employment, (*b*) prices of the goods manufactured? (U.L.C.I.)

3. What is a Holding Company? Can you assign reasons for the growth and development of such companies in recent years? (R.S.A.)

4. Distinguish between 'vertical' and 'horizontal' integration (or combination). Explain the reasons for these combinatons and describe the methods by which they are brought about. (R.S.A.)

5. Describe three kinds of shares which a large public company might issue. What are the special attractions of debentures from the viewpoint of (*a*) the firm and (*b*) the lender of the capital. (J.M.B.)

6. Explain the main methods whereby business firms combine together to form large-scale groups. (R.S.A.)

7. The XYZ Company Ltd, a newly formed company, issues 1 million Ordinary Shares of £1 each. Mr. James buys 1,000 of these shares and pays the sum of £100 for them. If the company

fails in six months' time, and owes its creditors £100,000 more than the assets will realise, how much must Mr James pay! Would it make any difference to your answer if the shares were Preference Shares? Explain fully.   (R.S.A.)

8. Outline the organisation of *either* the gas industry *or* the electricity industry. How does the government control the industry you have described?   (A.E.B.)

9. Although most businesses make profits there is always a risk of severe losses, which may even bring about the end of a business. What is the extent of the loss which would be sustained by (a) a sole trader, (b) members of a partnership firm and (c) holders of ordinary shares in a limited company? If a nationalised industry or public corporation incurs losses, upon whom do the losses ultimately fall?   (Oxford G.C.E.)

10. Large firms in the same industry often seek to combine into a larger single unit and have sometimes had the encouragement of the government in this. What are the advantages to be gained from such amalgamations and what are the dangers? Give examples.   (Oxford G.C.E.)

Chapter 18

Business Management

With the increase in the size of the business unit, the problem of management becomes more important; even in a small firm the owner must organise his work so as to obtain the best results, but with the growth of large-scale enterprises the management of the concerns becomes more complicated. The management of a large firm has become a specialised task, and the person who performs this function is known as the *Entrepreneur* or the Organiser.

Business management covers a large number of activities, which may be grouped under three headings:

(a) Planning. When a business is started, the Entrepreneur must have definite ideas of what he proposes to do. He must raise capital and use it in the acquisition of premises, machinery, tools, and raw materials or other equipment according to the nature of the business, and he must organise the sale of the product.

When the business has started, he must maintain the property of the firm, and supervise repairs and replacements. In addition, the question of output requires consideration whether to increase or reduce to meet fluctuations in trade and changes in fashion. He therefore requires gifts of foresight, judgement, anticipation and knowledge of markets. The coordination of such a variety of interests is a task which requires ability, and the larger the market the greater is the need for expert guidance.

(b) Control. The control of the employees of the firm requires tact and enthusiasm on the part of the Entrepreneur, who organises the work in such a way as to obtain the best results. He must find by experience the right proportions of skilled, semi-skilled and unskilled labour, and allocate duties so as to obtain full advantage of the divisions of labour. He should have a knowledge of human nature, and be able to obtain the best out of his employees by his own example and enthusiasm. In addition he will have to assess the amount of machinery and other fixed assets that he will require and apply Work Study methods in order to reap the maximum benefit from their application.

The larger the size of the business unit, the more impersonal it tends to become. This disadvantage may be overcome to some extent by the encouragement of skill and energy, and by the adoption of schemes to promote the social welfare of those in subordinate positions.

(c) **Risk-bearing.** A feature of modern industry is that production is ahead of demand, and it is the work of the Entrepreneur to estimate what the demand will be at some future date. He therefore requires all the information available regarding market conditions, and makes his plans and sets his employees to work months ahead of the time when the demand shows itself. This estimate of demand involves many risks: fashion may change, supplies of raw materials may be lacking, political events at home and abroad may change the anticipated demand. The Entrepreneur therefore undertakes the risks of production and if his anticipations are correct, he makes a profit.

The payment received by the Entrepreneur is composed of three elements:

(1) *The Wages of Management.* These represent a special form of wages for a special form of labour—viz. organisation.

(2) *Reward for Risks.* The Entrepreneur undertakes the risks of production, and his gross profit includes a payment for this service.

(3) *Net Profit.* The amount left after payment for the Entrepreneur's services of management and risk-bearing is known as the Net Profit, and represents a payment for the ability with which the firm has been managed.

2. THE INCIDENCE OF RESPONSIBILITY

Until the beginning of the nineteenth century, the typical business unit was small scale, and the functions of the Entrepreneur were well within the ability of the owner. Many small businesses of course exist at the present day, and are still managed by the proprietor: but with the growth of world markets, they have increased in size, and the typical unit is the joint-stock company. The functions of the Entrepreneur have therefore become more specialised. The planning, control and risk-bearing in a large concern are undertaken by different groups of individuals who being experts are able to advise the Entrepreneur so that he may be able to make the correct decision on projects involving perhaps many millions of pounds.

The incidence of responsibility may be shown by considering the various forms of business organisation:

(a) **Sole Trader.** A retail shopkeeper, electrician, plumber or professional man who runs his own business acts as his own entrepreneur. He organises the business, carries the risks which are attached to even the smallest forms of business units, and receives the whole of the profit (or suffers the loss) as a result of his enterprise.

(b) **Ordinary Partnerships.** The partners themselves are responsible for the planning and control of the business. Their numbers may permit some degree of specialisation of management which is not possible for the sole trader. They are individually responsible, however, for the risks of the undertaking, even to the extent of their private means.

(c) **Limited Partnerships.** In this form of business organisation, the planning and control of the business are in the hands of the *ordinary* partner or partners, of whom it will be remembered there must be at least one. In a limited partnership, the responsibility for risks is also divided: the ordinary partners are responsible for *all* the risks of the business, but the limited partners are only responsible up to the amount they have invested.

(d) **Joint-Stock Companies.** In these enterprises, the functions of the Entrepreneurs are divided to a much larger extent. The shareholders subscribe the capital, and therefore bear the risks of the business up to the *nominal* value of the shares they hold. The directors are responsible for the policy and planning, whilst the Managing Director or General Manager undertakes the duties of control. It is usual for the directors to be interested shareholders of the business and they combine risk-bearing with management.

(e) Co-operative Societies. The management is under-taken by a Committee elected by the members, and the decisions of the Committee of Management are carried out by a General Manager. The risks of the undertaking are borne by the members, each of whom has at least one share of the capital.

(f) Local Authorities. The management is in the hands of a Committee of the Council, which the ratepayers have elected. The policy of the Committee is carried out by paid officials of the undertaking, whilst the risks are borne by the ratepayers.

(g) State Undertakings. The management of such under-takings is in the hands of a Minister of the Crown, who is responsible to Parliament for the policy he adopts: the risks of the undertaking are borne by the taxpayers of the country.

The following table shows how the responsibility of manage-ing a business is divided:

Business Unit	Planning	Control	Risks
Sole Trader	Owner	Owner	Owner
Ordinary Partnership	Partners	Partners	Partners
Limited Part-nership	Ordinary Partners	Ordinary Partners	Ordinary Partners
Joint-Stock Company	Directors	Managing Director or General Manager	Shareholders
Co-operative Society	Committee of Management	General Manager	Members
Local Authorities	Committee of the Council	Local Government Officials	Ratepayers
State Under-taking	Minister of Crown	Parliament	Taxpayers

The entrepreneur may reduce some of his risks in the following ways:

(1) With the payment of a small premium he can arrange for the *Export Credits Guarantee Department* of the Department of Trade and Industry to cover some of the losses that may occur on the export markets.

(2) *The Specialist Markets and Produce Exchanges* enable the Entrepreneur to share his risks by buying or selling futures.

(3) *Insurance Companies* enable the Entrepreneur to protect himself against the material and immaterial risks of production. These include protection against fire, life, accident and marine risks in addition to loss of profits, bad debts, etc.

3. THE MANAGEMENT OF A COMPANY

The capital of a company is subscribed by the shareholders. It is not possible for the majority of them to take any part in its internal management since they may live far from the registered address of the firm, and may have no knowledge of the industry in which they have invested their money. In order to overcome these and other difficulties, the shareholders elect Directors whose duty it is to manage the concern, and to issue an annual report and balance sheet to the shareholders.

The following are the principal officials elected to serve the interests of the shareholders:

The Directors. Are chosen by the shareholders to conduct and manage the business. They may be regarded both as trustees and agents: from the former point of view, they are trustees of the powers which are committed to them and of the moneys which come into their hands, whilst as agents of the company, they are authorised by the Articles of Association to deal with other persons for and on behalf of the company. They usually receive a remuneration for these services which must be shown in the annual accounts.

The Directors are usually shareholders in the company, the minimum qualification being stated in the Articles of Association. This is not a legal obligation but a requirement of the Stock Exchanges before granting an official quotation for the company's shares.

The powers and duties of the Directors are determined by the Memorandum and Articles of Association, which include such points as the following:

(a) The Directors must meet periodically to transact the business of the company, either at appointed times or at times convenient to themselves.

(b) They are empowered to make contracts on behalf of the company. These must be within the objects of the company as stated in the Memorandum of Association.

(c) No Director in his private capacity can contract with a company of which he is a director unless special provision for this is made in the Articles of Association, and the action of the Directors must be ratified by the shareholders.

(d) As agents of the company, the duties of the Directors and their private interests must not conflict.

(e) The Directors are personally liable for any acts which are outside the scope of the company's activities, as stated in the Memorandum of Association.

(f) Directors, in addition to their liability as shareholders, are liable for negligence or fraud.

The work of the Directors is to supervise the working of the company and to obtain the best results for the interests of the shareholders. At their meetings, they receive reports and statistics from the Managing Director, and make criticisms and suggestions based on the information submitted to them. All matters of policy are decided by the Directors, who, in order to obtain first-hand knowledge, usually make themselves acquainted with the general routine of the business.

The Directors submit an Annual Report and Balance Sheet to the shareholders, and at the Annual General Meeting the latter are given the opportunity of making suggestions and criticising the management of the firm on the work of the previous year.

The Managing Director. Is usually elected by the other Directors and may also be their Chairman. When the Directors of a company have made decisions regarding the policy of the firm, it is his duty to see that their policy is carried out. The work of the Managing Director may be summarised:

(a) *Relation with Directors*. He gives full information to the directors regarding the working of the firm. In order to do this, he provides statistics and reports, and advises the directors on the possibilities of expansion or the adoption of new lines. The directors often rely on his knowledge of the inner workings of the firm to guide them in their decisions.

(b) *Organisation of the Firm*. He organises the work of the firm by dividing it into departments. Over each there is a manager, who is responsible for the allotted tasks. They receive instructions from the Managing Director who is available for advice and assistance if required. The departmental managers may sub-divide their departments into sections, and are responsible for the allocation of duties amongst the employees under their control. The Managing Director co-ordinates the work of the separate departments, always seeking improved methods in order to reduce the cost of production or distribution.

No two organisations are exactly alike in their method of control. A typical layout, however, could be on the following lines:

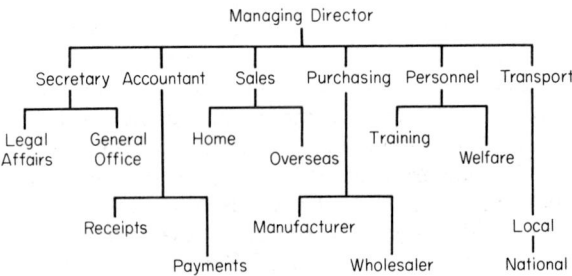

(c) *Control*. The successful Managing Director requires exceptional personal qualities in order to obtain the best results out of those under his direction. He should be able to form a sound judgment of the work of the men under him, and to give praise or blame with impartiality. This involves a study of the capabilities and characteristics of each member of his staff, in order to find the task for which each is best suited. When duties have been allotted according to the ability, temperament and personality of each employee, all routine matters should then be left to the department concerned. The Managing Director is thus free to deal with emergencies or matters of policy.

4. SELLING ORGANISATION

The organisation of sales varies from firm to firm according to the nature of the articles to be marketed; in a large firm, the selling department performs three services: (a) the execution of orders and the clerical work connected with it, (b) the control and direction of the work of the sales representatives, (c) the creation of a demand for the firm's goods by suitable methods of advertising and publicity.

The selling organisation of a smaller firm usually combines the above functions in one department and also may employ an *Advertising Agency* to undertake publicity on a national or international basis. A large firm will have additional departments as part of the selling organisation, such as those dealing with Consignments, Hire Purchase, and Mail Orders, etc. We may take the three services mentioned above as being typical to most selling organisations and examine their work more fully.

(a) The Sales Office

Location. Many buyers visit the headquarters of a firm as well as dealing through representatives. It is therefore important that the Sales Office should be situated in a convenient centre for transport.

Premises. The Sales Offices should attract customers by providing up-to-date and well-equipped rooms for their reception and interview.

Dealing with Correspondence. All correspondence should be promptly dealt with, especially as the customer often judges a firm by the following criteria:

(1) its promptness in dealing with replies to correspondence and execution of orders.
(2) the style and typescript of its letters, invoices, statements etc.

(3) the courtesy of its employees (particularly the switch-board operator).

(4) the goods or services it supplies.

Correspondence generally may be classified as follows:

(1) *Orders*. Are received from customers and from representatives. Full particulars are noted by the Sales Office, and sent to the warehouse for execution.

(2) *Enquiries*. Requests are frequently received from prospective customers for catalogues and information regarding the firm's goods. The Sales Office replies direct to the firm or individual making the enquiry: it informs the representative for the area from which the enquiry came, and arranges that the request for information be followed by a personal visit.

(3) *Reports from Representatives*. The Sales Office files the Special Report Forms it receives from the representatives. It also keeps records of the total sales, earnings and expenses of each. A card index system enables the Sales Office to keep a record of the firm's relation with each customer, and shows the amount and date of his purchases, and the date on which he was last visited. The Sales Office also periodically issues a sales bulletin or catalogue showing changes of price, and new lines.

(b) Control of Representatives

They are under the direction of the Sales Manager, from whom they receive instructions and to whom they send reports. A great deal of freedom is given to the representatives, especially when they are experienced, but they are required to consult the Sales Manager periodically on important matters affecting the policy of the sales organisation, such as the following:

(1) *Special Concessions*. The representative is given very little power to make concessions regarding the price. In former days, he had much more freedom in price-fixing than he has now: the standardisation of products in many industries enables price lists and catalogues to be issued. The larger the customers orders, however, the greater is the concession by way of *trade* discount.

(2) *The Granting of Credit*. He has much more freedom in

this respect, since he has a personal knowledge of the customer, and can therefore often form a better estimate of the status of a customer. Even so he cannot go beyond certain limits allowed by the Sales Manager.

(3) *Guarantees.* In introducing a new line of goods, or in soliciting orders from a new customer, a representative may be asked to give guarantees regarding the quality or performance of the goods. The Trade Description Act 1968 requires that there shall be no misrepresentation on the matter and the representative must be careful therefore not to mislead the customer in any way.

(4) *Claims.* A customer may demand credit for damaged or inferior goods, and in minor matters the representative is given a free hand. In claims involving a large amount, however, he is usually required to consult the Sales Manager.

(c) Publicity and Advertising. An important part of the work of the Selling Organisation is to create and maintain a demand for the firm's products. This may be done in several ways:

(1) By establishing a separate Advertising Department as part of the selling organisation, under the direction of an Advertising Manager. This method is employed where advertising is undertaken on a large scale. The Manager must have a knowledge of every phase of advertising; he must be familiar with the products and sales policy of his firm, and be well acquainted with market conditions and the activities of his competitors at home and abroad.

(2) The employment of an Advertising Agency, which will draw up the advertisement and attend to placing it in the Press or on Television, etc. The advertising agent usually designs the advertisement as he has a staff of designers who have specialised in commercial art. He is able to give expert advice regarding the value of the different forms of advertising for the goods of a particular firm.

(3) A scheme of co-operative advertising may be organised by a trade association, and the selling organisation of a firm may share the expenses of such an appeal to the public. A suitable slogan is invented, such as 'Eat More Fruit' and 'Buy

British Goods', and these phrases are displayed in retail shops
and in the Press, etc.

5. ADVERTISING

Aims. The object of advertising is to call the attention of the
public to a certain commodity and to induce them to buy it,
by convincing them that they want or need it and that it is
worth the price. An advertisement, therefore, must arrest the
attention, and, in addition, create a permanent impression:
the various means of attaining this double object depend
upon a knowledge of psychology as well as of commercial
methods.

Advertising has now become a necessary part of the expenses
of every firm which desires to maintain and extend its sales:
it has been estimated that in this country about £500 million
is spent annually on advertising. Statistics show that the
most advertised articles are patent medicines, toilet prepara-
tions and soaps, foodstuffs and tobacco.

Methods. No useful purpose would be served by giving a
long list of advertising methods—the student will be able to
make such a list for himself from his own observation. The
principal methods only need to be mentioned:

(1) *Newspapers.* The use of the Press for publicity is the
chief form of advertising. In adopting this method, the advertiser must consider the type of readers amongst whom the
newspaper or magazine circulates. The national newspapers
circulate throughout the country, and therefore have a great
advantage over the provincial papers from the advertiser's
point of view.

The type and form of an advertisement in a newspaper
requires consideration: increasing use is being made of colour
in both the national and provincial papers. In addition magazines afford themselves to the advertising of products perhaps
to a particular section of the population or society.

(2) *Television.* Commercial advertising is excluded from the
sound and television programmes of the B.B.C.; the Independent Broadcasting Authority, which receives no income from
licence revenue, broadcasts advertisements and receives

annual payments from the programme companies, which depend on advertising for their revenue.

The advertising policy of the I.B.A. is controlled by the provisions of the Television Act (1964), and by agreement with the Government certain classes of advertising are prohibited. An Advertising Advisory Committee has drawn up certain principles for television advertising, with a view to the exclusion of misleading or unsuitable advertisements from the programme. The cost of inserting advertisements in the I.T.A. service is borne by the advertisers, who, in a recent year, paid the programme companies about £100 million for advertising time.

(3) *Window-Dressing.* In all large towns, the owners of a business pay great attention to the use of the shop window as an advertising medium. Care must be taken in arranging the goods displayed: they should be easily reached, so that they can be taken out of the window if a customer wishes to examine them. The windows of a shop should not be overcrowded, and attention should be given to colour schemes where possible. In a large store, specialists in window-dressing are employed, and manufacturers frequently lend materials to display their products.

(4) *Posters.* The aim of a poster is to create a vivid impression, and many posters which are displayed on hoardings are of considerable artistic merit. In order to be effective, a poster should contain as few words as possible, in order that it may be read quickly. The use of slogans together with some design is particularly effective in this form of advertising.

(5) *Circulars, Catalogues and Free Samples.* This method is often used to advertise a new product. But it is necessary to avoid waste by seeing that they are sent only to persons who are likely to be interested in the product.

(6) *Mechanical Advertisements.* The use of mechanical signs for advertisement purposes ranges from costly electrically operated signs to small battery charged devices often found in retailers' windows.

The above list by no means exhausts all the methods of advertising: it is a highly developed art and new methods are constantly being employed.

Economic Value. At first sight, advertising appears to be an addition to the cost of an article, since the advertiser must include the expenses of advertising in the analysis of his cost of production. But it must be remembered that the aim of advertising is to increase the demand, and if this is accomplished, the cost of production is reduced. An increased demand enables a manufacturer to take advantage of large-scale production and we have seen in a previous chapter that one of the benefits of large-scale production is the lower cost per unit.

Similarly, in the wholesale and retail trades, an increase in the sales does not necessitate a corresponding increase in the number of sales representatives. In both cases, the fixed expenses of the firm, such as rent, rates, etc., have no relation to the volume of the sales. As a result, successful advertising enables a firm to produce an article at a lower cost; part of the reduction is retained by the advertiser to increase his profits, but the remainder of the saving is passed on to the consumer by selling the article at a lower price, and in this way the demand may be further increased.

It will be seen, therefore, that successful advertising benefits both the consumer and the advertiser.

The consumer benefits in two ways:

(1) he gains information regarding new products. The effect of an advertisement may not be immediate: a person frequently remembers an advertisement, and purchases an article when circumstances permit, or when he requires to renew his stock of a particular line of goods.

(2) he is able to purchase the article at a lower price, since part of the reduction in cost, due to increased output, is passed on to the consumer.

The advertiser benefits also because:

(1) he increases the demand for his goods; this leads to a larger output, reduced costs per unit, and increases his profits.

(2) because of the increased demand, the advertisement campaign pays for itself.

(3) advertising is a cheaper selling method than the employ-

ment of a large staff of representatives, who are costly to maintain.

(4) advertisements enable the producer to reach the consumer. They appeal *direct* to the consumer, and encourages him to demand the goods from the retailer.

(5) in certain lines of goods, the advertiser is able to set up a Mail Order Department. A large number of people in Britain read the national and provincial newspapers and communicate direct with the firms who advertise therein.

The Return from Advertisements. Many ways are adopted to measure the results of an advertising campaign. A coupon may be inserted as part of the advertisement, or such phrases as 'Dept. 27' or 'Box A' may be included in the address. By such means, the advertiser is able to tell where the prospective customer has seen the advertisement, and so to judge the relative values of different newspapers and magazines for advertising his particular line of goods.

But such tests are by no means conclusive: purchases may be made direct from a retailer as the result of recommendations etc. In order to obtain a more accurate statement of the results of advertising, a firm must prepare statistics showing the amount spent on advertising, the number of new customers, the increase in orders from existing customers, etc. From such statistics, an approximate estimate can be made of the effects of an advertising campaign.

QUESTIONS

1. Discuss the problems that arise when a wholesale and a retail business are combined under the same proprietor.   (R.S.A.)

2. What do you understand by Market Research? Expand your answer by a detailed description in the case of an example selected by yourself.   (R.S.A.)

3. How is a large joint-stock company managed and controlled? What powers are exercised in this connection by the shareholders?   (U.L.C.I.)

4. In large business houses, the commercial work of buying, selling, recording, etc., has to be sectionalised and the work of the staff specialised. Explain the nature of this sectionalising of the commercial work in some class of business house with which you are familiar.   (U.L.C.I.)

5. Choose four of the following and stating your reasons, indicate the type of advertising you might recommend for each:

(a) a small retailer.

(b) a mail order house

(c) the manufacturer of a new lawn mower

(d) the sale by the owner of his car

(e) a travel agency

(f) the promoters of a football pool.   (Cambridge G.C.E.)

6. If you were thinking of buying a retail business explain what information you would look for in the books of the business. What other data would you take into account in deciding whether the investment was worth risking or not?   (J.M.B.)

7. What is a board of directors in a public limited liability company? What does it do? To whom is it responsible? How does it direct the company?   (A.E.B.)

8. Explain the differences between the sole trader type of business and the public limited company, with reference to the ownership and management of capital.   (R.S.A.)

9. A large engineering firm has been situated in an industrial area for many years. It is now planning to expand. What considerations may influence its decision to build a new factory (a) in the same industrial area, (b) in a different area?   (R.S.A.)

10. What do you understand by the term *private enterprise*? Which of the following organisations are private enterprises: a public limited company, the B.B.C., the Co-operative Wholesale Society, the Bank of England, the Independent Broadcasting Authority, the Post Office, a commercial bank, a partnership, a building society, the London Stock Exchange, the Milk Marketing Board? State **one** characteristic which is common to all those which you have rejected.   (Oxford G.C.E.)

11. (a) How far do you think it is true to say that it pays a business firm to advertise and that advertising benefits the consumer?

(b) In view of the development of more modern methods of advertising, how do you account for the continued use of posters, especially on railway station platforms?   (Oxford G.C.E.)

Chapter 19

The Currency System

1. EVOLUTION OF MONEY

In the early days of history, primitive man had to satisfy many wants by exchanging the products of his own efforts for the products of the efforts of others: for example, the fisherman might exchange his fish for the skins of the hunter. The direct exchange of goods is known as *barter*, and even exists today among a few very primitive peoples of the world.

A system of barter on any large scale would be impracticable, under modern conditions, as it suffers from two principal defects:

(a) The double coincidence of wants is necessary before exchange can take place: the fisherman may have a surplus of fish, but the hunter may not want fish in exchange for his skins. Under such circumstances, the fisherman must find someone else who desires fish, and is able to offer in exchange commodities which the fisherman wants.

(b) Barter provides no standard of values: the fisherman and hunter may each want the commodity which the other has to offer in exchange, but no exchange will take place unless they can agree upon their relative worth. In addition, the difficulty of subdivision arises; the fish desired by the hunter may be worth more than two skins, but less than three.

The growth of exchange, as civilisation advanced, necessitated the use of a third commodity by which the value of all other commodities could be measured; this commodity is termed 'money', which was desired for its own sake as well as for its usefulness in facilitating exchange. Many different substances have been used as money—oxen and tea in China, bars of copper in Ancient Rome, rice in Japan, salt in Arabia and India, cattle in Africa and so on. All these commodities have a value in the eyes of persons using them, and have served as material for money.

But such commodities are bulky and perishable, and a more compact and durable commodity became desirable. The metals fulfil the requirements of compactness and durability, and because of their lightness and relative scarcity, gold and silver were universally offered in exchange for articles, because of both their acceptability *and alternative use* as ornament.

The stages in the use of the precious metals as money may be given as follows:

(*a*) A currency was used in which one or more metals were passed by weight alone: merchants carried scales with which they could weigh the metals offered to them.

(*b*) Uniform pieces were made of one or more metals; the weight and fineness being guaranteed by the issuing authority. This was the State which impressed a special stamp on the metal of given weight which allowed the merchants to count the coins instead of weighing them.

(*c*) The relative values of the metals used as coins was fixed.

(*d*) As confidence in the issuing authority grew, the use of precious metals became unnecessary so that today we are satisfied with promises to pay. Thus paper money and token coins made of alloys are universally accepted.

2. THE MEANING OF MONEY

Money is a commodity chosen by a community as a medium of exchange and as a measure of value of all other commodities and services: it must be universally acceptable in that community although not held for its own sake, but as a means of obtaining other goods or services now or in the future.

The term 'money' is used in a wider sense to include anything which serves as a medium of exchange, and therefore embraces bank-notes, cheques, bills of exchange and bank deposits. These circulating media are either *pieces of paper* which facilitate exchange, yet by themselves cannot be regarded as having any value, or bank deposits that may be easily transferred from one person to another by book entries. They *represent* value and are acceptable for that reason: this form of money is of great importance, coins being of secondary importance under modern conditions; money therefore as distinct from currency consists mainly of bank balances by means of which debts are settled by book transfers as the following table shows. The figures relate to the total deposits of the London Clearing Banks as well as the Scottish and Northern Ireland counterparts, the Overseas Banks in Britain, the National Giro, and the Accepting Houses of the City.

	1970 £ million	*1971* £ million	*1972* £ million
Notes in Circulation (in Britain)	3,860	3,800	4,280
Coin in Circulation	340	350	350
Total Currency in Circulation	4,200	4,150	4,630
Bank Deposits	32,250	44,000	61,470
Total Amount of 'Money' in Circulation	36,450	48,150	66,100

Money consists of:

(a) **The Coinage,** which is issued by or on the authority of the State, and includes:

(1) *Standard Coins*, containing the value of metal equivalent to the face value of the coin. Because of world price conditions there are few standard coins in circulation today.

(2) *Token Coins*, such as the cupro-nickel and bronze coins of this country: these are convenient sub-multiples of the monetary unit, and are not worth their face value.

Two 50p pieces, for example, are the equivalent of one pound sterling and can be exchanged for goods or services of that amount. As pieces of metal, however, they are only worth a small fraction of this sum.

(b) Representative Money. This form of money also acts as a medium of exchange, expressed in the terms of the monetary unit. It consists of:

(1) *Bank-notes.* The Bank of England has the sole right in England and Wales of issuing bank-notes subject to parliamentary control. In addition Scottish and Northern Ireland banks have limited rights to issue their own notes which apart from the amount allowed by legislation must be fully covered by Bank of England notes.

The student should study the wording closely on a bank-note. It will be seen that the issuing authority *promises to pay* the bearer the value of the note. In former times it was possible to exchange this value into a standard coin of equal amount. Nowadays the note can only be changed into another bank-note or the equivalent in token coins.

(2) *Negotiable Instruments and Bank Deposits* include cheques, credit cards and bills of exchange, which act as money, since they represent the right to specific balances in the hands of banks. Their use enables indebtedness to be settled by means of book transfers either within the same bank or between banks through the clearing system.

3. THE FUNCTIONS OF MONEY

The commodity used *as a base* for the calculation of the value of a currency *between countries* on the international markets is gold. Within a country, however, other forms of money are accepted. In both cases the money will have the following qualities:

(a) *It acts as a medium of exchange.* Goods or services instead of being exchanged directly for other goods, are exchanged for money which is exchanged again for other goods etc. Money therefore converts barter into sale and purchase, and becomes the universal third commodity for which all goods are exchanged.

(b) *Money acts as a measure of value,* since everything is exchanged for money. Thus exchange value becomes price, which is exchange value expressed in terms of money. The value of all commodities is measured by reference to gold or what it represents. This facilitates a comparison of the utility of different articles and thus simplifies exchange.

(c) *Store of Value.* Given stable conditions it does not deteriorate with time: the owner can keep it indefinitely so that he can exchange it at any time for goods or services in order to satisfy his wants.

(d) *Standard of Deferred Payments.* Under modern conditions, many payments are contracted to be made at some future date. In a *perfect* monetary system, the commodity chosen as the standard of value would have a steady value over a period of years: if this is attained, the value received at some future date will correspond to the amount due now.

Gold will not exert the same degree of influence on prices *within a country* as it is not possible to exchange its currency into gold. The internal currency, however, will as far as conditions allow attain all the qualities mentioned above.

4. PROPERTIES OF MONEY

In order to fulfil the above functions, a good money material must possess the following properties:

(a) *Acceptability.* The commodity chosen as the money material must be readily accepted in exchange for goods and services.

(b) *Portability.* It should be small in bulk so that it may be carried from place to place without inconvenience, difficulty or expense. This is less important to-day with the greater use of credit instruments such as cheques, bills of exchange and credit cards.

(c) *Durability.* It must not deteriorate in itself as a result of wear and tear.

(d) *Homogeneity.* All coins of the same metal or alloy must be of the same quality throughout; one coin must not be superior to another.

(*e*) *Divisibility.* It must be divisible into small units, and capable of being reunited without loss. The metals are superior to precious stones in this respect.

(*f*) *Malleability.* The metals or alloys are malleable and can be stamped with designs to show their value and origin.

(*g*) *Recognisability.* It is necessary that the material should be easily recognised and of such quality to prevent counterfeiting. Notice the difference in colour and size of the various coins now in circulation in various parts of the world.

(*h*) *Stability of Value.* A commodity which is subject to violent fluctuations in price is useless as money. In a time of rising prices, however, people tend to exchange their money for goods as they know that the purchasing power of the currency is diminishing. This creates more demand, prices rise further and the value of the currency falls once more.

5. PAPER MONEY

Most nations issue paper money in the form of bank-notes which are issued by the State through a Central Bank subject to legal control. Providing that there is no over-issue, paper money has many advantages:

(1) Its use saves the heavy cost of minting.

(2) There is no loss through wear and tear: the cost of printing the paper money is very small.

(3) Each unit of paper money is numbered.

(4) Larger denominations can be printed at little or no extra cost. These are more acceptable than high value coins.

Paper money is of two kinds:

(1) *Convertible.* When paper money is convertible, the holder has the right of changing it on demand into the standard metal: under these conditions, it performs the functions of good money to a high degree, providing the promise to repay is fulfilled immediately on demand.

(2) *Inconvertible.* The notes issued by the Bank of England and other Central Banks are now inconvertible because of the

high demand for gold throughout the world. In Britain the note issue is controlled by Parliament to guard against an over-issue which could have a serious effect on the economy. This has been witnessed in a number of foreign countries which have debased their currency in this manner.

6. THE MONETARY SYSTEM

Gold was adopted as the single standard of value in 1816; from 1344 to that date, silver and gold circulated together in various proportions. From 1931, however, the pound sterling has not been convertible into gold on the internal market of the country and token coins are accepted by the population which represent a promise by the British Government to repay on demand.

In 1971 Britain changed to the decimal currency system whereby the monetary unit of £1 was divided into 100 units called pence.

The major unit continues to be indicated by the '£' sign placed before the amount while the abbreviation of the smaller amount is 'p' which when expressed by itself is placed after the amount.

The decimal point and not the comma is the decimal sign which is placed opposite the middle of the figure. In the case of many machines however, this is not possible and the full stop on the base line can be used.

The following are the accepted ways of expressing amounts in decimal currency:

(a) *Amounts in whole pounds only*

£2, £25, £250, £2,500 *or*
£2·00. £25·00, £250·00, etc.

Note the use of *two* noughts after the decimal point where there are no pence.

(b) *Amounts in pence only*

7p, 11p, 78p, *or*
£0·07, £0·11, £0·78.

Note the use of *two* figures in each case after the decimal point.

(c) *Amounts containing both pounds and pence*
　　£2·07, £25·11, £250·78, etc.

Note the omission of the pence sign where the pound sign is used.

(d) *When writing cheques*, the amounts should be expressed in both words and figures in the following manner:

Amount in words	Figures
Seventy-eight pence	£0–78
Two pounds only	£2–00
Two pounds 08	£2–08
Two hundred and fifty pounds 78	£250–78

Note that in this instance the hyphen is preferable to the decimal point although the banks will accept the latter.

(a) The Coinage

Britain's decimal coins are divided into two groups as follows:

(1) *Cupro-nickel* coins represented by the 50p, 10p and 5p pieces. The seven-sided 50p piece is preferred to a note of similar value as the normal life of a low value note is usually only six months.

(2) *Bronze coins* represented by the 2p, 1p and ½p pieces. The contents of these coins is made up from proportions of copper, tin and zinc.

The weight of the coins except the 50p bears a relationship to the others in the group. The 1p piece for example is half the weight of the 2p whilst the 5p is half the weight of the 10p. Thus establishments dealing with large amounts of coin may weigh them on special scales rather than laboriously count each coin.

(b) The Note Issue. The Bank of England having a monopoly on the note issue in England and Wales is subject to conditions laid down by various Acts of Parliament: the amount of the issue is determined by the value of Government Securities in the possession of the Bank. This control is intended to give confidence in the present and future value of the currency. Notes of £20, £10, £5 and £1 are in circulation: the total value depends upon the time of year as a greater quantity is required at Christmas and holiday-times.

In addition Scottish and Northern Ireland Banks have the right to issue notes on a limited scale, but these are legal tender only in those countries although in practice they are accepted throughout Britain at their face value.

7. CREDIT

The term 'credit' is used in the business world with the meaning of confidence in another person or firm: goods and services are frequently transferred from one person to another without any value immediately being given in return. The person who parts with the goods or performs the services under such conditions is said to grant credit, which implies a belief that the debtor will meet his obligations fully in due course.

Credit may be granted in several ways:

(a) There may be an agreement to extend the time of a payment due for goods or services. Many tradesmen and professional men sell goods or perform services to their clients and do not demand payment until some time later. They *believe* that their clients will meet their obligations at the proper time.

(b) A joint-stock bank frequently uses part of its deposits in granting credit to its customers: although some form of security may be required, the bank has confidence in the integrity of the customers to whom it makes advances. The loan granted by the bank may take the form of an overdraft, a loan account or the discounting of a Bill of Exchange: the effect of the bank's action is to increase the total amount of the purchasing power of the borrower.

(c) One of the more usual methods of obtaining credit for consumer durables is through a **Finance House**. Their range of business is very wide and covers the lending of money for all types of durables, providing finance for agricultural or industrial use, granting personal loans to consumers, factoring and export finance, etc. Hence they are sometimes referred to as **Industrial Bankers**. Most of the finance houses are subsidiaries of other organisations such as the joint-stock banks or durable goods manufacturers. They obtain their funds principally from the London Money Market, smaller amounts being received from public deposits.

8. CREDIT INSTRUMENTS

Written evidence of debt is usually required by a creditor, and such documents are known as Credit Instruments, which create a right to wealth.

The principal credit instruments are Government Notes, Bank-notes, Cheques, Bills of Exchange, Promissory notes, Money Orders and Postal Orders. These instruments pass from hand to hand, and therefore create additional spending power for the community: their acceptability, however, depends upon the reputation of the debtor. Bank-notes are full legal tender for any amount by law, but cheques and bills of exchange circulate in a limited circle in which the names and reputation of persons concerned are well known.

Credit agreements are also important instruments in providing evidence of debt. These may be in the form of hire purchase, credit sale, conditional sale, lease, rental, contract hire or loan agreements. In fact they cover a wide field far beyond the scope of this book. The student should however note the distinction between *lender credit*—the granting of loans in the form of money, and *vendor credit*—the contract for the sale of goods etc. on credit terms. It is the total of these that is broadly referred to as credit and which has an important effect on the monetary policy of the country.

Credit instruments therefore act as *substitutes* for other forms of money: they economise the use of notes or coin which do not exist in sufficient quantities to finance trade. They enable production to be ahead of demand by facilitating the transfer of wealth to where it can best be used, and thus make large-scale enterprise possible. They also enable payment to be made at convenient times to both debtor and creditor.

On the other hand, the amount of credit is limited by the confidence in the monetary system by the community. Credit instruments give the right to repayment in the future whilst the number of notes in circulation depends upon the amount of Government Securities etc. in the possession of the Central Bank. An over-issue of credit instruments therefore may lead to unwise expansion of production, fluctuations in prices, and a subsequent lack of confidence in the monetary system. It is for this reason that the Government has the power to expand or restrict credit as necessary through the Treasury and Bank of England directives.

9. INSTALMENT SYSTEMS OF PAYMENT

There are few people who do not at some time in their lives purchase goods on credit. This enables them to have the goods at once and pay later by instalments out of earnings. There are three principal types of arrangements as follows:

(a) **Hire-Purchase:** the customer receives delivery of the goods on payment of a deposit: he agrees to pay the balance, with interest and service charges by weekly or monthly instalments over a certain period. Under the Hire-Purchase system, the goods are legally the property of the seller until the *last instalment* has been paid: in case of default in the payments, the seller can under certain conditions claim the goods from the customer. Thus the instalments paid by the customer are regarded as payments for hiring the goods.

There are, however, a number of legal safeguards attached to every transaction. The principal ones are:

(i) A customer who signs the agreement *at his home* has the right to cancel it within three days.

(ii) A customer who wishes to cease paying for the article may do so providing (a) he returns the article to the retailer; (b) he has paid at least half the purchase price.

(iii) Where more than *one-third* of the payments have been made, the article may only be reclaimed by the seller or finance company through a Court order.

(iv) In every transaction the *cash sale price* together with the hire-purchase price must be stated in order that the customer may calculate the additional cost.

(b) **Credit Sales:** the customer receives delivery of the goods upon payment of the *first instalment*, and agrees with the seller or finance company to pay further instalments weekly or monthly for a given period. By this method *the goods become the property of the purchaser on payment of the first instalment*: if payments are not continued, the seller of the goods cannot reclaim them. He must sue the customer in a court of law for the balance of the money due.

(c) **Lease, Contract Hire or Rental** agreements are of increasing importance in industry and commerce. This type of credit is not strictly a sale as the goods rarely become the property of the lessee. He uses them for a certain period of time, makes regular monthly or yearly payments and replaces them with newer models when necessary. This is particularly suitable for items of high cost, high depreciation or where taxation allowances make it worth while.

There are many other forms of consumer credit available to the consumer. These include credit extended by retailers on monthly or budget accounts, check trading and credit cards in addition to the granting of second mortgages for consumer purposes.

The total debt outstanding under hire purchase alone is over £2,000 million which covers articles such as cars, household equipment, electrical goods, etc. which gives some idea of the amount of credit outstanding in this country to-day.

Advantages. The advantages of payment by instalments under either of the above methods may be considered from two points of view:

(*a*) *To the Firm.*

    (1) Payment by instalments extends the sales of articles which are expensive; many such as cars, television sets, etc., have come to be regarded as necessities in every home, and a firm increases its turnover by offering facilities for payment by instalments.

    (2) The increased turnover causes the stock to be constantly changing, and reduces the risk that many articles will be out of date before they are sold.

    (3) The lender receives a high rate of interest on the money due to him. The transaction is usually financed by a finance company which specialises in providing

funds for hire purchase etc.; the retailer in most cases acts as an intermediary between the finance company and the buyer receiving a commission on the sale from the financier. Unless the retailer has large sums at his disposal, he would normally find financing expensive items by this method beyond his means. The retailer therefore has an arrangement whereby he in fact 'sells' the goods to the financier who 'lends' them to the purchaser until all the instalments have been paid.

(b) *To the Customer.*
   (1) He is able to have the use of the goods whilst he is paying for them.
   (2) People with small incomes find it easier to pay weekly or monthly instalments than to save the full amount before purchasing the goods. The customer can make his payments direct to the lender through the retailer or by using the bank giro system.

Disadvantages.

(a) *To the Firm.*
   (1) Under the hire-purchase system, the seller of the goods, or the finance company as the case may be, can subject to certain conditions take possession if the payments are not continued, but the goods will have deteriorated by use.
   (2) Under the credit sales system, the seller or finance company has the trouble of suing the customer before a court of law if payments have not been continued.
   (3) Both systems of payment involve additional expense to the seller, etc. since the payments must be collected and recorded.

(b) *To the Customer.*
   (1) The customer is often tempted to purchase goods beyond his means, and to agree to weekly or monthly payments which he can ill afford.
   (2) The customer is usually paying a high rate of interest for the privilege of paying by instalments. In addition, he is losing the interest which would accrue if he placed

his savings in a bank deposit or savings account until the amount necessary for his purchase was obtained.

(3) The customer may have a limited choice in buying goods by these methods. He cannot insist on good quality to the same extent as when he pays cash.

Whether payment by instalments is desirable depends upon the nature of the article purchased and the circumstances of the individual: where the article is both durable and necessary however the system is advantageous to both the buyer and the seller. Nevertheless a certain amount of caution is desirable before entering into too many contracts of this nature.

10. INDEX NUMBERS

One of the principal functions of money is to act as a measure of the value of goods and services: we give a certain amount of money when making purchases, and the amount we give depends on how much money is in circulation and the number of commodities for sale. The relation between the amount of money in circulation and the number of commodities varies from time to time, and consequently fluctuations in prices occur.

A rise in prices may be due to:

(a) An increase in the amount of money in circulation.

(b) The existing amount of money being used more frequently.

(c) A reduction in the number of commodities.

Similarly, a fall in prices will occur when the opposite to the above takes place.

This indicates the relationship which exists between the *quantity of money* in circulation, the *volume of goods* and *the price level*. The general level of prices varies from time to time, and attempts are made by means of **Index Numbers** to measure variations in the price level.

Many systems of Index Numbers have been employed, but the general principles of all are the same. A large number of commodities is taken, and the *average* price of each is multiplied by a number representing the importance of that commodity in our daily life. This is called the method of *weighted averages*, and the average of such weighted averages gives an index of the price level of all commodities. It is necessary for these averages to be weighted, as we spend much more of our income on food than we do on furniture, and therefore a rising price in foodstuffs is much more important than a corresponding rise in the cost of furniture.

The best-known Index Numbers are prepared by:

(a) *The Department of Trade and Industry*, whose Statistics Division prepares Index Numbers of Wholesale Prices, and collects a wide range of information relating to the trade and industry of Britain and other countries. In addition figures are given relating to the average earnings, unemployment, capital expenditure, etc.

(b) *The Department of Employment and Productivity* is responsible for the *Index of Retail Prices* currently in use and which was introduced in January 1962, using that year as the *base year* of 100.

This index number is calculated *on a monthly basis* using 1962 as the year for comparative purposes. Attention is focused on changes in demand whereby greater importance is given to the items on which large amounts are expended. Account is taken therefore of any seasonal change in both prices and demand by a change in the monthly weighting given to each item.

A continuous enquiry is in operation in order to keep a constant check on the weighting basis: over 11,000 private household addresses throughout Britain are visited in turn through the year by local officers of the Department: the householders at these addresses are asked to make detailed records of income and expenditure for fourteen consecutive days, and to provide details of long period payments, such as rent, electricity, insurance, cost of travel, etc. From this information (which is confidential), the *weighting pattern* of the Index of Retail Prices can be revised each January. Such an Index provides an accurate measurement of changes in prices of goods and services which consumers are purchasing.

Retail Prices Index. The importance given to the various categories can be assessed by the following diagram showing the comparison of amounts spent on each item out of income in the average home.

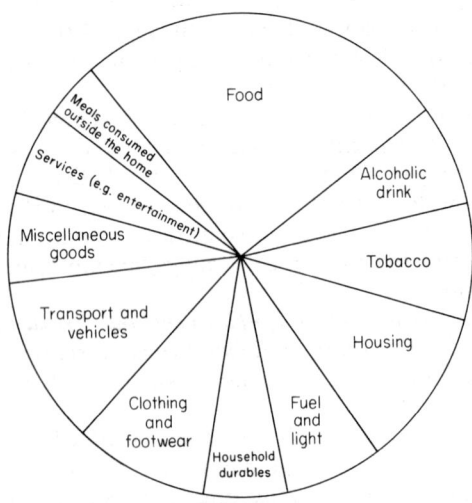

The Index covers the following main groups of items:

(1) *Food.* Information regarding retail prices of food and other items is obtained by the local officers of the Department. The difference in importance of the various items of food used is assessed. A considerable number of articles are weighted, and include meat, milk, fresh vegetables, bread, canned foods, sugar, butter, margarine, etc. From this information, the *average percentage increase* of food prices is calculated.

(2) *Alcoholic Drink.* Prices of beer, wines and spirits are obtained from firms of brewers, distillers and retailers.

(3) *Tobacco.* The retail prices of cigarettes, cigars and pipe tobacco are ascertained by direct enquiry from manufacturers.

(4) *Housing.* Information concerning the number of dwellings owned by local authorities and their rents, rates and water charges is obtained directly from the authorities

concerned. For other dwellings, information is obtained by visits to the tenants.

(5) *Fuel and Light.* The prices of coal, gas, electricity and oil are obtained from the retail outlets such as area boards and suppliers as well as from the various sample households.

(6) *Durable Household Goods.* Prices on such goods as furniture, carpets, domestic appliances, radio, television, pottery and glassware are obtained by personal visits made by officers of the Department to large retail stores.

(7) *Clothing and Footwear.* Information is obtained regarding the prices of all forms of clothing, hosiery and shoes. Enquiry forms are completed by retailers, which include co-operative societies, departmental stores and large multiple undertakings.

(8) *Transport and Vehicles.* The Index for this group is designed to reflect changes in the cost of buying, maintaining and running vehicles for private use, and also changes in fares and other transport charges. Information is obtained from vehicle manufacturers and dealers regarding the prices of both new and used cars of a given age, and from transport organisations concerning changes in fares.

(9) *Miscellaneous Goods.* The prices of such items as books, newspapers, sports goods, toys, soap, cleaning powders, etc., are obtained from retailers and trade associations.

(10) *Services.* Charges for services such as admission to theatres, postage, laundry, telephone, etc., are obtained locally by officers of the Department.

(11) *Meals bought and Consumed Outside the home* have been included in the system in view of the increasing number of meals taken in restaurants, cafés, etc.

The above results are combined in one average percentage result, which shows the increase in the cost of living *over a given period.*

The student is referred to the latest bulletin issued by the Department which will give the up-to-date figures and the *current* weighting attached to each of the above items.

(c) The *Central Statistical Office* collects statistics from various Government departments and assembles them in quarterly publications for easy reference. This information together with additional statistics provided from its own resources, enables the Central Statistical Office to provide Government, Industry and Commerce with the up-to-date information necessary for policy-making decisions.

(d) The *Business Statistics Office* of the Department of Trade and Industry collects and up-dates the main statistics which are published for reference purposes. Statistics are obtained from both the public and private sectors and include details of capital expenditure, stock holdings, consumption, investment, employment, production, overseas trade etc. In addition it is responsible for the continued development of a data bank which computer stores statistics and which is available for ready reference by interested parties.

QUESTIONS

1. What is barter? Enumerate the inconveniences of barter and the advantages of using money in trade.   (U.L.C.I.)

2. Describe the present currency system of this country and the part played in it by the Bank of England.   (U.L.C.I.)

3. State concisely the position and responsibilities of the Bank of England in respect of (a) the currency, (b) the Banking System in general.   (R.S.A.)

4. Explain fully what is meant by the statement that Bank of England notes are legal tender for any amount. What other forms may legal tender take?

5. Discuss the importance of hire-purchase to consumers and producers. What dangers to the economy may it sometimes bring?
(London G.C.E.)

6. Describe the services provided by Board of Trade division of the Department of Trade and Industry which assist the business world.   (London G.C.E.)

7. What is the difference between 'bank money' and 'legal tender'? What is meant by the phrase 'the value of money'? Explain whether the value of money has changed or not in this country in recent years.   (J.M.B.)

8. Every Friday, Messrs. Day and Knight pay out wages in cash amounting to £5,000. They draw cash from the local branch bank on Friday morning at 10 a.m. and pay their employees at 5 p.m. Their main difficulties are (a) security, and (b) the time taken in making up wage packets. Describe two methods they

might adopt to overcome each of these difficulties (four measures in all). (R.S.A.)

9. Mr. Buyer obtained a television set priced at £100 under a hire-purchase agreement. Explain how his rights or duties are affected in each of the following instances:

(a) After paying a total of £45, Mr. Buyer temporarily stops paying instalments because of illness.

(b) After paying a total of £20, Mr. Buyer wishes to end the agreement.

(c) The seller, hearing that the set has been damaged sends his representative to take the set away from Mr. Buyer.

(d) Mr. Buyer wishes to sell the television set to a friend before the instalments are completed. (A.E.B.)

Chapter 20

The British Banking Systems

I. DEVELOPMENT OF BANKING IN ENGLAND

The development of banking in England corresponds to the industrial development of the country. The following stages may be observed:

(a) **Foreign Bankers.** During the Middle Ages, the trade of England consisted chiefly of:

(1) *The export* of wool to Flanders in France where it was made up into cloth. This trade was in the hands of the Hanseatic League, a powerful group of merchants who established centres in the principal towns of Northern Europe. Their London depot was on the present site of Cannon Street Station, until they were expelled from England in 1589.

(2) *The import* of spices and silks from the East. These goods were brought to England by the Venetian Fleet, which made yearly visits to Northern Europe for nearly two hundred years. The imports were financed by the Lombards, whose name is still remembered in Lombard Street, the centre of British banking at the present day. The terms used in double-entry book-keeping and the law regarding negotiable instruments owe much to the influence of the Lombards.

The discovery of America and of a new sea-route to India at the end of the fifteenth century ruined the trade of Venice, and the growing activity of English merchants brought to an end the ascendancy of the Lombards in English finance.

(b) **The Goldsmiths.** English bankers took the place of the Lombards, and financed English trade to America. During the sixteenth and seventeenth centuries, the Goldsmiths developed banking in England in four ways:

(1) They first acted as custodians for money and valuables, and charged commission for their safe keeping.

(2) Receipts were given to the depositor, who could therefore pay his debts by transferring the receipt, instead of withdrawing the money from the Goldsmiths. His creditor could claim the money from the Goldsmiths, or have his account credited with the amount.

(3) If the deposit was large, the Goldsmiths issued several receipts of smaller denomination, and round sums. These could be used for the payment of debts of small amount; in these receipts we see the *origin of bank-notes*.

(4) The Goldsmiths learned by experience that the amount withdrawn was less than the amount deposited: the balance was left with them year after year. They could therefore make loans on good security and make a profit by charging interest. They were able to remit the charges for safe keeping, and to allow interest on the deposits.

The Goldsmiths lent considerable sums of money to the Crown on the security of the taxes; they suffered heavy losses however, through the refusal of Charles II and James II to recognise their claims, and they lost the confidence of the public. The need for a new institution to issue notes and to act as a Central Bank led to the foundation of the Bank of England in 1694.

(c) The Bank of England. When William III came to the throne in 1689, he wanted money to enable him to defend Holland against the French. His Dutch friends favoured a municipal bank in London on the model of the Bank of Amsterdam, but the City of London had lost money through investing charitable funds with the Goldsmiths, and the idea of a municipal bank was not popular.

William Paterson, a Scotsman, made the following suggestions:

(1) That a separate and independent bank should be founded.
(2) That the capital subscribed by the public should be handed over to the Government as a permanent loan at

8 per cent per annum, together with £4,000 towards the expenses of management.

(3) That a charter should be granted giving the bank the right to issue notes up to the amount of the Capital. The chief credit for the actual formation of the Bank is due to Charles Montagu and to Michael Godfrey whose influence in the City was vital to the success of Paterson's idea.

The loan of £1,200,000 was subscribed in ten days; a charter was granted and the Bank of England commenced business in the Mercers' Chapel, London, with fifty-four assistants. In 1734 it moved to the Threadneedle Street premises which is now its Head Office. The Bank of England was, therefore, not a State Bank, but a corporation, under Parliamentary control, with exceptional privileges.

The charter of the Bank of England was revised from time to time: the main landmarks in the history of the bank may be mentioned:

1711.   The charter granted in 1694 was renewed: Parliament allowed the Bank of England to be the only banking partnership *in England* to issue notes payable on demand. Other banks could be formed provided that they did not issue notes.

1826.   Banks with more than six partners could carry on business, including the issue of bank-notes, more than sixty-five miles outside London. The Bank of England was also authorised to open branches in the provinces.

1833.   An Act of Parliament authorised the establishment of joint-stock banks in London and within sixty-five miles radius of London, provided that they did not issue notes.

1844.   Bank Charter Act, dividing the Bank of England into two departments—the Issue Department and the Banking Department.

1921.   The Bank of England became the only bank in England and Wales with the right of issuing bank-notes.

1946.   Bank of England Act, which brought the bank under State ownership.

A full account of the work of the Bank of England is given in the next chapter.

(d) Private Banks. From 1694 to 1826 private partnership banks developed as follows:

(1) *In London.* The private banks could not issue notes, and therefore concentrated on deposit banking similar to the system used to-day. They also carried on the work of the Goldsmiths, and lent part of their deposits for financing trade by discounting bills of exchange and making loans on goods in the course of being marketed.

(2) *In the Provinces.* The growth of industry and trade during the eighteenth century led to the formation of many small private banks in various parts of England and Wales. These banks had the right of issuing bank-notes; loans were made in the form of notes, and as long as the credit of the bank and of the partners was good the notes passed as currency. The bank therefore received interest on the loan, and yet employed none of its own capital.

In periods of good trade, many banks issued a larger amount of notes than their reserves warranted, and frequently had to suspend payment when their notes were presented to them for cash: from 1814 to 1816 over 240 banks stopped payment and 89 failed, whilst in 1825, about 70 banks failed in a period of six *weeks*. The unregulated issue of bank-notes was one of th main causes of the Bank Charter Act of 1844; in that year, 279 banks in England and Wales issued notes.

Private banks have declined in importance during the last century for the following reasons:

(1) The Bank Charter Act (1844) made provision for the gradual concentration of the note-issue in the hands of the Bank of England.

(2) An Act of Parliament passed in 1833 permitted joint-stock banks to open in London, provided that they did not issue notes. Joint-stock banking rather than partnership banking therefore developed in England from 1834 onwards.

(3) Private banks amalgamated with the joint-stock banks, and so lost their right of issuing notes. The Barclay family, for example, has been connected with banking since 1674, and the bank bearing that name was formed late in the

nineteenth century by the amalgamation of twenty private
banks.

(4) The Limited Liability Act (1862) gave the advantage of
limited liability to all joint-stock enterprises, and thus encouraged that form of banking.

(e) Joint-Stock Banks. The growth of joint-stock banks
in England was due to the industrial changes which took place
during the latter part of the eighteenth century: the development of trade during the period 1750–1850 led to a demand for
increased banking facilities.

In England, no legal definition has been given of what is
meant by a bank: in most other countries, the law of banking
is codified, but in this country the law relating to companies
applies also to banking companies.

The Bills of Exchange Act (1882) refers to a bank as 'a body
of persons, whether incorporated or not, that carries on a
banking business'. In actual practice, however, the term 'bank'
is now taken to mean an institution which:

(1) receives money on deposit from the public;
(2) pays on demand by means of cheques;
(3) is a source of short, medium and long term loans.

The Limited Liability Act (1862) extended this principle to
banks. There followed a period of expansion and amalgamation
culminating in the formation of a few large banks with many
branches throughout the country. This had an added advantage
in that a depression in one part of the country did not have
such a damaging effect as previously.

Further amalgamations took place during the years so that
today banking in England is mainly in the hands of a few large
groups as follows:

	Branches
(1) Barclays Bank Group	3450
(2) Lloyds Bank	2400
(3) Midland Bank	3600
(4) National Westminster Group	3800

There are also several smaller banks outside the above groups
such as Williams and Glyn's Bank, The Co-operative Bank, etc.,

which have considerably fewer branches and are often local in character.

The principal advantage attached to the amalgamation of banking units lies in the creation of large increases in deposits. The bank is thus able to lend larger amounts to industrial firms which have amalgamated themselves in order to compete on equal terms with the principal firms and combinations of the world particularly in Europe, Japan and the United States. A number of banks have also extended their interests overseas. Barclays Bank, for example, has many connections abroad, principally through Barclays Bank International, a wholly-owned subsidiary company. The banks have agents in practically every country of the world through which their customers may transact business and receive advice on local trading conditions.

2. THE ENGLISH BANKING SYSTEM

The above account of the development of banking in England shows the way in which a unified system has evolved in this country. At the present time, banking consists of the following sections, all of which are interrelated and work together as one unit:

(a) The Bank of England, which is the pivot of the British Banking System, consists of eight departments, two of which, the Issue Department and the Banking Department, are concerned with the note-issue, etc., and which publish separate returns each week.

The Bank of England is the centre of banking throughout this country for the following reasons:

(1) It acts as the banker to the State: it keeps the Government accounts, manages the National Debt for the Government, and pays interest on loans raised by the Government.

(2) It is responsible for the note issue of the country being the sole bank of issue in England and Wales since 1921.

(3) It acts as the Bankers' bank: it holds the cash reserves of the other banks of the country, and is able to extend or restrict the amount of credit according to the needs of commerce.

(4) The joint-stock banks and finance houses accept the leadership of the Bank of England, which is therefore able to control credit in this country by directives given with Treasury approval. By this means, the Bank of England is able to exert a strong influence on the London Money Market.

(5) The Bank of England is a member of the London Clearing House: its membership enables the other clearing banks to settle their accounts by the payment of differences by cheques on the Bank of England.

(b) The London Clearing Banks. These banks have their Head Offices in London, and their representatives meet daily at the London Clearing House to exchange cheques and settle differences by 'cheques' on the Bank of England. The London Clearing Banks consist of the following groups:

(1) The Bank of England.
(2) The large group banks:
    Barclays, Lloyds, Midland and the National Westminster.
(3) Other banks, some of whom are subsidiaries to the above. These are Coutts, National and Grindlays, Williams and Glyn's.

The London Clearing Banks are closely connected with the Bank of England as follows:

(a) They keep a portion of their ready cash at the Bank of England: the amount to the credit of the Clearing Banks appears in the weekly return of the Bank of England under the heading of 'Bankers Deposits' (see page 277).

(b) The accounts kept by the Clearing Banks with the Bank of England make the Clearing House system possible, since differences can be paid by 'cheques' on the Bank of England.

(c) The Clearing Banks accept the leadership and recommendations of the Bank of England in the Money Market: the Bank of England Minimum Lending Rate is a factor in determining the discount rate on bills of exchange etc. It is also a factor to a limited extent in the determination of the base rates fixed by the Commercial Banks.

(c) Other Banks. Outside the London Clearing System are groups of banks which finance trade in a particular country or area: these banks are, however, members of the British Bankers' Association, which exists for the discussion of problems of common interest. They include:

(1) *Banks which are not members* of the London Clearing House and are either situated only in London or have a very few branches in this country. They include the Co-operative Bank, Reliance Bank, etc., who have arrangements with one of the Clearing House members to exchange cheques, etc., drawn on other banks.

(2) *Scottish and Northern Ireland Banks* have their own arrangements for the clearing of cheques, etc., drawn in Scotland and Northern Ireland. For cheques which are drawn on banks in England and Wales arrangements are made with one of the London Clearing House members.

(3) *Overseas Banks* of which there are two kinds:

  (*a*) Commonwealth Banks representing the interests of the Dominions, Colonies and Commonwealth and who have offices in London. Examples include The Bank of Montreal, The Standard Bank, etc.

  (*b*) European and Foreign Banks which take a prominent part in financing trade between Britain and the country they represent. All the major trading countries of the world are represented and examples would include The Chase Manhattan Bank, Moscow Narodny Bank, Credit Lyonnais, Société Générale, Deutshe Bank, etc.

  The Overseas banks will accept bills of exchange or documentary credits for their clients abroad. They will also collect bills in this country when they are due and remit the proceeds to their customers.

3. MERCHANT BANKS, DISCOUNT AND ISSUING HOUSES

These institutions are not banks according to the definition given above, since they do not accept deposits repayable on demand: a few however have close financial connections with the London Clearing Banks by way of shareholdings or interlocking directorates.

(a) Merchant Banks are also known as **Accepting Houses**

since they were mostly founded by men who commenced as merchants trading with other countries in such commodities as wool, cotton, tobacco, timber, etc. They have many foreign connections and their representatives abroad keep them informed of changes in industrial and financial conditions in other countries.

The merchant bankers, in addition to trading on their own account, frequently accepted bills for firms which were not so well known, and they found this side of their business so profitable that they gave up their commercial interests and became financial houses. Thus they are also called **Accepting Houses**; they earn a commission by accepting bills for other firms and on account of their world-wide repute, bills accepted by them are readily sold.

These institutions do not part with any money; they lend their good name only, charging a commission for their guarantee of payment when the bill falls due. The accepted bill may then be discounted by a bank or by a discount broker at a finer rate.

The importance of Merchant Banks is twofold:

(1) They circulate Bills of Exchange and in this way make the international payments for goods or services possible.

(2) The Merchant Banks act as financial advisers to many Commonwealth, European and foreign firms and governments. They arrange for their loans to be taken up in London and elsewhere. Their international reputation and accumulated experience makes them well qualified to render this service.

The joint-stock banks compete with the Merchant Banks for a share of their accepting business. A great deal of trade between Britain and the Commonwealth is financed by the Commonwealth banks which have offices in London, whilst the trade with the European Economic Community countries is financed by both the British and European banks having offices in both centres. Nevertheless the Merchant Banks of London are so well known on the international exchanges that an accepted bill bearing a name such as Baring's, Rothschild's, Samuel Montagu, etc., is as good as cash since these represent the very essence of the London Money Market.

The **Merchant Banks** also provide numerous other services to their clients. These include the operation of unit trusts, investment management, property investment and insurance from their branches in London and the provinces on the home market. Most of the larger Merchant Banks have subsidiaries or shareholdings overseas that provide entry into foreign markets. Thus the expertise of the City of London is used to finance multi-national companies whose requirements may amount to many millions of pounds.

(b) Discount Houses consist of several joint-stock companies and a number of private firms. As their name implies, they specialise in discounting bills of exchange. A large part of the world's trade is financed by bills drawn on London banks accepted for payment by the City Merchant Banks or Accepting Houses: they come to London for acceptance, and the owners satisfy their need for capital by borrowing from the banks or discount houses on the security of the accepted bills.

Discount Houses are willing to make loans on these: the amount depending on the name of the acceptor, time the bill has to run, and the current rate of interest. They obtain funds from four sources:

(1) Their own capital, which in many cases is considerable.

(2) The deposits of the public, which are accepted at interest: the Discount Houses compete with the banks for these which are not repayable on demand thus receiving a slightly higher rate of interest.

(3) They borrow from the joint-stock banks at a lower rate of interest than the general public, using the money to discount bills at a higher rate: such loans from the banks are for short periods, perhaps overnight or up to one month. The banks are therefore able to employ their funds in eligible assets (see page 300) and also have some control over the amount of capital available on the money market for short-term investments.

(4) If there are insufficient funds from the above, the Discount House may *at the last resort* borrow for a short period from the Bank of England. The rate of interest charged, however, would be higher than the other sources mentioned above.

Discount Houses, therefore, specialise in the discounting of bills, and relieve the banks of the risks attached to the variations in the demand for credit.

In order that the Bank may control this aspect of the Money Market, the Discount Houses agree to keep at least 50 per cent of their borrowed funds in certain specified categories of public sector debt. These include Treasury Bills, Local Authority Bills and Bonds and Local Authority Stock maturing in under 5 years.

(c) Issuing Houses. Specialise in the issue of new securities to large institutions and to the public: well-known Issuing Houses are Baring Brothers, Morgan Grenfell, N. M. Rothschild & Sons, J. Henry Schroder Wagg & Co., many of whom also act as Accepting Houses. The work of an Issuing House may be summarised as follows:

(1) They arrange the public issue of stocks and shares on behalf of British, European and foreign companies, corporations and governments.

(2) They specialise in both Community and foreign loans, which are raised in this country to enable a government or municipality to develop an area under its control. They also deal with domestic issues to a great extent, particularly with public joint-stock companies.

(3) Issuing Houses often act as sponsors and underwriters in order to guarantee the success of a share issue. They work in close connection with the London Stock Exchange, consequently a strict code is followed thus ensuring that the investor's interest is protected.

(4) They often privately assist small private companies to establish themselves by way of medium-term loans.

(5) Issuing Houses examine the merits of the proposed issue of capital before dealing. The success of a new issue may depend on the reputation of the Issuing House which markets the new securities.

(6) The Issuing House makes arrangements for underwriting the issue. The underwriters agree to buy any stock which is not taken up by the public which is then sold gradually either privately or through the Stock Exchange.

(7) In dealing with a foreign loan, the Issuing House obtains

the permission of the Bank of England before underwriting the issue.

Control by the Bank of England

The activities and dealings of the finance houses mentioned above are controlled by the Bank of England. The terms applying to the joint-stock banks set out on page 299 also apply to the finance houses with the following exceptions:

(a) Eligible liabilities do not include amounts borrowed from the joint-stock banks.

(b) The required day-to-day minimum reserve asset ratio is 10 per cent.

(c) The Bank of England reserves the right to call for Special Deposits at a higher rate if necessary.

(d) Finance Houses having eligible liabilities under £5 million are exempt from this control.

4. THE LONDON CLEARING HOUSE

Membership. The development of the cheque system in this country has necessitated the organisation of a clearing system: before 1775, cheques on other banks in London were presented by hand, but the labour of presenting cheques and receiving payment in cash or notes led to a room being taken in Change Alley as a meeting-place for bank clerks. The meetings were at first informal and unofficial, but the labour-saving advantages soon led to official recognition, and the acquisition of larger premises. At first, membership of the Clearing House was restricted to private banks, but the joint-stock banks were admitted in 1854. The Bank of England became a member in 1864: a complete list of the London Clearing Banks is given on page 262.

The Clearing House is managed by a Committee of the Clearing Bankers: it has only a few officers of its own, most of the work being done by the staffs of the clearing banks.

Clearing Procedure. There are two clearings each day, the first dealing with the Town clearing, the second dealing with the General clearing.

The Town clearing during the afternoon deals with cheques of £5,000 and over drawn on and paid into the branches in the City of London that day. The General clearing in the morning deals with the cheques under £5,000 from the City and all the cheques paid into the provincial branches on the previous day.

The Clearing House is organised into two departments, and each bank has several desks in each department.

(a) *The Out-Clearing Department.* The cheques paid into the *provincial* branches are sorted and listed before being sent overnight to the Head Offices in London. The following day, the Head Offices of each clearing bank will sort and list by computer the cheques drawn on other banks and the total claims found. The bundles of cheques are exchanged between the banks in the out-clearing department of the Clearing House.

Similarly the cheques over £5,000 paid into and drawn on the *City* branches are listed and the total claims found. These cheques are cleared through the Clearing House *on the same day* as they are paid in and represent a much greater amount in terms of sterling since they are drawn by the banks, insurance companies, stockbrokers, shipping companies and other financial institutions of the City of London.

(b) *The In-Clearing Department* receives the cheques from the out-clearing department: in this department, the banks deal with their own cheques handed over by the other banks. The cheques are listed again to verify the totals: they are then returned to the appropriate Head Offices, from whence they are sent to the respective branches for verification, etc., whilst details of the amounts are sent to the computer centre where the branch accounts are kept and debited to the customers account. A diagram of the full procedure can be seen on page 290.

(c) *Settlement.* At the end of each day, the Clearing House representatives of each bank prepare a Summary Sheet, showing the totals due to or from each bank. The balance between the banks is paid by means of a transfer on the Clearing Bankers' Accounts at the Bank of England.

The importance of the cheque system is shown by the fact that over three *million* cheques pass through the London Clearing House every working *day*. In addition the Clearing House deals with a considerable number of Bank Giro credits which are dealt with in a similar manner. These amount to over 350 million items in a year and once again the value of computers and electronic sorters can be seen.

Inter-Bank Computer Bureau. Forms part of the clearing procedure and maintained by the London, Scottish and Northern Ireland clearing banks. Its function is to facilitate the interchange of standing orders and direct debits between members on behalf of their customers.

5. DEVELOPMENT OF BANKING IN SCOTLAND

The banking system of Scotland differs in many respects from England: when the Bank of England was founded in 1694, Scotland had a Parliament of its own, and it was not until 1707 that the two Parliaments were united. As a result of history and political changes, there are many features in the Scottish banking system which are not found elsewhere in this country.

(a) Development. At the present time, the banking system consists of three banks:

(1) *The Bank of Scotland* founded in 1695 by an Act passed by the Scottish Parliament. This is the only bank established by Act of Parliament. Unlike the Bank of England, it was founded to aid commerce and industry, and not to render financial assistance to a government. In 1969 it extended its business by taking over the British Linen Bank which was founded in 1746.

(2) *The National and Commercial Bank* was formed in 1969 by the amalgamation of two old and well established Scottish banks—the Royal Bank of Scotland and the National Commercial Bank of Scotland. This group is now the largest in Scotland.

(3) *The Clydesdale Bank* was formed by the amalgamation of two banks—the North of Scotland Bank and the Clydesdale Bank. It has close connections with the Midland Bank.

All the Scottish banks have the benefit of limited liability, either according to the terms of their charters, or by registration under the Companies Acts; limited liability does not extend, however, to the note issues of any of the banks. They all have offices in London which look after Scottish interests in the City and which are used by the English banks for the exchange of cheques and notes.

(b) Characteristics. In many respects, Scottish bankers were pioneers, and from the early part of the eighteenth century adopted methods which were followed by English bankers at a later date. The characteristics of Scottish banking are as follows:

(1) Scotland did not develop a central banking institution. This is due to the fact that twelve years after the foundation of the Bank of Scotland the two countries were united by the Act of Union (1707). As a result, the Bank of England has always overshadowed the Bank of Scotland, and has acted as the Central Bank for the whole of Britain.

(2) The essential difference between English and Scottish banks is in connection with the issue of notes. This right brings the Scottish banks a certain amount of prestige over their English rivals and also acts as a cheap form of advertisement.

(3) The Scottish banks developed the system of branch banking during the early part of the nineteenth century. The Scottish people had great confidence in their banks, and they received interest on their savings by depositing their money in a bank. Since 1845, only two banks have failed in Scotland, and there are more branches per head of the population in Scotland than in England or Wales.

(4) The Scottish banks granted advances more easily and for longer periods than the English banks. Loans were often made on the personal security of the borrower which was of great benefit to manufacturers and traders.

(c) The Scottish Note Issue. The Scottish Bank Notes Act (1845) governs the issue of bank-notes in Scotland. The terms of this act were as follows:

(1) The right of issuing bank-notes was confined to banks already exercising the privilege. By forbidding the establishment of new banks of issue, the Act gave a monopoly of banking to the banks in existence in 1845. No new bank has been established in Scotland since that date.

(2) Each bank was authorised to have in circulation a certain amount of notes.

(3) Coin was not to be a reserve against notes, but was to be regarded as part of the general assets of the bank.

(4) The minimum denominations of notes was to be £1.

(5) Banks which amalgamated could continue to issue notes to the amount of their aggregate issue before amalgamation.

(6) Bank of England notes could circulate in Scotland, but *at that time* were not legal tender in that country.

The Act of 1845 fixed the fiduciary issue of the Scottish banks at £3,087,209, but this has been reduced, and at the present time the issue is £2,676,350, made up as follows:

	Authorised Fiduciary Issue
	£
Bank of Scotland . . .	1,289,222
National and Commercial Bank Group	888,355
Clydesdale Bank . . .	498,773
Total Fiduciary Issue . .	£2,676,350

Apart from this, the above banks may not issue any further notes unless they are covered by an equal value of Bank of England notes.

(d) The Scottish Clearing System

(1) *Note Exchanges.* The Scottish banks have an agreement not to issue the notes of another bank, and a system of note exchanges has been in force since 1752, when it was first adopted by the Bank of Scotland and the Royal Bank of Scotland.

At all towns in Scotland where there are two or more banks, an exchange of each other's notes takes place daily. Exchange vouchers are issued for notes handed over to another bank: these vouchers are forwarded to the head offices of the banks at Edinburgh, where a final settlement is made at the Clearing House.

(2) *The Clearing System for Cheques.*

(a) *Local Clearings.* Clearing Houses have been established in the principal cities and towns for the clearing of cheques and the exchanges of notes. The representatives of the various banks meet daily, and after dealing with the notes, the clerks exchange cheques on other banks and receive cheques on their own branch. The settling bank receives the balances due from the debtor banks, and pays the sums due to the creditor banks. These payments are made in the local clearings by means of a draft on Edinburgh.

(b) *The Edinburgh Clearing House.* Edinburgh is the centre of banking in Scotland. The same principle is used for the clearing of cheques and giro credits as at the London Clearing House.

The Scottish banks also have accounts at the Bank of England which as with the English banks is used for the settling of indebtedness with each other.

QUESTIONS

1. In what ways does the Scottish Banking System differ from that of England?

2. The Scottish people have been called 'Pioneers in Banking'. Illustrate the truth of this statement.

3. What is meant by 'clearing' a cheque? How is the Bank of England concerned in this process? (R.S.A.)

4. Describe the work of the London Accepting Houses (and other financial institutions) in the financing of foreign trade through bills of exchange. (R.S.A.)

5. 'Our economic system is based on credit.' Explain this statement bringing out the different ways in which credit is being used in the economic life of our country. (J.M.B.)

6. Why is it necessary to distinguish between a negotiable instrument and a non-negotiable instrument? In which of these two categories would you place a postal order, a dividend warrant to bearer, an uncrossed cheque, a share certificate, a cheque crossed 'not negotiable'. (R.S.A.)

7. What part is played by the Discount Houses in the British financial system? Do you feel that their continued existence is justified? Give your reasons. (R.S.A.)

Chapter 21

The Bank of England

1. CONSTITUTION

The Bank of England was founded as a private institution independent of any form of legal control except in regard to its powers of issuing notes and making loans to the State. The need for a State loan led to its foundation in 1694, when it was given the right of note issue in return. The original charter was granted for a period of twelve years, after which the Government might annul it on giving one year's notice: the charter was renewed from time to time, generally with the grant of additional loans to the State.

The constitution of the Bank of England was modified by the Bank Charter Act of 1844, which divided the Bank into two departments, and provided that the issue of notes should be kept distinct from the banking business of the Bank as follows:

(a) *The Issue Department* being solely responsible for the issue of notes.

(b) *The Banking Department* which acts as a bank of deposit, keeping accounts for the Government, British, European and foreign banks, financial houses and a few private customers.

The Bank now has practically no private customers but its responsibilities to the nation have increased during the last fifty years. As the Government's bank it deals with the control of the monetary system within Britain and also has a close link with the Treasury in connection with the foreign exchange markets of the world.

The Bank of England Act 1946 brought the capital stock of the bank into public ownership. Its chief terms were:

(a) The Bank to be managed by a board of directors known as *the Court* and comprised of the Governor, Deputy Governor and sixteen directors, all appointed by the Crown.

(b) The Governor and Deputy Governor to be appointed for a period of five years, the directors for a period of four years.

(c) The Court of Directors to meet weekly to consider recommendations of the various sub-committees and to be responsible for the implementation of monetary policy as put forward by the Treasury.

The bank is further subdivided into departments which specialise in particular fields. The most important are:

(a) *The Chief Cashier's Department* which deals with all the banking operations, exchange equalisation account, management and branch affairs.

(b) *The Accountant's Department* is concerned with the registers of stockholders who have lent money to the Government and the payment of dividends when due.

(c) *The Overseas Department* administers the Exchange Control regulations of this country and also advises the Treasury in its relations with other Central Banks and financial institutions abroad.

The Bank, whose Head Office is in Threadneedle Street, London, has eight branches in England—at Birmingham, Bristol, Leeds, Liverpool, Manchester, Newcastle-on-Tyne, Southampton and London (Law Courts) and one in Glasgow which is used for Exchange Control purposes only. These branches used to undertake ordinary commercial business, but this is no longer carried on: they act now as repositories for Government department accounts and as depots for currency for the joint-stock and other banks in their area.

2. THE NOTE ISSUE

The Bank of England has the sole right in England and Wales of issuing bank-notes. The largest is the £20 note the smallest being the £1 note. The *average* amount in daily circulation

(Top) The Bank of England, Head Office in London and (below) one of the smaller gold vaults. Each bar is worth about £5,000.

exceeds £4,600 million. The total amount in circulation, however, varies according to demand. At Christmas and holiday-times for example the amount needed rises as people require cash for the purchase of presents, etc.

The notes issued must be covered by Government securities held by the Bank of England. The Currency and Bank Notes Act 1954 fixed the *fiduciary issue* at £1,575 million giving the Bank power to increase this figure temporarily by asking Parliament for permission by means of a Treasury minute laid before the House.

Where an increase is required for longer than two years, a Statutory Order must be approved by Parliament thus assuring close Parliamentary control over the notes issued by the Bank of England.

Taking the Bank Return on page 277 as an example notes to the value of £4,800 million may be issued backed up by the fiduciary issue of the same amount.

The printing of the notes is controlled by the Bank's staff who also withdraw large numbers of worn-out notes each day. The provision of coin for circulation is the responsibility of the Royal Mint which is a separate Government department under the control of the Treasury and situated at Llantrisant in South Wales.

3. THE BANK RETURN

By the provisions of the Bank Charter Act of 1844, the Bank of England must publish each week a statement showing its assets and liabilities. This statement is published each Thursday, after the meeting of the Court of Directors. The student will find a copy of the return in the financial papers which are published every Friday.

The form of the Bank Return is determined by Act of Parliament, and is as follows:

BANK OF ENGLAND RETURN

ISSUE DEPARTMENT

	£		£
Notes issued:	4,800,000,000	Government Debt	11,015,100
In circulation	4,780,283,159	Other Government	
In Banking		Securities	4,344,039,798
Department	19,716,841	Other Securities	444,945,102
		Amount of	
	£4,800,000,000	Fiduciary Issue £4,800,000,000	

BANKING DEPARTMENT

	£		£
Capital	14,553,000	Government	
Public Deposits	14,766,387	Securities	447,640,820
Special Deposits	120,884,000	Advance and	
Other Deposits:		other Accounts	45,259,544
Bankers	181,534,453	Premises Equipment	
Reserves and		and other securities	107,774,802
Other Accounts	289,355,810	Notes	19,716,841
		Coin	701,643
	£621,093,650		£621,093,650

The following points in connection with the Bank Return should be noted:

(1) *Issue Department*

(a) Liabilities

1. *Notes Issued.* This shows the total amount of the notes that may be issued by the Bank; it is subdivided to show the number of notes in circulation and the value of notes held by the Banking Department. The latter figure can be seen in the Banking Department return and represents the amount of notes which could be issued in addition to the number already in circulation throughout the country should the demand arise.

(b) Assets.

(1) *Government Debt.* Upon each renewal of the charter, a further loan was made to the Government. No loans have been made since 1833, and the Government Debt to the Bank of England (not the National Debt) has stood at £11,015,100 since that date. This figure today is of historical interest but nevertheless it still serves as a security for the note issue.

(2) *Other Government Securities.* These include Government Loan Issues and Treasury Bills, and serve as the chief backing for the Fiduciary Issue.

(3) *Other Securities.* These consist of other first-rate securities, and of bank and trade bills of exchange.

The above assets cover the fiduciary issue which may not be increased without the prior approval of Parliament. Should an increase be sanctioned the extra notes in the circulation department would be offset by a corresponding amount in item No. 2 above.

(2) *Banking Department*

The Banking Department carries on the business of banking like any other commercial bank but is primarily concerned with Government business. It enjoys, however, an exceptional position, since it is the banker to the Government and acts as the bankers' bank.

(a) Liabilities.

(1) *Capital.* The capital of the Bank amounts to £14,553,000, and has remained unchanged since 1816; the stock is fully paid and is held entirely by the Treasury.

(2) *Public Deposits* include all balances standing to the credit of the British Government at the head office and branches of the bank; these balances include the Commissioners of the National Debt, the Inland Revenue, Customs and Excise, National Savings Bank accounts, etc., and will vary with the collection of taxes, etc.; they are reduced in amount when dividends are paid on Government securities or withdrawals made from National Savings Bank accounts, etc.

(3) *Special Deposits* are a percentage of eligible liabilities

(see page 295) which the commercial joint-stock banks and finance houses may be required to keep with the Bank of England as part of the Government's policy to control credit. A small amount of interest is paid to the depositors but the deposits cannot be withdrawn except by permission of the Bank of England.

During a period of credit restriction the amounts on special deposits are likely to be increased. This action prevents the commercial banks and other finance houses from lending to other sources.

(4) *Other Deposits* are divided as follows:

(a) *Bankers' Deposits* relate to the funds of British banks, which keep part of their assets with the Bank of England. This relates to the commercial banks cash reserves which are used for the withdrawal of cash when required and for the settlement of debts through the clearing house operations. The Government can through open market operations change this amount of the commercial banks holding with the Bank of England.

(b) *Reserves and Other Accounts* refer to the funds standing to the credit of those banks which operate mainly in European, the Commonwealth, and other countries. This section also includes the Banks unallocated profit and inner reserves as well as balances maintained by other Central Banks, merchant banks, finance houses, and the few remaining private customers of the Bank of England.

(b) Assets.

(1) *Government Securities*. Consist of the Bank's own investments in British Government Stock, together with the security given by the Government for its loans from the Bank to cover temporary shortages of funds—often referred to as *'ways and means'* advances. This section also includes Treasury Bills that have been discounted for its customers.

(2) *Advance and other accounts* include loans made to the Banks private customers. The Bank also lends money to the Discount Houses and Bill Brokers of the City by what is known as 'lender of the last resort'.

(3) *Premises, Equipment and other securities* include the Bank's own premises and equipment at net cost in addition to its investments in non-British Government Stock, such as European, Commonwealth or foreign securities. This section also includes the Banks investments in companies such as the Agricultural Mortgage Corporation and Finance Corporation for Industry etc.

(4) *Notes.* Bank-notes issued by the Issue Department but not in circulation are held by the Banking Department. They form a reserve available to supplement the notes in circulation should the need arise.

(5) *Coin* is the amount which is necessary to meet the day-to-day requirements of the Banking Department of the Bank of England only and not the amount in general circulation.

4. FUNCTIONS OF THE BANK OF ENGLAND

These may be seen from a study of the weekly Bank Return:

(*a*) The Bank of England is responsible for the note issue, being the only bank with this right in England and Wales.

(*b*) It acts as banker to the State in so far as:

(1) It receives the proceeds of taxation.
(2) Makes payments on behalf of the Government.
(3) Manages the National Debt for the Government.
(4) Pays interest on Government loans.
(5) It receives subscriptions for new loans which the Government may raise.
(6) Makes loans to the Government from time to time.
(7) Acts as the agent for the Government in carrying out its monetary policy and enforcing exchange control regulations.

(*c*) The Bank acts as the agent of the Treasury in the operation of the Exchange Equalisation Account. This is the account through which the Bank is able to control large fluctuations in the rate of exchange of the £ on the foreign exchange markets.

(*d*) It acts as the Bankers' Bank, since it keeps part of the cash holdings of the other banks.

(*e*) It is the centre of the Clearing House System, since all the clearing banks have accounts at the Bank of England. Differences in the amounts of cheques and giro credits cleared are settled by transfers on the clearing banks accounts at the Bank of England.

(f) The Bank of England by varying its own official Minimum Lending Rate causes the other financial institutions to review their rates of interest accordingly.

(g) It influences the London Money Market when buying or selling bills or securities according to the credit requirements of the market. This function is known as 'open market operations'.

5. THE BANK OF ENGLAND AS A CENTRAL BANK

In the twentieth century the merits of free trade were applied to banking, and greater competition between the banks and other financial institutions was regarded as being desirable. The increased use of paper money and credit instruments in world trade required some measure of control and this had to be in the hands of the State. Hence the establishment in each country of a Central Bank which is responsible for the control of credit and the issue of paper money. In most countries, a State bank had been founded to perform these functions, but in Britain there was no State bank in the true sense until 1946 although the Bank of England had been working in close consultation with the Treasury long before then.

From its foundation in 1694, the Bank of England acted as both a bank of issue and a commercial bank. Today it does not compete with the joint-stock banks for commercial business, but carries out the functions of a Central Bank. The theory of Central Banking has developed in comparatively recent times, and the solution of the monetary problems of the world depend, to a large extent, on the degree of collaboration of the Central Banks of the various countries.

The Bank of England maintains close relationships with the European and Commonwealth Central Banks, the Federal Reserve of the United States, and many others throughout the world. The Bank is also represented on various important high-level monetary institutions such as:

(a) The International Monetary Fund.

(*b*) The International Bank for Reconstruction and Development.

(*c*) The Organisation for Economic Co-operation and Development.

(*d*) The European Investment Bank.

(*e*) The Bank of International Settlements.

The *functions of Central Banks* may be summarised as follows:

(*a*) They must maintain the stability of the monetary unit: in order to do this, they have to possess the sole right of note issue, so that they can control the amount of notes in circulation, since this is an important factor in determining prices.

(*b*) They must have custody of the cash reserve, as the amount of notes issued at any given time depends largely upon these reserves.

(*c*) Central Banks should act as the bank having authority over all the other banks in the country, in order that they may control the amount of credit according to the needs of industry etc.

(*d*) Central Banks should be the Governments banks; Governments receive large sums of money from taxation etc. and make large payments for education, defence, social services, technology, interest on loans, etc. The volume of Government receipts and payments will cause disturbances on the money market, unless regulated by the Central Bank and adequate measures taken.

(*e*) Central Banks must possess the right to buy bills and securities for cash out of their own funds, when there is a scarcity of credit, and sell bills or securities when credit is plentiful. By this means, the Central Banks can influence the activities of the money markets of their respective countries.

(*f*) Central Banks must maintain balances in the principal monetary centres of the world, in order to settle indebtedness between nations.

Central Banks, therefore, must as far as possible act in the interests of both their Government and the world monetary system. Their primary consideration must not be to make a profit; they must be free from the influence of any particular section of the community, and keep free from the finer problems of commerce and industry in order that they may give impartial advice and help to the country they represent.

6. EXCHANGE CONTROL

The purpose of Exchange Control is to ensure that a country's receipts of foreign currency are used to the best advantage.

Before 1939 Britain received a high proportion of her total foreign currency receipts in the form of dividends and interest on considerable investments abroad. Today these do not amount to the same high proportion and Britain must rely on greater receipts from the sale of both goods and services in order to obtain foreign currency with which to purchase essential imports. Thus Britain (and most other countries) has to exercise some control over the use of her reserves of foreign currency.

The Bank acting as agent for the Treasury, is responsible for the administration of Exchange Control, and has set up a separate department to deal with its operation.

A great deal of the work is undertaken by the commercial banks and authorised dealers who for many transactions have power to authorise payments without reference to the Bank of England.

The Sterling Area and the Community.

Britain's early lead in international trade and finance was the chief reason why many countries used sterling as a base for international transactions and maintained much of their currency reserves in Britain. Thus the Sterling Area (or Scheduled Territories) became a currency area for exchange control purposes.

The Sterling Area today consists of the United Kingdom, Channel Islands, Gibraltar, Isle of Man and the Republic of Ireland. The currency arrangements are voluntary and there are no strict rules as to conduct between Governments. Most of their overseas trade is financed through London where they keep a large amount of their foreign reserves. Member countries usually sell their foreign currency earnings in London on the

Foreign Exchange Market, and purchase the foreign currency when required.

Controls. On accession to the European Economic Community in 1973 Britain agreed to a gradual run-down of balances held in London. Thus the sterling area, although still important in financing much of world trade has to be looked at in the wider context of Community affairs. Today London is regarded not only as an important European financial centre but as a banker to many countries both inside and outside the Community. Over the last few years the scope of Exchange Control has been greatly reduced: the chief controls still in force are as follows:

(a) *Transactions between residents* of the Sterling and Community Areas and residents outside it: control has been greatly relaxed, and the only remaining important restrictions relate to the movement of capital from Britain to countries *outside* these areas. There are still a few minor restrictions between residents *inside* the Sterling and Community areas but these will be abolished by agreement in due course, so that the currencies of each member country ultimately will become fully convertible.

(b) *Exports of goods* to areas outside the Sterling and Community areas are generally not subject to exchange control, except that they must be paid for within a limited time in an acceptable currency. The few controls that exist are imposed to supervise exports of military importance, to conserve materials and to prevent the export of national treasures, such as works of art, manuscripts, etc.

(c) *Imports.* Britain's entry into the European Community did not lead to the complete severance of connections with her old trading partners of the Commonwealth. Considerable amounts of food and raw materials etc, are still secured from these areas. Payments for these imports, together with imports from the Community area are largely free from monetary control although a few items are of necessity subject to specific import licences.

(d) *Overseas Travel.* Restrictions in the amount of currency and sterling notes that British travellers may take to countries *outside* the Sterling and Community areas exist from time to time. The reason is to conserve the amount of currency our travellers spend abroad, as this may strain the foreign currency reserves unless controlled.

7. THE EXCHANGE EQUALISATION ACCOUNT

The Bank of England acts as the administrator of the Exchange Equalisation Account. Its operation is largely determined by the exchange rate policies adopted by the Treasury which is the controlling authority.

Britain as a member of the European Economic Community and the International Monetary Fund undertakes to ensure that the rate of the pound to other currencies on the foreign exchange market, keeps within certain limits. If the pound should fall in value to say the dollar or French franc, the Bank *through the Equalisation Account* buys pounds and sells foreign currencies. This will have the effect of making pounds scarcer on the foreign exchange market and the price will remain constant or rise, depending upon the number purchased by the Bank. Conversely, if the pound should rise in price beyond a certain limit, the Bank will sell pounds in exchange for foreign currencies.

8. COMMUNITY DRAWING RIGHTS

In order to stabilise terms of trade, members of the European Economic Community have agreed to keep their currencies within certain limits on the foreign exchange markets. The members also operate a scheme of support where a member is experiencing balance of payments difficulties. A multilateral pool of drawing rights has been created made up from contributions of member countries according to agreed quotas. A member having *short-term* payments difficulties may draw from the pool agreed amounts as necessary.

The effect of the above is to stabilise the rate of exchange of the pound sterling on the foreign exchange market. Thus merchants buying or selling goods abroad are able to rely to a certain extent on a more stable rate of exchange when the time comes for payment.

QUESTIONS

1. Indicate the immediate effects upon the items in the weekly statement of the Bank of England when a stock is sold by the Bank on behalf of the British Government.

2. Why is the Bank of England Weekly Return of importance to the commercial world?

3. What is meant by a Central Bank? In what ways does the Bank of England fulfil the functions of such a bank?

4. How may changes in the rate of interest affect decisions made by businessmen? (R.S.A.)

5. In what ways does the Bank of England control the activities of the Joint-Stock Banks? (R.S.A.)

6. What are the main functions of the Bank of England? What part does it play in the cheque clearing system? (R.S.A.)

7. Explain the importance of the Foreign Exchange rates and show what effects might follow a rise in value of the pound sterling on theForeign Exchange Market. What methods are used by the Bank of England to keep the rates steady?

8. 'Credit was in short supply in Lombard Street and the authorities gave a moderate amount of indirect help.' Explain this statement. (R.S.A.)

9. Every business firm is in constant contact with its own bank, but very few firms have any direct dealings with the Bank of England. What then are the functions performed by the Bank of England which make it so important? (Oxford G.C.E.)

Chapter 22

Joint-Stock Banks

The services of a bank may be classified as (*a*) those which are fundamental, since upon the extent of these services the profit of the bank depends, (*b*) those which are supplementary; these include services which exist largely for the convenience of the customers of the bank.

(a) Fundamental Services.

(1) *The Collection of Deposits*. The large group banks of this country have thousands of branches, which collect the surplus funds of their customers and create a central fund out of which medium and short-term loans can be made. Two kinds of accounts may be opened.

    (*a*) *Current Accounts*, in which the money is repayable on demand, and is usually withdrawn by cheques drawn by the customer from his account.

    (*b*) *Deposit Accounts*, where the customer agrees to give an agreed period of notice before withdrawing the whole or part of the deposit. The usual period of notice is seven days, but larger sums of money are frequently placed with a bank on fixed deposit for any period up to six months. As time is necessary for the withdrawal of funds out of these accounts, the use of cheques is not allowed. Withdrawals have to be made on a special slip provided by the branch bank.

(2) *Source of Loans*. Experience has shown that only a portion of the deposits need be kept in hand to meet the demands

of the bank's customers: the balance can be used to make loans of various kinds. These are charged interest.

The loans take the following forms:

(a) An agreed amount may be added to the credit of a customer's current account, against which he is permitted to draw cheques, and he will repay the loan by regular instalments, usually out of weekly or monthly earnings to a separate loan account.

(b) A fluctuating overdraft may be allowed, up to a certain maximum figure. This is the more usual type of overdrawn account for business purposes and a cheaper method of borrowing than (a) above.

(c) Bills of Exchange may be discounted by the Bank. The banker purchases the right to receive the *full* payment of the debt represented by the bill when it falls due. He purchases the bill for its present value paying the borrower the gross amount less interest and other charges.

The type of security demanded by banks for loans and advances is discussed later in this chapter.

(3) *Agents for Payment.* The principal banks of this country are members of the London (or Edinburgh) Clearing House, who also act as agents for the smaller banks. The importance of the cheque in modern society can be seen in that over 750 million pass through the London Clearing House alone each year.

The holder of a *current account* is entitled to use a cheque book with which to make payments out of his account. A cheque is an unconditional order to the bank and *branch upon which it is drawn* to make the payment of the stated amount to the person named as the payee or his agent.

The most usual type of cheque in daily use is the *crossed cheque* which affords the drawer a considerable degree of protection should it be lost. The effect of the crossing provides a means of tracing a stolen cheque as a crossed cheque must be paid into a bank account and cannot be cashed over the counter. An *open cheque* on the other hand is one which bears no crossing and may be cashed over the counter of the branch bank *on which it is drawn*. An open cheque that had been stolen therefore could be cashed by the wrongful owner, unless of course, the drawer had instructed his branch bank in time to 'stop' payment on it.

Computer Banking. The increased use of cheques passing through the banking system has resulted in the installation of computer centres by all the principal banks.

The following chart traces the passage of entries to and from a customer's account. The student should study carefully the passage of entries to and from his account and note how these ultimately appear on the statement he receives.

The computer centre is linked by land line to a number branches of the same bank and is in direct contact with the clearing department of Head Office. The modern banking process eliminates the need for each branch to keep its own separate customers accounts.

A bank computer installation.

THE MODERN BANKING PROCESS

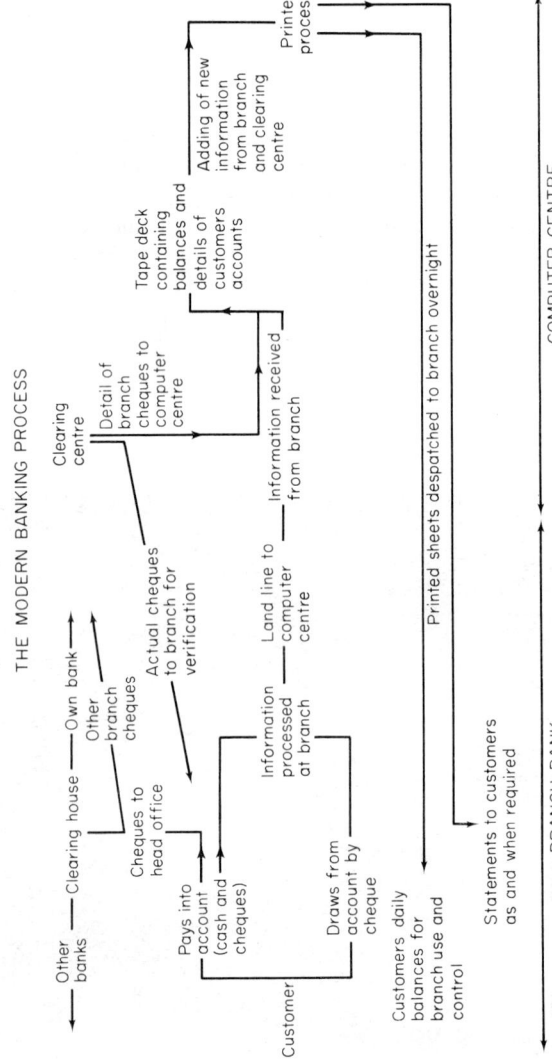

(b) Supplementary Services.

(1) *Acceptance of Bills.* The large number of commercial firms in the various countries of the world makes it impossible for each firm to know the status of every other firm with which it may have occasion to deal. The names of the principal banks in every country however are well known, and banks frequently accept bills for their customers. The extent of the liability is included under the additional note 'contingent liabilities on account of customers' on every joint-stock bank balance sheet (see page 293). The banks of course require security covering the amount of the bills, and charge a commission for the use of the bank's name.

(2) *Dealings in Foreign Exchange.* Banks collect bills on behalf of their customers: this frequently involves the conversion of one currency into another. They also deal on the highly specialised foreign exchange markets on behalf of their authorised customers. The amounts outstanding at any given time are printed in the banks balance sheet as an addendum. The principal banks have affiliated institutions, agents and correspondents abroad, and therefore finance a great deal of the import and export trades on behalf of their customers.

(3) *Documentary Credits.* An increasing amount of world trade is being undertaken by this means. An arrangement is made between say a London bank and an agent bank in another country whereby the exporter receives payment for goods on production of the shipping documents. Thus the importer's bank may allow a period of credit to give the importer time to sell the goods.

(4) *Letters of Credit.* World-wide letters of credit can be issued up to any amount, whilst traveller's cheques of various denominations can be cashed in any country of the world through the agency system. In issuing these documents, the bank substitutes its credit for the inferior credit of the customer.

(5) *Investments.* A bank undertakes to carry out the purchase or sale of securities (stocks and shares) on behalf of its customers: the bank employs a firm of stock-brokers to carry through the business, and shares the commission with the broker. The bank also undertakes the safe keeping of its

customers' securities, and attends to the collection of dividends as they become due.

(6) *Custody of Valuables.* Banks are willing to safeguard the valuables of their customers: these may consist of jewellery, deeds of property and documents, etc.

(7) *Executor and Trustee Business.* There is a separate department to deal with this specialist class of business. The administration of a deceased person's estate often requires special knowledge, and a bank allows itself to be nominated by any of its customers as executor.

Similarly, a bank permits its customers who are large investors to have their securities registered in the name of the bank's nominees, and undertakes an *investment management* service.

(8) *References.* A bank is willing to act as a reference for any of its customers: the enquiry, however, must *always* come through another bank.

(9) *Night Safes.* These are provided to enable shopkeepers and tradesmen to deposit cash after the bank has closed. Customers are provided with a wallet which can be locked, the customer having one key and the bank another. Cash and cheques are entered in the customer's paying-in book, and the locked wallet is placed in the night safe until the next business day.

(10) *Banker's (or Standing) Orders and Direct Debits.* Banks undertake the regular payment of subscriptions, insurance premiums, etc., on behalf of their customers.

(11) Numerous other services are given by all the principal banks which include the provision of credit cards, factoring services through subsidiary companies, information departments that are particularly useful to exporters, sale of particular unit trusts, keeping of company share registers, purchase and sale of foreign currency, attendance at shows and fairs, cash dispensers for use by customers when the bank is closed, etc.

2. ANALYSIS OF BANK BALANCE SHEET

The study of the balance sheet of a joint-stock bank shows the principles on which British banking is conducted; it shows the sources from which a bank obtains funds, and the uses to which these funds are put.

All limited joint-stock banks are required by law to compile a balance sheet twice per year, and copies must be forwarded to the Registrar of Companies every February and August: a copy of the current balance sheet must also be exhibited in the public part of every branch of the bank.

The following is a simplified balance sheet of a joint-stock bank: the figures are only approximate, and many details have been omitted (e.g. a full statement of the investments):

BALANCE SHEET AT 31ST DECEMBER 19..

Liabilities	£	Assets	£
Capital:		Cash in hand and at	
Authorised £100 m.		Bank of England	130 m.
Issued	78 m.	Money at Call and	
Reserve Fund		Short Notice	359 m.
including undistri-	202 m.	British Government	
buted profit		Treasury Bills	49 m.
Current, Deposit and		Bills of Exchange	
other Accounts	2,176 m.	and refinanceable	
		credits	237 m.
Contingent Liabilities		Cheques in course of	
on account of cus-		collection	76 m.
tomers £451,808,000		Special Deposit with	
		Bank of England	33 m.
Contracts for the Pur-			
chase and Sale of		Advances to Cus-	
Foreign currencies		tomers	1,044 m.
£1,455,726,000		Investments	433 m.
		Bank Premises	95 m.
	£2,456 m.		£2,456 m.

RESERVE ASSETS STATEMENT

Eligible Liabilities	£1,818·2 m.	Reserve Ratio 14·1%
Reserve Assets	£256·3 m.	

(a) Liabilities.

(1) *Capital.* The authorised capital is the maximum amount which the Bank is permitted to issue under its Memorandum of Association: the issued capital is that portion of the author-ised capital which has actually been sold to shareholders. The

shares issued are sometimes of different denominations (e.g. £25, £20, £5), but they may be freely purchased or sold on the Stock Exchange.

(2) *Reserve Fund*. This fund includes the share premium and capital reserves together with other reserves and undistributed profits built up by the bank over a period of years.

(3) *Current, Deposit and other Accounts*. Represent money entrusted to the bank by its customers; most of this money is repayable on demand or at short notice. The bank must therefore keep its assets in a liquid state, in order that the normal demands for repayment may be met. Experience has shown, however, that only a proportion of the deposits are likely to be withdrawn over a certain period: the remainder can be used in making loans (advances) at a higher rate of interest than that allowed to depositors.

(4) *Contingent and Other Liabilities* include amounts on which the bank may be liable on customers acceptances, etc. as detailed on page 291.

(b) Assets. The assets of the bank are set out in the order in which they may be realised: a bank must keep a certain proportion of its assets in a liquid form, so that in emergencies it may obtain a flow of money into the bank and thus be able to meet all demands.

(1) *Cash in Hand and at the Bank of England*. Banks keep in hand a certain amount of 'till money' in the form of notes and coin, in order to meet the daily requirements of their customers. They also keep an account with the Bank of England, and further supplies of cash can be obtained by drawing on this account, when necessary. The Bank of England account is also used to settle indebtedness between member banks at the Clearing House.

(2) *Money at Call and Short Notice*. Represents money lent in the money market to discount houses, bill brokers, bullion brokers, stockbrokers, stock-jobbers and other British banks. This money is repayable at varying periods of from one day to one month, and consequently, the bank's cash reserve can be rapidly increased by calling in this money.

(3) *British Government Treasury Bills* are government 'Bills of Exchange' that are issued weekly through the Discount

Houses on the London Money Market to finance government expenditure. They are usually for a period of three months making an ideal and secure investment for the bank. As they mature for payment at different dates, the bank knows when it will receive repayment with interest.

(4) *Bills of Exchange and refinanceable credits.* These form an ideal investment for the banker: the amount is clearly stated, they are not subject to depreciation, and they are for comparatively short periods.

The bills which a bank is prepared to purchase are of the following types:

- (*a*) Local Authority Bills—short term finance having the backing of the ratepayers and guaranteed for repayment.
- (*b*) Commercial Bills, there being two kinds (1) Fine Bills—those drawn by well known, undoubted creditworthy companies and (2) Other Bills that are drawn by traders known only in a limited sphere.

(5) *Cheques in course of collection* are the cheques that have been received at branches and are awaiting payment from the other banks through the Clearing House procedure. These items will be added to the bank's balance at the Bank of England within a short time.

(6) *Special Deposit* with the Bank of England. In order to restrict bank lending the Treasury through the Bank of England has power to call the joint-stock banks to place part of their deposits in a special account at the Bank of England. A small amount of interest is allowed but the funds may not be withdrawn without Treasury permission when the restrictions on credit are eased. It should be noted that the amount of the deposit provided by each bank is not part of the liquid assets for reserve purposes.

(7) *Advances to Customers.* The loans or advances made to customers represent about 45–50 per cent of total deposits and are the principal source of profit for the bank. Interest and commission charges are made on these loans every half year, the amount depending upon (a) the type of loan (b) the amount (c) the base rate (d) the security offered and (e) the customer's standing in the eyes of the bank. The form and analysis of these loans are detailed on page 299.

(8) *Investments*. These include British Government and Commonwealth Stocks, the Stocks of Public Boards and Local Authorities as well as investments in subsidiary banking, finance and hire-purchase companies. Investments, however, are subject to fluctuations in value, and cannot be immediately realised in case of emergency: on the other hand, they often yield a high rate of interest, and show a substantial margin of profit. Investments by the banks in finance houses have the added advantage in that customers not eligible for bank loans may be offered alternative facilities in subsidiary companies.

(9) *Bank Premises*. The principal banks have very many branches, and their premises often occupy the chief sites in the centre of many towns. The actual value of the land and premises however usually exceeds the value shown in the balance sheet.

3. LOANS AND ADVANCES

A bank makes a large portion of its profits by making loans and advances to its customers: it lends part of its deposits to those who are able to use them, earns interest on the loans etc., passes some of the interest back to the depositors and recoups its profit out of the rest after all expenses have been paid.

The interest charged by each bank on its loans and advances is dependent on its *Base Rate*. Each bank expresses its lending rates independently in relation to its base rate which it determines in the light of current commercial and market conditions.

In making a loan, a bank must take several precautions:

(*a*) *Security*. The banker must bear in mind that he is *lending other people's money*, and that any loss, due to failure to repay the loan will fall on the bank. The banker must be cautious and make full enquiries regarding the standing of the borrower. On the other hand, if he is too timid in making loans, he is reducing the profits of the bank. Some form of security is usually demanded, but the competition among banks compels every bank manager to make loans to customers backed only by their personal undertaking to repay them. The form of security is dealt with later.

(*b*) *Liquid Assets*. The bulk of the funds available for loans is obtained from the deposits of customers, and as most of these are liable to be withdrawn at short notice, the assets held by the bank against them must be easily realisable.

(c) *Length of Time.* The type of loan often determines the length of time given for repayment. Advances to businessmen in the form of overdrafts are usually for short periods. These are granted for a period of not more than twelve months and at the end of that period are subject to review. Loans of a more personal nature and term loans however are usually for much longer periods, in a few cases up to 10 years. The amount charged on these various types of loans is based upon the base rate applied by each bank.

(d) *The Purpose of the Loan.* The banker is entitled to enquire as to the purpose of the loan: he must take care not to make loans for speculative purposes. It is very often difficult to distinguish between speculation and enterprise, but the control over branch managers by the Head Office of a bank reduces the danger of making loans that are not for legitimate trading purposes. During periods of restrictions on credit however the bank may not be able to give a loan which in normal times would be acceptable.

Every manager is able to lend money to his customers up to a pre-determined limit. Any amount in excess of this must be referred to higher authority, usually District or Head Office.

Form of Loan. The loan granted by a bank may take one of several forms:

(a) *Overdraft.* When an overdraft is arranged, the customer is authorised to draw cheques on his *current account* up to a fixed limit: interest is charged on the *daily* balance. The customer can therefore reduce his debt when he has funds in hand. An overdraft is often used to finance the sale of goods on credit, since the amount borrowed can be reduced as payment for the goods is received. The interest charged on this borrowing is between 1 and 3 per cent over base rate.

(b) *Loan Account.* When a definite sum is advanced by the bank, the amount of the loan is debited to a *Loan Account*, and credited in the current account of the customer. It will be noticed that the amount of an overdraft fluctuates, but the amount of the Loan Account is fixed until repaid by regular monthly payments. This is usually a more expensive method of borrowing and is between 3 and 5 per cent over base rate.

(c) *Term Loans*. Medium and long term loans are available for periods from two years up to ten years. These are usually for financing business enterprises, finance for shipbuilding and export credits, assisting with house purchase etc. The interest charged on these loans is assessed on base rate but variable depending upon the amount of risk involved.

(d) *Discounting Bills*. Banks are always willing to discount bills of exchange, provided that they are satisfied with the standing of the parties to each bill. The customer is credited at once with the *net* value of the bill, the bank collecting the full amount on maturity.

Forms of Security. The various kinds of security accepted by a banker may be summarised:

(a) *Stocks and Shares*. These are regarded as attractive forms of security, since they are easily realised in case of need: gilt-edged or blue-chip securities are preferred, other securities being valued by the banker on their merits but usually consist of *public* joint-stock company shares. The bank, as a rule, does not advance more than 80 per cent of the market value of the securities, since it must allow for possible price changes.

(b) *Guarantees*. A debt due by a customer to a bank is often secured by a guarantee given by one or more persons on his behalf. The guarantor is liable on the loan up to an agreed amount until payment of the debt has been effected. The guarantee must be in writing and signed by the guarantor: specially printed forms are provided by the bank for this purpose.

(c) *Freehold Land*. The title deeds to land and property are also regarded by banks as good security against advances. To mortgage the property, however, may be a costly process; it is necessary to investigate the title deeds and to prove the customer's title. Banks may require the security to be valued by a qualified valuer although usually this is undertaken by the branch manager.

(d) *Life Policies*. After a life policy has been in existence for a certain period, it acquires a *Surrender Value*: the advance on a life policy, therefore, will not exceed the surrender value. The bank will investigate the conditions of the policy, and require a legal assignment.

(e) *Documents of Title*. The existence of goods stored in this country or undergoing some process of manufacture is often evidenced by documents of title, such as a *Warehouse Receipt* and a *Bill of Lading*. Such documents are often accepted by a bank as security against an advance.

The bank, however, must take a number of precautions in accepting documents of title; the value of the goods is liable to fluctuations, for example. The bank may therefore demand a *Letter of Hypothecation*, which conveys to the bank the full right to the goods, and authorises the bank to dispose of the goods in default of repayment of the loan.

4. ANALYSIS OF BANK ADVANCES

The following table sets out the total loans and advances made by the financial institutions of the City to both home and overseas residents.

	1969 £m	1971 £m	1972 £m
Manufacturing Industries	3,058	3,670	4,773
Construction Industries	994	1,281	1,857
Property, Hire Purchase etc.	936	1,555	3,393
Distribution, Service, Professional	1,726	2,204	3,111
Personal	873	1,404	2,641
Overseas residents	2,886	6,530	7,879
TOTAL LOANS AND ADVANCES	£10,473m.	£16,644m.	£23,654m.

5. JOINT-STOCK BANKS AND THE BANK OF ENGLAND

Far reaching changes in the control of monetary policy took place in 1971 affecting the financial markets of this country. As regards the banking system, the following measures are now applied by the Bank of England:

(a) all banks are required to hold on a day-to-day basis a

minimum of 12½ per cent of their eligible sterling liabilities in certain specified reserve assets. (For finance houses, the figure is 10 per cent)

(*b*) to place such amount of Special Deposits with the Bank of England as the Bank may call from time to time.

Eligible Sterling Liabilities are composed of the following items:

(*a*) All current and deposit accounts of British and overseas institutions and residents payable on demand or mature for payment in under two years.

(*b*) Certain other deposits including sterling balances held in Britain and obtained by transfer from foreign centres.

The total of eligible liabilities in the Bank balance sheet on page 293 amounts to £1,818·2 m.

Reserve Assets consist *only* of the following items:

(*a*) Balances actually held by the joint-stock bank on account at the Bank of England. (This does not include cash held in the tills of the joint-stock banks). These balances must be a minimum of 1½ per cent of the Eligible Liabilities above.

(*b*) British Government Treasury Bills.

(*c*) Money at call with the London Discount Market including overnight loans to brokers on the gilt edge market.

(*d*) Investments in British Government securities maturing within one year.

(*e*) Local Authority bills having an original maturity of under six months.

(*f*) Certain Commercial Bills accepted by approved institutions.

The figure given for these items in the balance sheet on page 293 is £256·3 m.

The ratio may therefore be calculated as follows:

$$\frac{256\cdot3}{1818\cdot2} \times \frac{100}{1} = 14\cdot1\%$$

Whilst the above is over the required minimum, this represents a 'cushion' to meet seasonal fluctuations and calls by the Authorities for further special deposits.

The effect of such measures has been:

(*a*) To make a more competitive banking system. The banks and other institutions are free from the cartel type lending and interest rates.

(*b*) The introduction of a more flexible method of control by the Authorities over the monetary markets as a whole, ending quantitative ceilings on lending by directives based on arbitrary dates.

(*c*) The availability of wider monetary terms for the consumer.

(*d*) The restriction of the Bank of England operating on the gilt edge market of the Stock Exchange. The Bank will only deal in the following circumstances:

(1) Except on very special occasions it will only buy from the financial institutions gilt edge stock having one year or less to maturity. This measure prevents the institutions from increasing their cash balances at the Bank by circumventing the Reserve Asset requirement above.

(2) The Bank reserves the right to buy or sell securities as necessary on the gilt edge market in order to carry out its open market operations.

6. THE AMALGAMATION OF BANKS

The advantages which are claimed for the policy of amalgamation may be summarised as follows:

(*a*) Local banks cannot compete with the larger joint-stock banks, unless they perform some special type of service, such as the National Savings Bank or the Trustee Savings Banks.

(*b*) The extension of the area of a bank's activities is a convenience to trade, since the presence of branches in different parts of a country avoids the inconvenience and expense of employing agents.

(*c*) Larger banks have greater resources: their reserves are better managed and advances can be made on a more generous scale. The amalgamation of industrial firms has led to a need for larger loans in order to finance trade in competition with rival foreign firms.

(*d*) Concerted action in time of emergency is more easily obtained when there are a few large banks.

(*e*) A large bank with thousands of branches is able to establish a more efficient organisation, and to co-ordinate the work of various departments. The reserves may be better managed, and a greater degree of uniformity in the granting of loans can be attained.

(*f*) Amalgamations have led to improved foreign connections: branches have been established abroad, subsidiary companies have been formed, and an international system of banking established.

(*g*) The large banks have extended their sphere using part of their capital and expertise by investment in merchant banks and finance houses.

The following disadvantages have been suggested against amalgamations:

(*a*) *Reduction of Capital*. The shares of the absorbing bank are usually worth more than those of the smaller bank, and the exchange of shares in the amalgamated concern results in a reduction of the nominal capital compared with the total of the capital of the separate banks.

(*b*) *Reduced Competition*. Banks compete in the Money Market, in order to find profitable investments for their funds, but amalgamation makes possible a greater degree of co-operation and agreement amongst themselves and restrictive practices may appear.

(*c*) *Danger of Monopoly*. Many fear that amalgamations may lead to the formation of a 'money trust', and that any abuse of its power would have serious national effects.

(*d*) Large banks have less knowledge of local requirements: their organisation is centralised and their work is directed from the head office.

QUESTIONS

1. What is the relation of the joint-stock banks to the Bank of England?　　　　　　　　　　　　　　　　　　　(U.L.C.I.)

2. Indicate the circumstances in which a man in need of money might seek (*a*) a bank loan, (*b*) a bank overdraft and (*c*) a loan from a building society; give examples so as to make clear the differences

in the requirements which these forms of borrowing are designed to satisfy. What kinds of security would a bank and a building society expect the borrower to provide? (Oxford G.C.E.)

3. Discuss the merits of overdrafts from (*a*) the customers' point of view, (*b*) the bankers' point of view, as a means of affording temporary financial accommodation for traders. (R.S.A.)

4. 'The cheque-paying banks.'—What do you understand by this term? Explain, in some detail, the organisation which permits the cheque to be used as the general method of effecting payments in business in this country. (R.S.A.)

5. What are the significant differences between a bank overdraft and a bank loan? How does a bank try to make sure that it will be repaid if the customer defaults? (London G.C.E.)

6. Distinguish between a bank overdraft and a bank loan. When might a bank manager recommend his customer to have one rather than the other? (Cambridge G.C.E.)

7. What facilities are offered by the commercial banks in Britain to the commercial community, and how do the banks obtain the resources necessary to provide these facilities? (R.S.A.)

8. Describe *four* methods by which a debt can be paid. Outline the advantages and disadvantages of each method. (A.E.B.)

9. Which are the principal clearing banks? How does the clearing system work? What particular advantages does it give to the business world? (A.E.B.)

10. What is a cheque? Discuss its importance as a means of payment showing how the interests of the drawer are provided for and protected. (A.E.B.)

11. The receipt of deposits and the advancing of loans and overdrafts are the chief functions of a modern Bank. Discuss this and state briefly any other functions banks perform. What limits are there, if any, to the amounts banks can lend? (R.S.A.)

12. It is sometimes said that banks can create money and credit. Give your views on this statement. (R.S.A.)

13. Philips, a business man receives a crossed cheque in payment of a debt owing to him by Roberts. What should he do in *each* of the following circumstances?

(*a*) the cheque is post-dated three weeks ahead.

(*b*) the cheque is payable to Roberts and drawn by Simms, but Roberts has endorsed it 'Pay P. Philips' with his signature.

(*c*) the cheque after being paid into Philips' bank account, is returned to him by his bank marked 'Refer to drawer'?

(Oxford G.C.E.)

Chapter 23

The Money Market

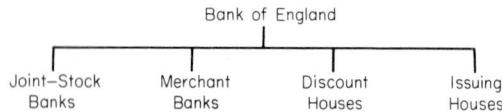

Bank of England

| Joint–Stock | Merchant | Discount | Issuing |
| Banks | Banks | Houses | Houses |

The Money Market refers to any place where money is dealt in as a commodity. There are money markets in all the principal commercial centres of the world, including London, Paris, Frankfurt, New York, Tokyo, Toronto, Melbourne, Wellington, Singapore etc., linked by teleprinter and satellite networks. The *Money Market is world-wide*, and changes in one centre quickly react elsewhere. It is often quoted as the nearest approach to a perfect market, since credits by author- ised dealers can be transferred with ease from one place to another, and the cost of this transfer is comparatively small.

The **Money Market** may be described as a place where money is borrowed: by 'money' is meant the right to the *use* of money or credit. The activities of the Market would be more exactly described if it were called the 'Loan Market', where loans are arranged by direct negotiation or by the discounting of bills. The greater part of the funds is provided by banks and financial houses, who lend their surplus funds for short periods to firms and brokers who specialise in the discounting of bills.

The London Money Market is in the neighbourhood of the Bank of England and Lombard Street, but unlike any other market, *it has no building of its own*: the area round the Bank of England is a convenient meeting-place for borrowers and lenders, and in it are situated the head offices of the British banks, the London offices of European, Commonwealth and foreign banks, the Merchant Banks and the establishments of bill brokers and discount houses.

2. THE LONDON MONEY MARKET

For many years, London has been regarded as one of the principal financial centres of the world.

The chief reasons for London's financial supremacy are:

(*a*) Over the last three hundred years, London has benefited financially from the *geographical position* of this country; Britain is near enough to the Continent to reap all the benefits of trade; London has developed as the centre for international payments and has been called 'the strong-box of Europe'.

(*b*) The internal history of this country has been more peaceful than that of any other country of Europe: the people of Britain gained economic and political freedom before those of any other country, and therefore developed industry and commerce early.

(*c*) Britain has developed territories abroad, and this country's monetary system and laws are therefore used or adapted in many parts.

(*d*) British traders have become known all over the world, and have gained a reputation for fair dealing. Many large firms and British banks lend their names to other firms in this and other countries, and the bill on London is used to finance trade between many countries of the world.

(*e*) Britain is poorly endowed with minerals, etc., and has had to rely to an increasing extent on the 'giving of services' to the rest of the world in order to pay for essential imports. These services include the highly specialised money market.

(*f*) The necessity of setting up machinery for dealing with international payments led to the development of the Money Market in London. The reputation of the financial institutions of this country resulted in the London Money Market being regarded as the most important in the world.

3. MEMBERS OF THE LONDON MONEY MARKET

There is no 'membership' of the Market in the same sense as there is membership of, say, the Stock Exchange. It was developed by the principal banks and finance houses of the country, and the admission of any new firm depends upon the opinion of the existing members, who are guided by the view that the Bank of England takes of the newcomer.

The principal members of the London Money Market are as follows:

(a) The Bank of England. Is often described as the pivot of the Money Market, and has enormous funds at its disposal. It keeps not only the Government Funds, but also part of the surpluses of the commercial banks: the joint-stock banks keep balances at the Bank of England because, in emergency these may be turned into notes on demand. The funds at the disposal of the Bank of England enable it to influence the Money Market whenever it chooses to exert its power as a Central Bank.

(b) The London Clearing Banks. In addition to the Bank of England, the clearing banks have large funds at their disposal for loans on the Money Market. They use their funds in making loans at call or short notice, and in discounting bills of exchange, but of course they must keep their reserve ratios over the required minimum required by the Bank of England.

(c) Other Banks. The provincial banks of this country, and the banks of Scotland and of Northern Ireland are also closely connected with London, and contribute to the supply of funds available for loan on the London Money Market, again subject to minimum reserve ratios.

(d) The European, Commonwealth and Foreign Banks have offices or agents in London; these banks are both borrowers and lenders, according to their requirements. On account of their international position, their activities are largely determined by the relative rates of interest in this country and abroad. These banks also are required to keep minimum reserve ratios on a day-to-day basis.

(e) Merchant Banks. With the growth of foreign trade, certain large firms have become so well known and enjoy such good credit that smaller firms are willing to pay them a commission for the use of their names. The smaller firm therefore arranges that its creditors should draw bills on the Merchant Bank or Accepting House, and for this privilege they pay a commission: the smaller firm often obtains better terms from its creditors, to whom it offers a first-class acceptance. These institutions therefore help to finance the import and export trade of this country by guaranteeing the payment of bills accepted by them.

(f) Discount Houses arose on account of the custom of giving credit to a buyer of goods: the buyer accepted a bill of exchange, which could be discounted for its present value. Discount Houses specialise in this form of business: many of them have large resources of their own, in addition to money which they borrow on the Money Market against approved security.

Discount Houses also deal to a large extent in the purchasing of *short-term* local authority bonds and bills carrying a higher rate of interest than Treasury bills in addition to local authority stocks maturing in under five years.

(g) Bill Brokers may act either as agents or as principals.

(1) *As agents*, they act as middlemen between those who have bills to sell and those who wish to purchase bills for investment. Their profits consist of the commission which they charge to one or both parties.

(2) *As principals*, they give their own cheques for the bills which they buy; they borrow funds from the Money Market and make their profit out of the difference between the rates at which they can borrow, and the rates at which they can discount bills. Firms acting as principals have an account at the Bank of England, since when money is scarce it may be necessary to borrow from the Bank.

Bill brokers are therefore specialists in bills of exchange; they have acquired expert knowledge regarding the standing of parties to them, and at the same time provide the commercial banks with investments which are liquid and provide good security.

(h) Stockbrokers come into the Money Market for short-term loans with which to pay for stocks they have bought on behalf of their clients. The loans are made on the security of the stock, and are repayable at the next fortnightly settlement

(i) Building Societies form an important section of the Money Market. They are corporate bodies subject to control by the Registrar of Building Societies and various Building Societies Acts. The funds of a society are derived mainly from the general public who invest in shares or deposits. Building societies lend on a long-term basis on the security of private dwelling houses for owner-occupiers. The total amount on loan to the public exceeds £5,000 million.

(j) Insurance Companies. Vast funds are accumulated by the Insurance Companies from the premiums collected from policy-holders. A great deal of these are invested on the London Money Market in Government Stock and Joint-Stock Company shares. Insurance companies are often willing to lend on a long-term basis to both the public and private sectors of industry in order to finance particular projects.

(k) The Post Office, through the National Savings Bank and the National Giro, accumulates large sums which are lent to members of the London Money Market on a short-term basis.

4. DEALINGS IN THE MARKET

Billbrokers visit the head offices of the principal banks and finance houses each morning, and seek the following information:

(a) Loans. The brokers are informed by the banks what existing loans can be renewed, how much is to be called in, and how much new money is available. When a broker is informed by a bank that it wishes to call a certain sum from him, he will try to arrange a new loan with another bank, and if successful, he will transfer the security for the loan from the first to the second bank.

The visits of the various brokers to the banks enable both sides to form an estimate of the conditions of demand and supply for money, and if necessary to adjust existing rates of interest. The rates charged for loans often vary during the course of the day; money may come on the market later in the day, and if supplies are scarce, it may command high rates of interest. When the joint-stock and other banks are calling in their loans extensively, the brokers may be compelled to borrow from the Bank of England, and the market is then said to be '*in the Bank*'.

(b) Bills. On their morning visits to the banks, the brokers make enquiries regarding bills for sale and wanted. The Clearing Banks purchase large numbers, since they form an ideal investment for their surplus funds and in certain cases may form part of their reserve assets. The merchant bankers and accepting houses both buy and sell bills, according to their requirements or according to orders which they have received from their foreign clients. The European, Commonwealth and Foreign banks receive from their clients abroad a large number payable in London which are sold to the City brokers.

The rate of discount depends on the number offered, and the supply of money: when there are few bills to be discounted and money is plentiful, the rate of discount is low, and therefore favourable to the seller. Similarly, when a large number is offered for sale, and money is scarce, the rate of discount is high, and favourable to buyers.

The principal classes dealt with on the London Money Market are as follows:

(1) *Trade Bills*. These are drawn by one commercial house on another, and their value depends on the reputation of the firms that are parties to them. They are backed by goods in the course of being marketed, but the reputation of any commercial house is inferior to that of an important bank, and thus a higher rate of discount is charged.

(2) *Bank Bills*. Are bills which have been accepted by a bank; the term is also often used to refer to bills where the bank is the drawer or the endorsee. Bank bills are used to finance foreign trade. An importer, whose reputation is not known abroad, may arrange with his bank to accept a bill on his behalf. These are therefore discounted at a lower rate, on account of the additional security.

(3) *Treasury Bills*. Government income from taxes and other sources is not received at an even rate throughout the year and therefore the Treasury has to borrow in anticipation of revenue. Much of this is done by means of Treasury Bills.

They are issued by the Treasury, and payable three months after date. The rate of interest is fixed at the time of issue to the Discount Houses. Between them the Discount Houses ensure that their combined bids are sufficient to meet the Government's requirements each week and thus the Government is assured of a ready market for its bills.

The banks do not bid for Treasury Bills, but buy the amounts they require from the members of the Discount Market.

5. MONEY MARKET RATES

Many rates of interest are quoted in the Money Market:

(a) The Minimum Lending Rate is the official rate at which the Bank of England will discount approved bills or make loans against approved securities for a minimum period of seven days for institutions such as the Discount Houses in the City. The rate is fixed at the weekly meeting of the Directors every Friday morning, and is therefore a flexible rate that will respond to the changing conditions of the money market.

(b) Deposit Rate paid by the joint-stock banks is influenced by the Base Rate determined by individual banks. The rate paid on deposits is usually $1\frac{1}{2}$–2 per cent below this rate, thus determining the *minimum rate* at which they can lend money on the Money Market, since the banks must at least cover the interest which they pay to their depositors. Larger sums placed on deposit with the banks will usually command a higher rate of interest.

(c) Call Money Rates are those charged by the banks for money at call or short notice. Most of the money is lent by the Clearing Banks to the Discount Houses and Bill Brokers, and the loan is more or less permanent, though the banks have the right to recall the money at any time. As such money is on fixed deposit with the banks, the rate of interest charged is about 1 per cent above the base rate, but the actual rate depends upon the demand for funds and the amount of money available.

(d) Market Rate is the rate of discount at which members of the Money Market will purchase the various classes of Bills of Exchange and Treasury Bills. The market rates depend upon the relation between the supply of money, and the number of bills offered: the rates are above those charged for call money, but they cannot rise above the Bank of England minimum lending rate, for if the market rates were above the Minimum Rate, sellers of bills would discount their bills at the Bank of England at the lower rate.

6. THE BANK OF ENGLAND AND THE MONEY MARKET

It is usual to speak of the control of the London Money Market by the Bank of England, but such control would necessitate the control of the other money markets of the world. It is more exact to refer to the *influence of* the Bank of England on the Money Market; the aim of the Bank is to prevent frequent fluctuations in prices through variations in the amount of money available, and in pursuing such a policy, the Bank receives the support of the joint-stock banks and other financial institutions.

The Bank of England influences the volume of funds available in the Money Market in the following ways:

(a) Bank Minimum Lending Rate Policy. This consists of raising or lowering the Bank of England's Minimum Lending Rate according to the estimated monetary needs of the country. The effectiveness of producing these changes depends on the reaction of the financial institutions in making corresponding changes to the other rates of the Money Market.

The effects of an increase in the Minimum Lending Rate are:

(1) *Foreign Funds.* London Bills become cheaper to buy since an increase in the rate of discount reduces their present value: there is a movement of foreign funds from centres abroad for investment here, whilst foreign holders of London Bills find it more profitable to allow them to mature, instead of selling them. The above influences create a demand for sterling which improves the value of the pound on the foreign exchange market and in normal times causes an influx of foreign currency into this country.

(2) *Money Market Conditions.* An increase of the Bank Minimum Lending Rate may be accompanied by an increase

in the rates of the Money Market, since loans become more expensive. Less call money is borrowed at the higher rate, and fewer bills are discounted. In addition, merchants sell stocks of goods held on borrowed money, and the funds of the Money Market are further replenished.

(3) *Prices.* An increase in the rate leads to a *fall in prices* as more commodities are offered for sale in order to avoid higher rates of interest on borrowed money. The fall in prices makes the country a good market to buy in, and a bad one to sell in: exports therefore increase, and imports *in the short term* are reduced.

In common with prices generally, the prices of Stock Exchange securities fall, in order to adjust the yield to the new rates of interest: speculative securities held on borrowed money are sold, on account of the increased cost of borrowing.

The raising of interest rates therefore builds up the reserve of foreign currency held by the Bank in the Exchange Equalisation Account, since it causes an inflow of money from abroad, and economises the use of money at home.

The aim of the Bank of England in normal circumstances is to keep the interest rates as low as possible for two reasons:

(*a*) a low rate encourages trade activity.

(*b*) the Government is the largest borrower and high interest rates result in higher taxation in order to pay the increased rates.

A reduction in interest rates has the opposite effects to those stated above. A low rate means cheap borrowing and *a rise in prices*, and these considerations encourage manufacturers to extend their businesses.

Changes are made as little as possible, since these have important effects abroad. In order to deal with internal monetary problems, the Bank uses further controls such as 'open market' policy, calling of special deposits and the reserve asset ratios.

(b) 'Open Market Policy.' Is the name given to the activities of the Bank of England to adjust the conditions of the Money Market as follows:

(1) *When funds are plentiful.* Under these circumstances, there are more lenders than borrowers, and rates of interest

tend to fall. This may lead to a withdrawal of foreign funds invested in this country, and thus affect the rate of exchange.

In order to reduce the supply of money available for loans on the Money Market, the Bank of England may advise the Government to increase the weekly amount of Treasury Bills, in order to absorb the surplus funds. In addition, the Bank may sell for cash some of its holdings in bills and securities, and by this means further reduce the amount of funds available on the Money Market and with the joint-stock banks. Thus the balances held at the Bank of England by the financial institutions will fall which may affect the reserve ratios of individual banks, thus forcing them either to restrict their lending or increase their base rate.

(2) *When funds are scarce.* Funds may be scarce on the Money Market for several reasons; unexpected withdrawals may take place from London, or traders may demand increased credit facilities from their banks. Again, the number of bills to be discounted may be larger than usual. As a result of the scarcity of funds, the rates of discount will rise.

Under such circumstances, the Bank of England purchases certain bills or securities for cash, thus relieving the Market of its surplus bills and increasing the available funds. The reduction in the number of bills to be discounted and the increase in the funds of the Money Market as well as the balances of the financial institutions at the Bank of England, will cause a reduction of rates.

(c) Special Deposits. The Bank of England may call for special deposits from certain financial institutions. This has the effect of forcing the banks etc. to restrict their loans and assess the reserve ratio. It will lead to a shortage of lendable funds in the City that has to be controlled by the price mechanism or base rate applied by the banks on their customers' loans.

QUESTIONS

1. What institutions are concerned in the use of short loans in the London Money Market? Give a brief description of the part played by each. (R.S.A.)

2. Consider the importance to businessmen of the Bank of England weekly return and of the Base Rate. Examine the

significance of the latter in some detail, and indicate its relation to the other Money Market rates. (R.S.A.)

3. What do you understand by the term 'base rate'? How is this applied and what effect does it have on the businessman?

4. A manufacturer in the United Kingdom wishes to export machinery priced at £10,000. What would you advise him to do to secure payment and what methods of payment would you suggest?
(A.E.B.)

5. What is the composition of the London Money Market? What activities does it engage in, and from what sources do its members obtain the finance required for such activities? (R.S.A.)

6. Compare the main functions of commercial banks and merchant banks. (R.S.A.)

7. London has been described as the financial centre of the world and the pound sterling as an international currency. What were the circumstances which brought about this position?
(R.S.A.)

Chapter 24

The Marketing of Securities

I. STOCK EXCHANGES

A market where stocks, shares and other kinds of securities are bought and sold is called a **Stock Exchange**: the Stock Exchange in London is the most widely known centre for securities in Britain, and forms part of the united market that includes a number of exchanges in the provinces. The Stock Exchange deals in securities of government and commercial undertakings all over the world, and is in close contact, by means of the telephone, telex and cable, with the principal stock exchanges abroad such as Paris, Brussels, Amsterdam, Zurich, New York, Milan, Singapore, Melbourne, Tokyo, etc.

The market for securities is therefore the best example of a world market: many are in universal demand, they are perfectly graded and although subject to exchange control, can easily be transported from one country to another. The improvements in communication that have developed has very nearly attained the ideal of a perfect market—that there should be one price for a commodity throughout the market whether on a local or international basis.

2. THE STOCK EXCHANGE IN BRITAIN

In 1972 the London and Provincial Stock Exchanges were unified under the title The Stock Exchange governed by one Council. Thus members wherever they are situated are all subject to the same rules and participate in equal privileges. The largest of the exchanges or units is in London having the greatest number of members and quoted securities although since federation members may seek permission to deal on any exchange in Britain. A closer look at the federation shows the following groups:

(a) The Stock Exchange in London

Dealings in stocks and shares became a recognised occupation during the second half of the seventeenth century, when a large number of joint-stock companies were formed. These received

The Stock Exchange—London

a great impetus in this country through the growth of the National Debt, and when the Government granted a charter to the Bank of England.

The continued growth of the East India Company and other joint-stock enterprises made it necessary to organise facilities for the buying and selling of securities, which at first took place in the Royal Exchange or in one of the coffee-houses near the Bank of England.

The most famous of the coffee-houses was Old Jonathan's, and in the early eighteenth century this coffee-house was regarded as the headquarters of all dealers in stocks and shares. In 1748, Old Jonathan's was burnt down and on the same site the New Jonathan's was erected. By 1773 the New Jonathan's Coffee House decided to change its name, and had the words 'The Stock Exchange' written up over the door. Members paid a small subscription, drew up rules, and appointed a Committee of Management. It is interesting to note that the motto of the Stock Exchange—'my Word is my Bond'—which typifies the work of the Stock Exchange and indeed that of the City of London.

Today the Stock Exchange in London is housed in a 26-storey building, 321 feet in height completed in 1973. This building houses the trading floors, administrative offices of the Council and the offices of about 200 member firms.

(b) In the Provinces

Since federation in 1972 by the formation of a unified exchange, dealers are on equal terms with those on all other exchanges in Britain, so that terms relating to one are equally applied to all. The units outside London are to be found at the follow ng centres:

(a) *The Scottish Unit*, in Glasgow linking the exchanges of Aberdeen, Dundee and Edinburgh.

(b) *The Northern Unit*, linking the Huddersfield, Leeds, Liverpool, Manchester, Newcastle, Oldham and Sheffield exchanges.

(c) *The Midlands and Western Unit*, linking those of Birmingham, Bristol, Cardiff, Nottingham and Swansea.

(d) *The Belfast Unit*.

(e) *The Irish Unit* centred in Dublin.

(*f*) *The Provincial Unit* catering for all provincial brokers not attached to any other unit.

The dealers have a detailed knowledge of the local securities dealt in, have greater reserves through themselves amalgamating in many cases with partnerships on neighbouring exchanges, and are able to specialise to a greater degree on particular stocks.

The Stock Exchange publishes an official list of quoted securities and is under the control of one Council, there being working committees dealing with day to day arrangements at each unit. Through federation brokers in any one market have access to all the other markets and also brokers may open offices in whatever centre they wish.

Management. The Stock Exchange is controlled by a Council of 46 unpaid members most of whom are members of the London administrative unit. The Government broker is an ex-officio member and of the remainder, one-third of the committee retire annually but are eligible for re-election by members of the exchanges. Administration is carried out by the following:

(*a*) *The Council* which is responsible for the overall control of the Exchange working in close co-ordination with the administrative units at each centre.

(*b*) *The Administrative Units* at each unit having responsibility for the maintenance of an efficient market place where the public through brokers and jobbers can deal in stocks and shares safely and quickly. They are also responsible for the discipline and conduct of the members of the Exchange, and for deciding what securities shall be quoted.

(*c*) *Committees* are appointed to assist in the administration of each unit and the recommendations of the Committees are submitted to the Council for approval. These include committees dealing with property upkeep, finance, rules, disputes, etc. The Quotations Committee however is of particular importance and is centred only in London being comprised of members from each unit. Its task is the vetting of applications from joint-stock companies who wish to have their share prices quoted on the Stock Exchange.

Membership of the Stock Exchange is very exclusive and consists of about 4,600 brokers and jobbers most of whom deal in London. To become a member, the following conditions must apply.

(*a*) A candidate must be over the age of 21.

(*b*) No one is eligible for membership who has been more than once bankrupt and who has not obtained a complete discharge.

(*c*) A candidate is required to obtain a Proposer and Seconder who are not under any financial obligation in the case of the candidate's default. They must each be members of four years' standing and must have at least two years personal knowledge of the candidate.

(*d*) Candidates for membership must obtain a nomination from a retiring member before applying for admission. The cost of nominations fluctuates and is determined by the Council from time to time.

(*e*) New members must pay both an entrance and a nomination fee whilst all members pay an annual subscription for the privilege of membership.

(*f*) New members must be approved by a three-quarters majority of the Council.

Members employ a number of clerks in their offices; authorised clerks (red or yellow buttons) are allowed on to the trading floor and are allowed to deal on behalf of their firms but not on their own account. Unauthorised clerks (blue buttons) are also allowed on the floor but may not deal.

3. BROKERS AND JOBBERS

The members are divided into two classes—stock-brokers and stock-jobbers.

The jobbers work on the floor of the House and *deal only with the brokers*, who act for the outside public. When a person desires to buy or sell securities, he must therefore first instruct a stock-broker concerning his requirements; *the broker* (or his authorised clerk) will then go to the appropriate unit and find a jobber dealing in this class of security whereupon if he is satisfied as to the price etc. does business according to the instructions of his client.

The market at any one of the administrative units is divided into sections for ease of operation and is typically as follows:

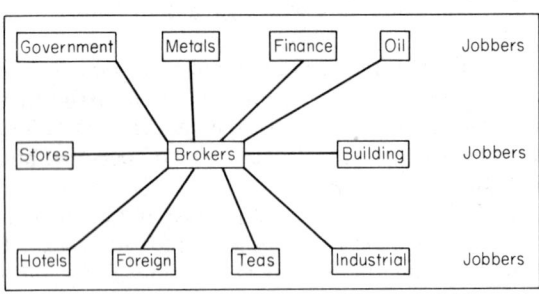

The Organisation of the Market

The division of members into brokers and jobbers has the following advantages:

(*a*) The necessity of employing a broker when buying or selling securities *protects the interests* of the public. The jobber is a specialist in the types of securities in which he deals, as he will deal *with only one kind of security*, e.g. shares of Property Companies, or shares of Engineering Companies, etc. It is to the advantage of an investor to employ another specialist who knows the technicalities of the market, to act on his behalf.

(*b*) There is a great variety of securities dealt in on the Stock Exchange: the Official Price List which is printed daily deals with very many separate securities amounting to many thousands of millions of pounds. *Jobbers specialise* in a few securities which they are always prepared to buy or sell, and the floor of the Exchange is subdivided into 'markets' where jobbers dealing in the same kinds of securities congregate. Many different jobbers deal in the same types of securities; there is competition between jobbers for the orders which the brokers bring in. This specialisation enables jobbers to estimate the supply of and demand for the various types of securities.

(c) The broker always acts in the interests of his client. He usually informs his client of the name of the jobber with whom he has dealt. A jobber is forbidden by the rules of the Exchange to receive orders direct from the public but only from an authorised broker.

(d) The brokers perform many services for their clients in addition to the actual buying and selling of securities. Transfers of stock have to be registered, and share certificates have to be obtained from the company whose shares the client has purchased. In addition, he frequently gives advice to his customers regarding investments, and sends circulars, price lists and prospectuses to his clients.

4. METHOD OF DEALING

When a person wishes to buy or sell securities, he must first of all instruct a broker. Most people when dealing on the Stock Exchange deal through their branch bank's brokers. The broker goes to the Exchange and asks the jobber to state a price for the stocks or shares concerned. *The broker does not say whether he wishes to buy or sell*; if he did so, the jobber could name a low price to a seller of stock, and a high price to a buyer.

The jobber names, therefore, *two prices*—such as 56–58— meaning that he is prepared to buy the stock named at 56p, and to sell it at 58p. If the broker thinks that the buying price is too low, or the selling price too high, he will make enquiries of other jobbers who are near at hand and specialising in the same stocks. When the price is satisfactory, the broker will then declare that he wishes to buy or sell so much stock at the figure quoted. The difference between the two prices quoted is called the *Jobber's Turn*: the difference between the buying and selling prices is wide when the broker names stock which is not often dealt in, for if the jobber buys stock which is not in great demand, he will only offer a low price as it may be some time before he sells it. In the same way, if the jobber contracts to sell such stock, he will want a higher price, since he may have difficulty in obtaining it before the time for delivery arrives.

When the broker agrees to the price quoted, each party to the transaction makes a note of the purchase or sale, and the bargain is checked next day in a room in the Stock Exchange where the clerks of the jobbers and brokers meet for that purpose.

Dunworth & Cuell *Stockbrokers* Bought by Order of D. Aylen Esq For Settlement 29th September				Throgmorton St. London EC2N 1HP 18th September 19 –	
No	*Security*	*Price*	*Stamp*	*Commission etc*	*Total*
79	Beta (Holdings) Ltd at 1·33	£105·07	£2·00	£4·10	£111·17
	Subject to the regulations of the Stock Exchange			Signed Dunworth & Cuell	

The Contract Note

Within a few days, the broker sends to his client a *Contract Note*, showing:

(a) the price at which the business has been done,

(b) the amount of the Broker's Commission (usually a percentage of the buying or selling price),

(c) the amount of the Contract Stamp Duty,

(d) the amount of the Transfer Stamp.

Until the settlement day arrives, the broker's client who has bought stock does not pay any money (unless he has purchased Government Stock): whatever happens to the price of the stock on the exchange, he pays the agreed amount as stated on the contract note (£111·17 in the above example). If a previous settlement day has just passed, he may enjoy a fortnight's credit before payment is due.

5. THE SETTLEMENT

In some cases, such as dealings in British Government Stock, transactions are carried out for immediate payment, and securities are transferred at once, but the majority of transactions are for the account. Stock Exchange settlements take place *twenty-four times per year*—twenty accounts are for a period of two weeks each, and four accounts for three weeks each.

Each settlement occupies the following days:

(a) **Contango Day** is the day in which members who desire to postpone settlement of their bargains carry them over to the next fortnightly account. A 'making-up' price is fixed on the first day of the Settlement, and at this price transactions are carried forward to the next account. The charge for the privilege of carrying-over is called a Contango.

(b) **Ticket Days.** Two days are allowed for making out tickets giving particulars of each transaction. These are passed from the broker to the jobber and state:

(1) amount and name of the security bought.
(2) the price.
(3) the name and address of the broker's client who has bought shares.

The process of passing tickets is facilitated by the work of the Settlement Department, which acts as a Clearing House. Each member prepares a list of his purchases and sales of stock. Thus a member who has *sold*, say, £1,000 more of a particular stock than he has purchased is brought in contact with a member who has *bought* £1,000 more of that stock than he has sold. A separate ticket is therefore not necessary for every transaction; a large number can be settled by the transfer of differences in the amount of stock.

(c) **Pay Day** is the last of the four Settlement days, when all members who have to deliver securities must hand them over in exchange for payment. Differences must be paid by cheques on a bank which is a member of the Bankers' Clearing House. Ten days of grace are allowed for the delivery of registered securities, but no period of grace is allowed for payment. Any member who fails to meet his obligations is declared a defaulter.

6. TYPES OF SECURITIES

The securities dealt in on the Stock Exchange may be divided into three classes—stocks, shares and bonds.

Stock consists of the capital of a company or the amount of a government or local authority loan which has been issued so as to be divisible at the will of the purchaser. Although the unit of stock is usually £100, any quantity, such as £463·61 worth, can be bought or sold.

Shares consist of the capital of a company which has been issued in a number of fixed portions and cannot be subdivided. The capital of a company is usually divided into portions of 50p, £1, £5 or £10, although smaller and larger divisions are often found.

Bonds are promises to pay a certain sum of money with interest and are usually issued in multiples of £100. They may be redeemable either at a fixed period or at some future date to be determined by a government, local authority of joint-stock company. Other bonds are irredeemable, which means that the borrower will continue paying interest for a considerable time.

Debentures are similar to bonds but are applicable only to companies, and are usually issued with the assets of the company as security.

Securities may be classified also according to the following methods of transfer from seller to buyer.

(a) Inscribed Stock. The names of the owners of British Government inscribed stock are in the registers kept at either the Bank of England or the National Savings Bank. When any of this stock is sold, the seller (or his representative) completes a form stating the name and other details of the buyer as evidence of his agreement to transfer. No certificate is issued; the inscription of the buyer's name in the Register is the only recognised evidence of ownership.

(b) Registered Securities are the property of the persons entered as owners in the registers of the issuing body: every company is legally compelled to keep a register of shareholders. The owner of registered stocks (or shares) receives a certificate stating that he is owner of so many shares or so much stock; the nominal value of the shares is given as well as the numbers. When sold, the seller only will sign a *Transfer Deed*, made out by the selling broker, and this, together with the *Share Certificate*, is sent by the broker to the office of the company in order that the necessary alterations may be made in the Register. The old certificate is cancelled, and a new one is made out and sent to the purchaser.

Certificate No. 1234   500 Ordinary Shares
Beta (Holdings) Limited.
Registered Office
120 Portsdown Avenue, Manchester

Capital £1,000,000
Divided into 250,000 6% *Preference Shares and* 750,000 Ordinary Shares of £1 each.

This is to certify that *John Brown Esq. of 38 South Road, Winchester* is the Registered Holder of *Five hundred pounds* of fully paid *Ordinary Shares* in Beta (Holdings) Limited subject to the Memorandum and Articles of Association of the Company.

Given under the Common Seal of the Company 4th October 19 . .

A specimen share certificate.

(c) Bearer Securities. Many bonds are issued payable to bearer: when sold, these are transferred by merely handing them over to the buyer. *Coupons* are attached to the bonds and at the appropriate time the holder applies for payment by sending a dated coupon to the government or company which has issued the bond.

Bearer securities are transferred by mere delivery, and as a result stamp duty is not paid on every transfer. The sale of registered securities is complicated by the question of payment of dividend, especially when the books of a company have been closed for this purpose, but in the sale of bearer bonds the dividend coupon is received by the buyer with the bond itself. Bonds also make good security for loans, since possession of the bond is a good title to them.

On the other hand, the anonymous nature of bearer bonds has its disadvantages: the Government or company issuing them has no register of the holders, and cannot therefore send, in the case of a company, reports and balance sheets, with the same regularity as to registered shareholders. Furthermore, if bonds are lost, they are more difficult to recover than registered securities.

Exchange Control regulations, however, require the holders of all foreign bonds to deposit them at a bank in order that the payment of the foreign currency dividend is received into the Exchange Equalisation Account held at the Bank of England. The Government then pay the holder the appropriate amount of the dividend in sterling.

7. SPECULATION

Although the majority of transactions on the Stock Exchange are for investment purposes, many are of a speculative nature; in such dealings, the buyers and sellers of securities often have no intention of making or accepting delivery.

Speculative transactions may be classified as follows:

(a) Bulls. In a 'bull' transaction, a speculator *buys* stocks or shares in the hope that they will *rise in price* before the next settlement. He may have very good reasons for his anticipation. The usual contract for the purchase of securities is made out, but of course no money is due until the next settlement day. If, in the meantime, the shares rise in price, as anticipated, the buyer sells them at the increased price; when the settlement day arrives, both transactions of buying and selling are settled by the payment of the difference between the buying and the higher selling price. This sum (less commission) is due to him from the broker with whom he dealt. The 'bull' dealer has made a profit on the transaction without the outlay of any money as the following example shows:

15th June 19 –	Purchase of 1000 shares in A Ltd at £1·20 each	£1200
23rd June 19 –	Sale of the above shares at new price say £1·40 each	£1400
	Profit on deal (ignoring all charges etc.)	£200

(b) Bears. In a 'bear' transaction, a speculator may have good reasons for expecting a *fall in the price* of certain stocks or shares. He therefore *sells* these through his broker to a jobber: if the anticipated fall in price takes place, he will buy the shares at the lower price in order to hand them to the broker on settlement day. When the fortnightly settlement arrives, the difference between the selling price and the lower buying price is due to the speculator from the broker.

In both 'bull' and 'bear' transactions, if the forecasts of the speculator are wrong, the speculator must either carry over his bargains by payment of a contango, or pay the difference due to the jobber.

(c) Stags. When a *new issue* takes place, the public is invited to apply for shares, and frequently the number applied for exceeds the number to be allotted. Over-subscription often results in the shares being sold at a premium when they come on to the market. A stag is the name given to a person who anticipates the over-subscription of an issue of new shares, and applies for a large number with the object of selling them at a profit as soon as possible. For example, £5 shares may be issued on such terms as £1 per share on application, and two further instalments of £2. A stag applies for a large number of shares, and remits £1 for each share. The popularity of the new issue may cause the shares to rise to say £1·20 on the Stock Exchange: the 'stag' sells his shares at this price, ceases to be liable for further instalments and makes a profit (ignoring all charges) of 20p per share.

(d) Options. An option is an arrangement made with a jobber (through a broker) whereby the jobber guarantees to buy or to sell a definite amount of a certain security at a fixed price during a specified period, without any obligation to accept or make delivery. The commission paid to the jobber for this guarantee may be regarded as an insurance against price movements. Options are of three kinds:

(1) *Call Options.* Is the right to *buy* a certain amount of securities at a fixed price for a specified period. A broker may know, for example, that within the next three months, he may want to buy £1,000 worth of certain shares, but desires to have some idea now of the price of the shares. He can, therefore,

go to a jobber and ask him to guarantee to sell him the shares he wants to buy at a price which he names, say £1 per share. The jobber will state his charge for such a guarantee, and if agreeable, the broker will pay the amount quoted. The broker can now go to the jobber at any time during three months, and purchase £1,000 worth of the shares at the price agreed upon—viz. £1,000. If the shares have advanced to say £2 each, the broker has gained £1 per share; his net profit will be paid to him, less the amount of the option money which he paid to the jobber.

If the shares have decreased to 75p, on the other hand, he may forego his option and buy the shares at that price.

(2) *Put Options*. A put option is the right to *sell* a certain amount of a security at a fixed price for a specified period. A broker may know that within the next three months he may want to sell £1,000 worth of a certain share, and so he may go to a jobber and ask him to guarantee to buy it from him at a certain price, say 50p per £1 share. For this guarantee, he pays a certain amount to the jobber, to whom he may go at any time during the period of three months and receive £50 for each £100 worth sold. If the shares have fallen much below 50p the broker will make a profit by selling at the higher price. If the shares have risen above 50p the broker may sell his shares in the open market, and forego his option.

(3) *'Put and Call' Options*. A 'put and call' option, or a Double Option, is the right to sell or buy a certain amount of a security at a fixed price during a specified period. For the guarantee of a fixed price, whether buying or selling, the broker pays a double commission to the jobber. As in the above examples, the broker may during the period of the option either buy or sell the securities at the guaranteed price. If price movements are favourable, he may forego his option, and buy or sell at the prevailing market price.

8. THE OFFICIAL LIST

Each unit of the Stock Exchange publishes daily an Official List, containing the names of securities in which they have a particular interest, together with their latest prices. The Stock

Exchange *Daily* Official List is published in London and contains the names and quotations of nearly 10,000 securities. This paper and the Official Lists published by the other units give a full description of each security, stating in various columns the amount of the authorised issue, the amount actually issued, the amount paid up, the rate and date of the last dividend payment, the gross yield, etc.

The Stock Exchange protects the investing public by investigating the good faith of every company which applies for permission to deal. Before an official quotation is given, members must be satisfied that the Memorandum and Articles of Association are in order, and that other legal formalities have been complied with. When an official quotation is granted, the company must send three copies of its Annual Report and its published accounts to the Secretary of the Stock Exchange.

An abridged version of the official lists appear in the leading daily financial papers. The student is well advised to make a careful study of these lists and to note the changes that occur in the quotations from time to time.

The following table illustrates the principal points:

Stock Exchange Quotations

THIS YEAR'S		STOCK	CLOSING PRICE	+ OR —	LAST DIV %	GROSS YIELD	P/E RATIO
HIGH	LOW					%	
2	23	Alpha	23–25	− 3	—	—	—
1	120	Beta (Holdings)	130–133	—	15	11·3	26·6
2	36	Gamma 'A' Ordy (25p)	40–42	+ 2	10	5·9	3·2
9	89	Delta 5% Preference	96–97xd	− 1	5	5·2	—
5	42	Delta Ordinary (50p)	59–60	+ 3	20	16·6	12·0

A brief study of the above shows:

(*a*) This year's highest and lowest prices of the named stock from January 1st to the current date.

(*b*) The name of the stock in alphabetical order. Unless otherwise stated the stock is quoted in £1 units.

(*c*) The closing price in the daily paper is *yesterday's price*, the highest price being the client's buying price. Note that the price quoted for Delta Ltd. 5% Preference Shares is '*ex-dividend*' meaning that the dividend has recently been declared to the shareholders, and that the *seller* of the shares is entitled to the dividend payment when paid. Where a dividend is shortly due to be announced a price will be quoted '*cum dividend*', which will be paid to the *buyer* of these shares.

(*d*) Column 5 shows the increase or decrease recorded yesterday on the previous day's price.

(*e*) Column 6 shows the actual percentage dividend declared by the directors and paid to the shareholders. This figure is based on the *nominal value* of the shares.

(*f*) Column 7 shows the percentage dividend to the shareholder based upon the *market price* of the share, calculated as follows:

$$\frac{\text{Nominal Value} \times \text{Dividend}}{\text{Market Price}} = \text{Yield \% on cash invested.}$$

(*g*) Column 8 refers to the price/earnings ratio which is a more acceptable method of calculating the value of an investment, particularly since the introduction of corporation tax. This figure informs the investor *the number of years* it would take to recover the cash price of the investment from dividends paid, assuming that the profits remained constant and that no further shares were issued.

This is a more exact assessment of the company than the gross yield, as a company may not want to distribute all of its profits in the form of dividend to the ordinary shareholders. If this was the case then the gross yield would either be very low, or non existent.

The price/earnings ratio can be calculated from the following formula:

$$\frac{\text{No. of ordinary shares issued} \times \text{Current buying price}}{\text{Profits available for distribution to the Ordinary shareholders.}}$$

From the table on page 329 assume that Beta (Holdings) have issued 100,000 *ordinary shares* and that the profit available to these shareholders is £5,000 then the ratio is:

$$\frac{100,000}{5,000} \times \frac{133}{100} = \frac{133}{5} = 26 \cdot 6$$

Similar calculations are made for the remaining *ordinary shares* in the table.

Assuming the issued ordinary shares in Gamma is 1 million and the available profit for distribution is £131,250, the student should calculate the price/earnings ratio and check the answer in column 8.

Likewise, assume that the issued ordinary share capital in Delta is 250,000 shares and the available profit to these shareholders is £12,500. Calculate the ratio at the ruling market price.

9. THE PRICES OF SECURITIES

The prices of securities constantly fluctuate: the Daily Official List published by the Stock Exchange and the lists given in the principal morning newspapers show the prices at which bargains were made on the Exchange *during the previous session.*

The principal factors which affect the prices of securities may be summarised:

(*a*) The most important factor is the relation of demand and supply. If the supply of a security remains unaltered, and the demand for it increases, its price will rise: similarly, if the demand decreases, the price will fall. The supply is more or less fixed by the Memorandum of Association which limits the amount of stock that can be issued: one has therefore to study the factors which affect the demand for a particular security.

(*b*) The price of a commodity will affect the price of shares of firms producing that commodity: for example, a high demand for the product or a discovery of new sources should reflect itself in the expectation of profits available for distribution.

(*c*) The rate of interest affects the price of securities: an investor is more likely to choose securities giving a high yield rather than a low one. In addition dividends which are expected to be announced shortly may cause the price to rise slightly.

(*d*) The safety of the principal: this depends on the nature of the undertaking and the efficiency of its management. The Chairman's report and future prospects of the undertaking are important factors to be considered. Foreign investments are usually considered more uncertain than home investments, and perhaps a higher rate of interest has to be paid to insure against the additional risk.

(*e*) The purchasing power of money affects the price of securities. An increase in prices is equivalent to a reduction in the purchasing power of money, and the price of securities will tend to rise.

(*f*) Rumours will affect the price of securities: the market is particularly sensitive to mergers, take-over bids and amalgamations.

(*g*) The date of maturity of a bond which is redeemable will cause it to increase in price as the due date approaches.

(*h*) The supply of capital seeking investment and the demand for capital for new issues may affect the price of existing securities. If new capital is limited, the transfer from old to new will cause a fall in price of the old, since more of these securities will be offered for sale in order to reinvest the proceeds in the new. Similarly, Government borrowings will tend to depress the price of existing loans.

(*i*) Political conditions may affect the price of securities, since the actions of governments may increase or decrease confidence which is an essential element in promoting investment.

10. UNIT TRUSTS

A Unit Trust is one in which the funds consist of investments determined at the time of formation, and except under special circumstances remain unaltered for the period of the trust. The investor who buys sub-units in the Trust is in virtually the same position as if he had bought a small holding in each of the securities which constitutes the Trust unit. The Unit Trust Movement began in 1931, since when many have been formed in order to popularise investments in Stock Exchange Securities with small investors.

(a) Method of Working

(1) A trust deed is drawn up, and a Bank or Insurance Company acts as trustees. Managers are appointed who are specialists in the field of finance and who sell the units to the public.

(2) A panel of securities is drawn up; the list may include 75–100 high-class securities, including Government Funds, Insurance, Banks, etc., to a value of, say, £1,000,000.

(3) The total is divided into perhaps 500 units, each unit being therefore worth £2,000.

(4) Each unit is divided into 2000 sub-units each worth £1: the sub-units are offered to the public, and their prices are quoted on the financial pages of the leading newspapers. The minimum purchase may be, say, 100 sub-units, and fees for commission, registration and Stamp Duty must be paid. Thus a small investor who purchases 100 sub-units has a small interest in all the securities possessed by the Trust.

(5) As each unit is sold, the Trust is able to purchase another unit on the Stock Exchange.

(6) The cost of running the Trust is covered by making an initial charge which forms part of the price of a unit, and by taking an annual service charge out of profits.

(b) Advantages. The Trust possesses the following advantages for the small investor:

(1) It enables him to invest in Stock Exchange Securities with the same degree of safety and with the same earning capacity as has always been available to the more wealthy.

(2) Risks are spread by investment in many different classes of securities.

(3) Sub-units can be sold whenever desired.

(4) The income is distributed half-yearly.

(5) Certificates are issued to investors in respect of each sub-unit purchased.

(6) The association of a Unit Trust with a bank or insurance company is a guarantee of its soundness.

(7) The investor is often able to obtain insurance cover through the unit trust whilst he is a member.

II. INVESTMENT TRUSTS

An investment trust is a joint-stock company registered with limited liability and is constituted to invest its subscribed capital in stocks and shares *of other companies*. Members of the public are invited to take up shares in the trust, their contributions being invested in certain securities on the stock market. Profits made through buying and selling these shares on the Stock Exchange and dividend receipts are distributed among the shareholders in accordance with the number of trust shares they each have bought.

QUESTIONS

1. What factors affect the prices of British Government Securities? (U.L.C.I.)

2. What special features in respect of organisation characterise the Stock Exchange? What are 'contango' and 'backwardation' respectively? (R.S.A.)

3. Distinguish carefully between 'inscribed', 'registered' and 'bearer' stock. Assuming the stock is quoted on the London Stock Exchange, explain how, in each case, transfer of title is effected from one holder to another. (R.S.A.)

4. The Stock Exchange is often described as a 'perfect market'. Give a sufficient description of its work to justify this attribute, and point out how the division of its members into brokers and jobbers may be considered to help towards the attaining of this perfection. (R.S.A.)

5. Describe the process by which you would purchase through the Stock Exchange, 100 Ordinary Shares in a British industrial company whose shares are quoted on the Stock Exchange. (R.S.A.)

6. Suppose you own stocks and shares of a nominal value of £6,000 which are £1 units, quoted at 80p. You wish to sell these and with the proceeds purchase as many shares as possible in another company whose shares are quoted at 48p. How many shares would you be able to buy? (Ignore all charges.)

7. Mr. Clark has £5000 to invest in debentures or preference shares. He can buy 6 per cent debentures at par, or 8 per cent preference shares at 125, both in the same company. Which should he buy? What considerations, other than cost, should influence him. (R.S.A.)

8. You are a shareholder in a public limited liability company. You wish to sell part of your holding. How can this be done? Would your answer be different if your holding was in a private company? (A.E.B.)

9. Describe the work of the Stock Exchange and discuss its importance to industry and the government. (A.E.B.)

10. The balance sheet of a limited company contains the following items: 20,000 *Ordinary Shares* of £1 each, 10,000 6¼ per cent *Redeemable Preference Shares* at £1 each, *General Reserve* £20,000, 100 5 per cent *Debentures* at £100 each. Explain the meaning of the terms in italics and the differences between these forms of capital (A.E.B.)

11. A business has the opportunity to expand and requires 50 per cent more fixed capital immediately. In **each** of the following cases, describe **one** method you would recommend for financing the expansion where a business is run by (*a*) a partnership, (*b*) a public limited company, (*c*) a state controlled corporation.

(Oxford G.C.E.)

Chapter 25

Methods of Payment in Foreign Trade

1. IMPORTANCE OF CREDIT

The exchange of goods and services between individuals in different countries of the world makes it necessary to devise methods by which debts can be settled quickly and easily.

It will be remembered that in the *internal trade* of a country, notes, coins and cheques are used for everyday transactions between business firms and individuals. In the home trade, such a system has been made possible by the development of a national system of banking, and by the establishment of the Bankers' Clearing House where mutual indebtedness is settled.

In the same way, Euro-dollars and credit instruments such as the foreign Bill of Exchange, are used to settle indebtedness between merchants in *international trade*. The system although often subject to exchange control has been made possible by the development of what is virtually an international system of banking, whereby banks in one country have their branches or agents in all the important trading centres of the world, and balances may be adjusted largely by book entries.

2. THE MEANING OF CREDIT

Credit has been defined as the 'confidence of man in man', and where this confidence exists, the seller of goods is willing to give the buyer time for payment. A retailer is allowed a period of time by the wholesaler before payment is due, and similarly, the customer is often allowed by the retailer to settle his accounts weekly or monthly. In these and similar examples, credit is allowed because of the *confidence* which one party to the transaction has in the other. The system of payment by cheque has developed on account of this confidence that a person offering a cheque in payment of a debt has the right to settle his indebtedness in that way.

Confidence in other people depends on collective experience: a man gains a reputation among his business associates by the methods on which he conducts his affairs. The reputation of an individual or business concern may be excellent in his own town or country, but in other countries the business may be unknown.

Banks and financial houses however, are known all over the world, and a credit instrument issued by them is universally acceptable. British banks and finance houses enjoy a reputation second to none, and they are able to lend their names to smaller firms, thus making a credit instrument acceptable all over the world.

A British merchant, therefore, uses the reputation of his bank in settling his accounts abroad: he negotiates his foreign bills through a bank in order to make them acceptable to a foreign merchant. Credit, from this point of view, is the substitution of the superior credit of a bank for the inferior credit of the individual.

3. AN INTERNATIONAL BANKING SYSTEM

Banks act as the clearing house for the world's debts in three ways:

(*a*) They keep accounts with other banks abroad and feed these accounts by remitting all credit instruments bought here from local customers. For example, if an American merchant buys goods from London, he pays for the goods by purchasing from an American bank a bill of exchange payable in London: in such a case, the American bank receives the money and places it to the credit of the British Bank which has accepted the bill. When the bill reaches London, the British bank pays the exporting merchant.

A development in the field of international indebtedness has been the increased use of **Euro-dollars.** These are U.S. dollars deposited in London commercial banks by citizens and institutions of the U.S.A. Considerable sums are involved, their main uses being:

(i) to finance export goods sold on credit

(ii) providing short-term loans on international markets

(iii) providing longer term loans for investment.

(b) Even if the owner of a foreign Bill of Exchange does not sell it to a bank, the bank will collect his debt for him in a foreign centre and remit the proceeds to him in this country. When a British exporter has sent goods abroad, he therefore hands the Bill of Exchange *with the other documents* to his bankers for collection: the bank forwards the bill to its agents abroad, and obtains acceptance or payment of the bill before surrendering the Bill of Lading, etc. In due course, the foreign importer pays the bill, and the proceeds are placed to the credit of the British bank. Upon receiving this information, the bank in this country pays the British exporter by crediting his bank account at the branch where he keeps his account.

(c) If a foreign importer pays the money of his own country into his bank, the British bank deals with the question of the exchange of foreign currencies, and pays its customer the equivalent amount in British money.

In the import trade, similar methods are used by banks, the examples given above being reversed. The bank uses the balances which it has accumulated abroad for the payment of debts due to foreign merchants who have sent goods to this country.

As a result of a world-wide banking system, very little money is used in financing international trade. Foreign Bills of Exchange have been called *'the money of International Trade'*.

4. CHIEF CREDIT INSTRUMENTS

The various forms of credit instruments differ from each other in the speed by which the right to money can be transferred from one place to another. The principal forms of credit instruments are as follows:

(a) Telegraphic Transfers. Telegraphic or Cable Transfers are orders for payment sent by telegraph or cable: it is therefore the quickest method of transferring money from one centre to another. Banks and many large industrial concerns have the permission of the Bank of England to keep funds available in different countries of the world, and by this means money can be paid out in another centre *on the same day* as instructions are received by the bank in this country.

In a telegraphic transfer, it is of course impossible to send a signature in writing and therefore a system of private codes is used to enable the bank abroad to test the genuineness of the instructions which it receives. The telegraphic transfer is the safest and quickest mode of transferring funds, and is therefore the most expensive method of credit remittance.

(b) Mail Transfers. Are orders for payment sent by letter or Air Mail through the usual postal system. The system of mail transfers also depends upon a bank or industrial concern having funds abroad on which it can draw. A mail transfer therefore performs the functions of a cheque in the home trade, but unlike a cheque, it is not transferable.

A British importer may arrange for a mail transfer at a bank by paying cash: the bank will gain interest on the money until the date of the arrival of the mail transfer in the foreign centre. A mail transfer is a slightly cheaper method of transfer.

(c) Guaranteed Mail Transfer. In an ordinary Mail Transfer, described above, there is slight element of doubt as to when the transfer will arrive in the foreign centre: the document may have to wait a few days for a mail-boat or plane, and circumstances may arise which may delay its arrival. Meanwhile, the foreign creditor is uncertain as to when he will be paid, and the delay in payment means loss of interest on the money.

In a Guaranteed Mail Transfer, the bank undertakes that the money shall be paid over on a *fixed date*, irrespective of the arrival of any ship or plane. The bank has funds abroad to enable it to do this: as an additional precaution, the bank often sends instructions by deferred cable rates—i.e. the Cable Company sends the telegram at a lower rate during slack hours.

(d) Foreign Bills of Exchange. As in the home trade, the *seller* of goods may draw up a Bill of Exchange and send it to the buyer for his payment or acceptance. This form of credit instrument is dealt with in the sections which follow.

5. FOREIGN BILLS OF EXCHANGE

A Foreign Bill of Exchange differs from an Inland Bill in the following respects:

(a) It is made out in sets of two or three.

(b) It is payable at sight or so many days after sight, whereas an Inland Bill of Exchange is payable at a definite date.

(c) If dishonoured, a foreign bill *must* be protested—i.e. a notary public (usually a solicitor) must be employed to present the bill a second time and to attach a certificate stating that the bill has been presented by the notary public and has been dishonoured. In the case of an inland bill being dishonoured, the protest is optional.

(d) A Foreign Bill of Exchange, unlike an inland bill, usually has other documents attached to it, such as the Invoice, Bill of Lading, Insurance Policy, Certificate of origin, etc.

The *seller of goods* draws the bill of exchange on the buyer (or his bank): if for example, James Smith, a London merchant, has sold goods to William Bishop in New York, the former would draw up a Bill of Exchange in the following form, and send it to New York for acceptance:

York Road,
London, EC2 3AB

$1200.   *2nd Aug. 19..*

   Sixty days after sight of this FIRST of Exchange (second and third of the same tenor and date being unpaid), pay to my order the sum of Twelve hundred dollars, value received.

To Wm. Bishop Inc.,   JAMES SMITH.
   New York.

Upon receipt of the above Bill of Exchange, the buyer of the goods would accept it by writing across the face of it 'Accepted, payable at the Federal Bank, New York', and signed by William Bishop or an authorised agent of the firm.

METHODS OF PAYMENT IN FOREIGN TRADE 341

The accepted bill would be returned to London where it may be discounted by James Smith if the reputation of the acceptor is good enough: this means that a British bank would purchase from James Smith the right to money in New York.

The difficulty, however, lies in the fact that all traders are not well known; their reputation is local or national and as a result, it is usual to obtain the acceptance of a bank or accepting house instead of that of a trader. By such an acceptance, the bill becomes negotiable anywhere, since the reputation of a bank is known all over the world.

Foreign Bills of Exchange therefore fall into two classes:

(1) *Trade Bills*, which are drawn up and accepted by merchants, as in the example given above.

(2) *Bank Bills*, which are drawn up by a merchant (usually the seller of goods) but accepted by a bank or accepting house on behalf of the buyer.

6. BANK CREDITS

A Bank Credit is one opened by a banker stating the conditions on which he will accept bills drawn by a foreign merchant who sends goods to this country. The British importer approaches a banker or an accepting house, and arranges that it shall accept bills drawn on him either for a single transaction or for his year's trading. A credit limit is agreed upon, provided that the bank is satisfied with the security offered. A small commission is charged for this service, and by its acceptance the bank *guarantees the payment* of the bill to the foreign merchant. This enables the foreign merchant to discount the bill at a lower rate of discount.

Bank credits are of two kinds:

(a) *A Confirmed Credit* states that the issuing bank guarantees the payment of the bill provided that the terms of the credit are carried out. This type of credit is therefore the safest guarantee of payment to the foreign merchant.

(b) *An Unconfirmed Credit* carries no such guarantee by the issuing bank: it is therefore of no protection to the foreign merchant. A lower commission is charged for this credit, and they are used between firms having long-standing business relations where there is little doubt as to whether payment will be made.

Opening a Credit. A British merchant wishing to import goods from abroad fills in a special form at his bank giving the following particulars:

(1) the name and address of the foreign merchant.

(2) the amount of the credit.

(3) the period of the credit.

(4) whether bills are to be drawn on the bank or on the British merchant.

(5) if bills are to be drawn at sight or for so many days after sight.

(6) whether the credit is to be confirmed or unconfirmed.

(7) whether the credit is to be advised to the foreign merchant by cable or letter.

(8) the exact nature of the documents to be surrendered.

(9) the nature, quantity, quality and description of the goods to be shipped.

(10) the port of shipment.

If the bank agrees to open a credit, advice is sent by cable or letter to the foreign merchant or to his bankers.

Using the Credit. When the foreign merchant receives advice of the credit, he ships the goods and prepares the necessary documents. These include:

(1) the Bill of Exchange, which is drawn on the British bank.

(2) the Bill of Lading, which is necessary to enable the British merchant to obtain the goods from the shipping company.

(3) the Invoice stating the price of the goods, etc.

(4) the Insurance Policy and sundry documents such as Certificate of Origin, etc., where required.

The foreign merchant then sells the bill to his local bank, which will readily purchase a bill guaranteed by a British bank. Thus the foreign merchant receives immediate payment for his goods.

The bank abroad will forward the bill with the documents

attached to the British bank for its acceptance and payment: the latter will credit the account of the foreign bank with the amount due when the bill has matured.

The British importer will obtain the Bill of Lading by paying the Bill of Exchange, and claim the goods from the shipping company in due course.

7. DOCUMENTARY CREDITS

To obtain a documentary credit, an importer approaches a bank and fills up a form giving full particulars of the proposed transaction. The importer agrees to pay bills drawn on *himself*: the bank agrees to discount such bills.

The foreign exporter is then notified that a documentary credit has been opened in his favour and so is able to sell the bill and obtain payment when the goods are shipped. He forwards the bill to the British bank, with the usual shipping documents attached, and upon their arrival the importer is able to obtain the Bill of Lading upon acceptance or payment of the bill.

The British bank also receives a *Letter of Hypothecation* from the importing merchant: such a document conveys to the bank the full right to the goods if the Bill of Exchange is not honoured: it authorises the bank to deal with the goods in any way it may consider necessary—to pay for freight storage and insurance of the goods and to sell them if necessary. The bank is authorised to use the proceeds in discharge of the importer's indebtedness, and if the amount realised is insufficient, the importer is responsible for the balance.

The distinction between a bank credit and a documentary credit must be clearly understood: in a *confirmed* bank credit, the *bank* is responsible for the payment of the bill. In a *documentary* credit, the *importer* is responsible—the bank merely agrees to make advances on the bill to the importer.

When new relations are opened up between firms in different countries, the seller usually asks the buyer to arrange for payment by means of a bank credit. When such relations become established, the seller agrees to draw a bill on the buyer, who thus avoids the cost of a bank credit. The seller of goods first draws bills payable at sight, and gradually extends the period of credit as he becomes better acquainted with the firm abroad.

QUESTIONS

1. Describe in detail the ways in which British banks help to finance foreign trade. (U.L.C.I.)

2. What is a Foreign Bill of Exchange, and in what respects does it resemble and differ from an Inland Bill of Exchange? Prepare a specimen Foreign Bill. (U.L.C.I.)

3. Explain fully the help afforded by the Government to the export trade of this country. Why is it necessary to extend the export trade?

4. Describe the work done by London Accepting Houses and bill brokers in the financing of foreign trade. Give examples to illustrate your answer. (R.S.A.)

5. 'To the British exporter the most desirable of all methods of payment is the establishment in his favour of an Irrevocable Documentary Credit which is also "Confirmed".' Explain this statement. (U.L.C.I.)

6. What are (a) the main sources of information available to firms engaged in overseas trade, (b) the means of payment used for this trade? (R.S.A.)

7. Give a definition of a documentary credit and describe its general nature. Explain in outline the role of the banks when this method of payment is used. (A.E.B.)

8. S. Smith & Co. in London purchase goods valued at £10,000 from J. Jones of New York and it is agreed that settlement will be made by means of a two months bill of exchange. Outline the procedure to be followed in this method of settlement. What reason can you give for a bill of exchange being used instead of other means of payment? How does a bill of exchange differ from a cheque? (Oxford G.C.E.)

Chapter 26

Foreign Exchange

I. INTERNATIONAL INDEBTEDNESS

International indebtedness arises on account of the exchange of goods and services between persons or firms in different countries of the world. Amongst primitive communities, payment was made by barter; the improvements in transport and communications have, however, created a world market, and as we have seen, London is an important financial centre of the world.

Foreign Exchange may be described as the business of *exchanging* currencies: merchants in one country are always making claims on the currency of another country in order to pay for goods which they have purchased or for services which have been performed for them.

There are many methods of settling international indebtedness:

(*a*) *Gold Bullion* may be sent by the Central Banks when settling international indebtedness. The Bank of England, for example, would remit gold out of the Exchange Equalisation account to another Central Bank. Nowadays there is little gold movement in international trade as most countries prefer to build up balances before adjusting the exchange rates of their currencies in order to counteract large surpluses or deficits. Members of the European Economic Community however have agreements with each other not to change their respective rates outside given limits without consultation.

(*b*) *Bills of Exchange.* A Foreign Bill of Exchange may be accepted by the buyer of goods, or by a bank on his behalf.

(*c*) *Bankers' Drafts.* When trade relations have become

established between merchants in different countries, the seller of goods may agree to accept the buyer's *banker's* cheque in payment.

(*d*) *Telegraphic Transfers*. These form the quickest way of transferring money from one country to another. Money is paid into one bank, and paid out of another bank abroad on the same day.

(*e*) *Mail Transfers*. Such transfers are sent by letter to the agent of the bank or financial house abroad. Where a Guaranteed Mail Transfer is used, the bank undertakes to make payment abroad on a fixed date, irrespective of the arrival of the mail-boat or plane.

(*f*) *Securities*. Many stocks and shares are international and can be bought or sold on all the principal stock exchanges of the world. Merchants can therefore purchase these securities in the home market, and send them abroad for sale, and credit the proceeds to their accounts with banks in other countries. Similarly, by purchasing securities abroad, funds may be transferred to this country. Such methods are *only used by financial houses* when, after allowing for expenses, the net proceeds are greater than those obtained by any other form of remittance.

(*g*) *Interest Coupons*. Coupons for the payment of interest on many international securities are payable to bearer at any foreign centre. Exchange dealers are always ready to buy such coupons, and use them to transfer funds abroad.

(*h*) *Accounts Abroad*. Many large firms keep accounts with banks in other countries, and by this means they are able to make payments abroad by drawing on the funds which they have accumulated elsewhere.

It must be remembered that in all the above examples the permission of the Bank of England is required for the transfer of funds *outside* the Sterling Area unless carried out by an authorised dealer.

2. THE ORGANISATION OF FOREIGN EXCHANGE

The organisation of Foreign Exchange is essentially an extension of the internal credit system to the wider field of international settlements. The use of credit instruments, such as cheques, economises the use of currency in the home trade; similarly, the organisation of Foreign Exchange economises the use of currency over greater distances between the various countries of the world. Debts owing by individuals in one country are *set off* against the debts of individuals in another country, just as banks at home cancel debits and credits on each other through the various clearing houses. As a result of this cancellation, time, trouble and expense are saved, and the necessity for the transfer of balances between countries is largely avoided.

The London Foreign Exchange Market consists of:

(a) Authorised banks and finance houses which maintain foreign exchange departments, and are regular dealers in foreign currencies. A network of private telephone lines links together foreign exchange departments of authorised banks and finance houses, whilst the extension of the system of international telephones, radio and telex communication has made the whole world one market for financial and exchange purposes.

(b) Foreign Exchange Brokers, who act as intermediaries in bringing buyers and sellers together. The brokers install and maintain at their own expense private telephone lines to the banks and finance houses, and specialise in the currencies of particular countries. They are bound by the rules of the Brokers' Association, which forbid them to deal on their own account or to charge commission in excess of a standard scale.

The improvements in communication have made a recognised meeting-place unnecessary for the Foreign Exchange Market. It is under the control of the London Foreign Exchange Bankers' Committee, assisted by a Committee of the London Foreign Exchange Brokers' Association. These committees regulate the working conditions of the market; any bank or finance house may become a member of the market without restriction, so long as it has the permission of the Bank of England.

The function of the Foreign Exchange dealer is to facilitate the exchange of the currency of one country into that of another country. The rate of exchange is the number of units of one currency which will exchange for a given number of units of another currency: for example, if a dealer will give 10 francs for £1, the rate of exchange between London and Paris is said to be £1 = 10 francs. The dealer will not always give the same number of francs for £1; the supply of francs may be limited, or the demand for French currency may be larger than anticipated.

The rate of exchange between two countries varies from day to day and even from hour to hour, according to the world demand and supply for a particular currency. In addition the market is concerned not only with the *spot* (present) rate of exchange but the forward rate also. Merchants and dealers are anxious to cover themselves against future changes in the rate and make arrangements for the purchase or sale of foreign currency now for an agreed rate in, say, three months' time.

The problems of foreign exchange are due to three reasons:

(1) *Monetary Units.* Different units of money have been adopted in each country as the standard of value: the units vary and the value of one currency in terms of another must be calculated.

(2) *Distance.* Currency or bank balances in one centre may have to be transferred to another centre for making payments.

(3) *Time.* The transfer between two centres involves a loss of interest whilst the money is in transit. In addition, the time element is important when the money is due at some future date.

Because of the variety of transactions in foreign exchange, various rates of exchange are quoted for each type of business done.

3. FOREIGN EXCHANGE WITHOUT THE GOLD STANDARD

When a country is not on the Gold Standard, we have seen that gold cannot be obtained for export, and that the paper money which circulates in that country cannot be exchanged for gold at the Central Bank. Under such conditions, the rates of exchange cannot be controlled by movements of gold from country to country except by the use of the Exchange Equalisation

Account under the control of the Central Bank. When two countries are off the Gold Standard, the rates of exchange between those countries depend on the relative purchasing power of their currencies.

(a) The Purchasing Power Parity. This theory states that the value of one currency in terms of another is determined in the long run by their relative purchasing powers: therefore the rate of exchange tends to rest at a point which expresses equality between the purchasing powers of the two currencies.

Suppose, for example, that a metre of silk costs £1 in England and 10 francs in Paris: under these conditions the rate of exchange would be 10 francs = £1.

(1) For, if the rate were above 10 francs to the £1—let us say 12 francs—it would pay anyone in Paris to buy silk in Paris at 10 francs per metre, sell it to England at £1 per metre, and then change the £1 into francs at 12, thus making a profit of 2 francs per metre (ignoring transport charges etc.)

(2) If the rate were 9 francs, it would pay anyone in Paris to change 9 francs for £1, buy silk in England at £1 per metre, and sell the silk in Paris for 10 francs, thus making a profit of 1 franc per metre.

If either of the above conditions prevailed for any length of time, the number of people anxious for profit would restore the rate of exchange to a position at which the price levels were equal. The purchasing power theory suggests that rates of exchange can only differ from the point of equality of price levels by the cost of transporting goods.

(b) Comments on the Theory. It provides a *working basis* to show the principal factor which determines the rate of exchange between two countries without the Gold Standard. The theory, however, has the following defects:

(1) The comparison of price levels in different countries is difficult, since the relative importance of many commodities varies in different countries.

(2) People in different countries distribute their incomes differently, and therefore a comparison of price levels is misleading.

(3) The price level, for purposes of comparison, should be

based on goods that enter into foreign trade: but these are difficult to separate.

(4) Currency conditions affect the purchasing power of two or more countries. The value of paper money is partly determined by the monetary policy of the Central Banks.

The relative purchasing powers of the currencies of two countries, show what the rate of exchange should be under conditions of free trade on the commodities that enter into trade between the two countries. The actual rate of exchange may differ from the relative price levels according to the balance of trade at any time.

4. EXCHANGE QUOTATIONS

Funds may be sent from one country to another in various ways, and many forms of remittance may be purchased. For each form of remittance, different rates of exchange are quoted in the Foreign Exchange Market; the rates vary according to the time which elapses before payment, the amount of risk involved, and the trouble and expense incurred.

All the leading newspapers publish a list, giving the rates of exchange ruling in London *on the previous day*. The majority of the rates quoted are for telegraphic transfers, and give the highest and lowest prices at which business was transacted.

The rates quoted in the Foreign Exchange Market are as follows:

(a) Sight Rates. These are also known as Cheque Rates and Short Rates of Exchange, and cover cheques and bills payable on demand, or having only a few days to run before maturity.

(b) Forward (Long) Rates. Are quoted for bills having, as a rule, either one or three months to run before they fall due. They are based on the Sight Rate, making allowances for:

(1) Interest at the discount rate ruling in the foreign centre for the time the bill has to run before maturity.

(2) An additional expense on a long bill.

The Forward rate is therefore usually cheaper than the Sight Rate, since the money is not payable until some time in the future, during which period interest is lost by the purchaser of the bill. The effect of quoting a cheaper rate of exchange is that the purchaser of the bill pays for it the Present Value of the bill.

(c) Cable Rates. These rates, which are also known as Telegraphic Transfers (T.T.), are the most important and may be regarded as the basic rate of exchange between two currencies. Cable rates are quoted for remittances sent by bankers to their agents abroad authorising the transfer of funds to third parties. These rates are dearer than Sight Rates, since there is no loss of time or interest, and the cost of the cable is small.

(d) 'Tel Quel' Rates. Is a rate of exchange which has been adjusted to suit a bill 'as it is'. The Forward rate is quoted for bills which have a fixed period to run, such as three months. Many bills, however, have a shorter or longer period to run before maturity, and for such, a special rate is quoted by calculating a new rate from the Sight Rate, to allow for the loss of interest until the bill matures. This special rate is known as a Tel Quel rate, since it is quoted for one particular bill.

5. FLUCTUATIONS IN RATES OF EXCHANGE

Variations in the rates of exchange between two countries may be due to the interaction of many factors, which may be analysed as follows:

(a) Trade Conditions. These refer to the relation of imports and exports, the value of which is obtained from the returns published by the Department of Trade and Industry. We may examine the effects on the rates of exchange of (1) a surplus of imports, (2) a surplus of exports, and for purposes of illustration confine our attention to the trade between Britain and France.

(1) *Surplus of Imports.* If Britain has imported more from France than she has exported to that country, there will be an increased demand in London for Bills of Exchange or banker's drafts payable in Paris. The price of bills or bank drafts in London will therefore rise, which means that for every pound sterling a British merchant will obtain fewer francs than

previously. The exchange rate will move against Britain, or in other words, the quotation of francs per £1 will go down.

(2) *Surplus of Exports*. If Britain has exported more to France than she has imported, there will be an increased supply in London of bills drawn on Paris, and therefore the price of these bills will fall. The exporters in this country will receive more francs for each pound sterling: the rate of exchange will move in favour of Britain, i.e. the quotation of francs per £1 will go up. We may conclude, therefore, that fluctuations in rates of exchange are primarily due to fluctuations in imports and exports; if a country's exports exceed its imports, the value of its currency will increase compared with the value of other currencies.

(b) Financial Influences. Large sums of money are transferred from country to country for various reasons: the transfer increases the demand for Bills of Exchange, etc., payable in the country receiving the money, and thus affects the rate of exchange.

Money is due from one country to another for the following reasons:

(1) *Freight Payments*. Large sums are due to Britain for the services as listed under the heading of invisible exports.

(2) *Interest Payments*. Britain invests large amounts of money abroad and interest payments are received annually on the investments which are made by both Government and private enterprise.

(3) *Commissions and Premiums*. Commissions are due to agents in this country for their services to foreign merchants: similarly, premiums are remitted to Britain for risks insured against with British companies.

(4) *Profits*. With the growth of international combines, profits are remitted to this country from branches and subsidiary companies abroad.

(5) *Banking Operations*. The international system of banking which has developed during the present century exercises a most powerful influence on exchange rates.

(a) Balances and funds are moved from one centre to another, to cover their commitments abroad. This causes an increased demand for bills which are purchased by the banks.

(b) Increased rates of interest cause a flow of capital from other centres with lower rates of interest. As a result, the rate of exchange on the centre with the higher rate of interest is improved.

(6) *Stock Exchange Operations.* With the growth of international combines, many securities are dealt with on all the Stock Exchanges of the world. If, say, American securities are bought in this country, there is an increased demand for dollars in order to pay for them.

Coupons attached to securities are often payable, when due, in more than one centre. They are therefore cashed in the most profitable place, depending upon the rate of exchange.

(c) Currency Conditions. The conditions of a country's currency affects the rate of exchange in the following ways:

(1) If notes have been issued with no reliable backing, the purchasing power of the currency will fall.

(2) If the currency is worn or debased, more will be demanded in exchange for a foreign currency.

(d) Speculation. Foreign currency may be bought or sold in the expectation of a rise or fall of the rate of exchange. The improvements in communications have made easier the simultaneous buying and selling of the same currency in two or more markets. Professional dealers make a profit by *Arbitrage operations*: these consist of buying in a centre where a currency is cheap, and selling in a centre where it is dearer. By means of the telephone, a dealer may buy francs in Paris at, say, 12 to the £, and sell them in London at 10 to the £.

The effect of Arbitrage operations is to equalise rates of exchange, since the increased demand for cheap currency sends up the price.

6. ELIMINATION OF EXCHANGE RISKS

It is obvious that, when a bill of exchange is expressed in foreign currency, due at some future date, the holder of the bill may be involved in considerable loss through exchange movements: a bill for 600 francs is worth £60 when the rate is 10 francs to the £, but if the franc falls in value and is quoted at 12 francs to the £, the same bill is only worth £50. There are three methods by which risks of loss through exchange fluctuations may be avoided, viz. the use of Exchange Clauses, the purchase or sale of Forward Exchange, and the opening of Foreign Currency Accounts.

(a) The Use of Exchange Clauses. An Exchange Clause may be defined as one included in the wording of a bill in order to fix the method of arriving at the rate of exchange at which the bill must be paid by a foreign creditor of this country. The following are examples of Exchange Clauses:

(1) *Exchange as per Endorsement.* The effect of this is to enable the bank to whom the drawer sells the bill to fix the rate of exchange at which the bill is payable. The bank pays the drawer or holder of the bill its full face value, without any deduction for discount or other charges.

(2) *Payable without Loss in Exchange.* This clause has the effect of ensuring that the drawer in this country receives the full amount of the bill, less discount (if any) for the time the bill has to run.

(3) *Payable at the Collecting Bank's Selling Rate for Sight Drafts on London.* Empowers the Collecting Bank to fix a rate at which it is willing to sell a Sight Draft on London for the amount of the bill.

Other Exchange Clauses, largely variations of the above, are used in connection with the trade of particular countries.

(b) Forward Exchange. The purchase or sale of Forward Exchange is an application for the principle of 'Futures' to exchange dealings. A merchant who has a payment to make in a foreign centre at some future date may settle the rate of exchange with his banker *now*, and so be free from concern regarding fluctuations in rates of exchange. Similarly, a merchant who has money to receive from a foreign centre at some future date arranges *now* with his banker the rate he will receive for foreign currency when it is paid.

By the use of Forward Exchange, an importer knows the *exact* cost of the goods imported, since he can purchase forward the amount of foreign currency he will require at a given rate of exchange. Likewise an exporter knows the proceeds of his sales of goods abroad by a forward sale of the foreign currency.

(c) Foreign Currency Accounts. A trader may accept payment from a foreign creditor in foreign currency, and with the permission of the Bank of England open an account with a foreign bank in each country in which he transacts business. He can therefore convert the foreign currency into sterling at a favourable opportunity, or he may use it to pay for his own purchases of goods from that country. If the balance of a Foreign Currency Account becomes too low, it may be increased by purchases of the currency; if it becomes too large, the balance may be reduced by selling the foreign currency and remitting the proceeds to his bank in this country.

Foreign Currency Accounts cannot be considered as absolute safeguards against losses in exchange: the value of the currency in such accounts depends upon whether the movements of rates of exchange are favourable to the holder, and this depends upon variations in the exchange value of the currency. They require expert operation, since an element of speculation may enter into them, but they are most useful to those whose normal trading or financial activities make it unnecessary to convert the currency into sterling except at infrequent intervals.

Various steps have been taken to prevent extreme fluctuations of exchange rates. The Exchange Equalisation Account for example which is operated by the Bank of England, goes some way towards checking extreme fluctuations in these rates.

QUESTIONS

1. Describe how a British merchant may protect himself against loss on exchange when he is arranging for the future supply by foreign manufacturers of goods, the prices of which are quoted in foreign currencies. (R.S.A.)

2. Explain the difference between spot and forward rates in the Foreign Exchange Market. What are T.T. rates? (R.S.A.)

3. Explain briefly the motives for exchange control. What methods may be adopted?

4. London has been described as the financial centre of the world and the pound sterling as an international currency. What were the circumstances which brought about this position?

(R.S.A.)

5. A British importer receives a consignment of canned ham from Holland for which he must pay net cash against documents. He will only be able to sell the goods in smaller lots ex-warehouse and needs finance for the transaction. In what forms and against what security could he obtain finance from his bank? (R.S.A.)

6. Many well-known firms with overseas subsidiaries hold large balances with banks overseas. They profitably transfer these funds from centre to centre according to various factors. What are the reasons for this and explain how such action may be against national interests.

7. One of your competitors in the European Economic Community has suggested a closer link between his retail outlets and your export business. What are the chief points you would consider before accepting or rejecting this offer? Would your answer have been different if the suggestion had came from the U.S.A.?

Appendix I

ROYAL SOCIETY OF ARTS
SINGLE-SUBJECT EXAMINATIONS
COMMERCE
STAGE II (Intermediate)—
THURSDAY, 24th JUNE, 1971

[TWO AND A HALF HOURS ALLOWED]

FIVE *questions are to be attempted.*

1. In Britain, privately owned industries (public joint stock companies) exist side by side with nationalised industries (public corporations). Give three examples of each and state the work done by those you select.

2. The number of brokers in the London Stock Exchange has increased by about 15 per cent in the last few years but the number of jobbers has decreased by more than one-third, and there are now about four brokers to one jobber.

    What are the functions of jobbers and brokers and why do you think the number of jobbers is decreasing?

3. Various terms such as c.i.f. are used in quotations and invoices in connection with overseas trade in order to make perfectly clear what is included in the price quoted. Explain fully the meaning of c.i.f. Write down three other such terms and explain their meaning in detail.

4. Describe the advantages and disadvantages of transport of freight either
    By rail
OR
    By canal.

5. Explain the following:
clearing banks;
special deposits;
advances to customers;

base rate;
bank liquidity.

6. Some people say that advertising is a waste of money while others say that it pays to advertise. Discuss.

7. Explain what is meant by the following terms used in insurance:
(a) Consequential loss.
(b) Employers' liability.
(c) Public liability.
(d) Fidelity guarantee.

8. Complete the following table to give the information required:

Type of Retail Trade Unit	Distinctive Feature	Owned By	Example with which you are familiar	Advantage to Owner	Advantage to Customer
Small Shop					
Departmental Store					
Multiple Shop					
Co-operative Society					
Voluntary Chain					
Mail Order Business					

ORDINARY NATIONAL CERTIFICATE IN
BUSINESS STUDIES, 1971

(Joint Examination Scheme of the Royal Society of Arts
and the London Chamber of Commerce)

STRUCTURE OF COMMERCE

THURSDAY, JUNE 17

[THREE HOURS ALLOWED]

FIVE *questions to be attempted.*

1. Describe the chief sources of capital available for both public corporations and public liability companies.

2. When two car manufacturers combine they expect to enjoy certain commercial and economic advantages. What are these advantages? What advantages, if any, can the consumer expect to enjoy?

3. As a prospective customer, compare the services offered by the National Giro with the Giro systems provided by the commercial banks.

4. "The totally unnecessary costs of advertising have inevitably led to high prices and in turn to the establishment of consumer protection bodies." To what extent is this statement true?

5. Describe the changing roles of sea and air transport in the carriage of goods to and from the United Kingdom and indicate some of the contemporary problems and developments associated with these two forms of transport.

6. A member of the public wishes to use £10,000 to buy the shares of a company quoted on the London Stock Exchange. Explain the machinery for the purchase of these shares and indicate the role of the intermediaries concerned in the transaction.

7. Indicate the effects on the export trade and related services by Britain joining the European Economic Community.

8. "The full advantages to the consumer of mass production are only now being realised with the growth of mass selling." Discuss this statement with reference to the various types of large scale retail business.

9. (*a*) Outline the general principles upon which insurance is based.
   (*b*) Explain why some insurance policies are issued in the names of many underwriters.

ASSOCIATED EXAMINING BOARD

for the General Certificate of Education

November Examination, 1971 – Ordinary Level

COMMERCE

[TWO AND A HALF HOURS ALLOWED]

Answer FIVE *questions.*

All questions carry equal marks.

1. (a) What is meant by the statement 'insurance is a pooling of risks'?
   (b) What are the essential elements in a contract of insurance?
   (c) Describe any business risks which are uninsurable.

2. Show briefly how a public limited company differs from a public corporation in regard to (i) ownership (ii) control (iii) raising of capital (iv) disposal of profits.

3. What documents normally pass between a retailer and a wholesaler during a business transaction? Explain the **purpose** of each of these documents.

4. Why is foreign trade of great importance to the United Kingdom? Describe the ways in which exporters may obtain orders from abroad.

5. What are the differences between (a) retail markets, (b) wholesale markets, and (c) commodity markets? Explain how these markets assist in production.

6. Describe the type of traffic undertaken by (a) tramp steamers, (b) cargo liners and (c) passenger liners. How are (i) the Baltic Exchange, and (ii) Lloyd's concerned with shipping?

7. Describe the services offered by the joint-stock banks to the business man.

8. Explain the difference between:—

    (a) Industrial and commercial occupations.

    (b) Registered letter service and recorded delivery service of the Post Office.

    (c) Dividend and interest.

    (d) A hire purchase agreement and a credit sale agreement.

    (e) *ad valorem* duties and specific duties.

9. Describe the various ways in which manufacturers can advertise their goods. How is the consumer protected against misleading and false advertising?

UNION OF EDUCATIONAL INSTITUTIONS

Ordinary National Certificate in Business Studies

STRUCTURE OF COMMERCE

WEDNESDAY, 16th JUNE, 1971

1400 – 1700 HOURS

Answer SIX *questions.*

All questions carry equal marks.

1. (a) What is meant by the term specialisation in or division of labour?
   (b) State its advantages and disadvantages.

2. Compare a Public Corporation with a Public Limited Liability Company.

3. How would you define the term "capital" in respect of a business?
   In a limited company how would you distinguish between
   (a) Authorised Capital and Issued Capital.
   (b) Fixed and Circulating Capital.
   (c) Capital owned and capital employed.

4. (a) State the advantages and disadvantages of Air Transport.
   (b) What is "containerisation", and how far is it a threat to air transport especially in exporting goods?

5. What are the characteristics of a multiple retail organisation? What advantages has such an organisation over other types of retail outlet?

6. Give a general account of the ways in which Consumers are protected by
   (a) legislation,
   (b) Government Departments, and
   (c) voluntary organisations.

7. State the main features of futures (terminal) and auction commodity markets, giving reasons for the existence of both and naming the main examples of both.

8. Give an outline account of the four branches of Insurance.

9. (a) Describe the cheque system.
   (b) Briefly describe the work of the London Clearing House.

10. What are the methods by which a British exporter may obtain payment for goods sold abroad?

11. Commercial activities are not restricted to the actual buying and selling of goods. Describe the other auxiliary activities which may be regarded as branches of Commerce.

12. Write an account of the speculative procedures used in the Stock Exchange and give one example of a way in which they can be reduced.

ROYAL SOCIETY OF ARTS
SINGLE-SUBJECT EXAMINATIONS

COMMERCE
STAGE II (Intermediate)

FRIDAY, 28th JUNE, 1968

[TWO AND A HALF HOURS ALLOWED]

FIVE *questions are to be attempted.*

1. Why must the objects of a company be stated carefully in the Memorandum of Association? What other documents has a company to prepare before it can commence business?

2. Chambers of Commerce, Trade Associations and the Confederation of British Industry are all concerned with the promotion of trade. Discuss the work of any two of them.

3. 'Although the wholesaler is less important today than formerly his functions have still to be carried out'. What are these functions and who carries them out?

4. Select two of the following and distinguish between the terms:
   (a) Customs and Excise Duties.
   (b) Flags of convenience and flag discrimination.
   (c) Charter Party and Bill of Lading.

5. Discuss briefly the Common Market *or* Describe the operation of (a) the World Bank and (b) the International Monetary Fund.

6. What is meant by an unfavourable balance of trade? How can it be corrected?

7. Give the meaning of (a) freight liner trains, (b) development areas, (c) automation.

8. The Bank of England controls the monetary policy of the country by making changes in the *Minimum Lending Rate*, by *open market operations* and by means of *special deposits*. Write brief explanatory notes on the three phrases in italics.

Appendix 2

Metric Weights and Measures

Length

10 millimetres	= 1 centimetre
10 centimetres	= 1 decimetre
10 decimetres	= 1 metre
10 metres	= 1 decametre
10 decametres	= 1 hectometre
10 hectometres	= 1 kilometre

Weight

10 milligrammes	= 1 centigramme
10 centigrammes	= 1 decigramme
10 decigrammes	= 1 gramme
10 grammes	= 1 decagramme
10 decagrammes	= 1 hectogramme
10 hectogrammes	= 1 kilogramme

Area

100 sq. millimetres	= 1 sq. centimetre
100 sq. centimetres	= 1 sq. decimetre
100 sq. decimetres	= 1 sq. metre
100 sq. metres	= 1 sq. decametre
100 sq. decametres	= 1 sq. hectometre
100 sq. hectometres	= 1 sq. kilometre

Capacity

10 millilitres	= 1 centilitre
10 centilitres	= 1 decilitre
10 decilitres	= 1 litre
10 litres	= 1 decalitre
10 decalitres	= 1 hectolitre
10 hectolitres	= 1 kilolitre

Metric Equivalents

LENGTH

British to Metric

1 inch =	2·54 centimetres
1 foot =	30·48 centimetres
1 yard =	0·91 metres
1 mile =	1·61 kilometres

Metric to British

1 millimetre =	0·039 inches
1 centimetre =	0·39 inches
1 metre =	39·37 inches
1 kilometre =	0·621 miles

WEIGHT

1 ounce =	28·35 grammes
1 pound =	0·454 kilogrammes
1 cwt =	50·8 kilogrammes
1 ton =	1·016 tonnes

1 gramme =	0·035 ounces
200 grammes =	7 ounces
1 kilogramme =	2·2 pounds
1 tonne =	0·984 tons

CAPACITY

1 pint =	0·568 litres
1 quart =	1·136 litres
1 gallon =	4·544 litres

1 litre =	1·76 pints
5 litres =	8·8 pints
10 litres =	2·2 gallons

Appendix 3

The Principal Currencies of the World

Country	Currency	Country	Currency	Country	Currency
Algeria	Dinar	Hungary	Forint	Nigeria	Naira
Argentine	Peso	Iceland	Krona	Norway	Krone
Australia	Dollar (Aust)	India	Rupee	Pakistan	Rupee
Austria	Schilling	Indonesia	Rupiah	Poland	Zloty
Bahamas	Dollar (Bah)	Iran	Rial	Portugal	Escudo
Bahrain	Dinar	Iraq	Dinar	Singapore	Dollar (S)
Belgium	Franc (Bel)	Israel	Pound (I)	S. Africa	Rand
Bolivia	Peso	Italy	Lira	Spain	Peseta
Brazil	Cruzeiro	Jamaica	Dollar (J)	Sudan	Pound (S)
Burma	Kyat	Japan	Yen	Sweden	Krona
Canada	Dollar (Can)	Jordan	Dinar (J)	Switzerland	Franc
Chile	Escudo	Kenya	Shilling	Tanzania	Shilling
China	Renminbi	Kuwait	Dinar	Trinidad	Dollar (T)
Colombia	Peso	Liberia	Dollar (L)	Tunisia	Dinar (T)
Cyprus	Pound	Libya	Dinar (L)	Turkey	Lira (T)
Denmark	Krone	Luxemburg	Franc	Uganda	Shilling
Finland	Markka	Malaysia	Dollar (M)	U.A.R.	Pound (E)
France	Franc (Fr)	Malta	Pound	U.S.A.	Dollar
Germany (Fed)	Mark	Mexico	Peso	U.S.S.R.	Rouble
Gibraltar	Pound	Netherlands	Florin	West Indies	Dollar (WI
Greece	Drachma	New Zealand	Dollar (N)	Zambia	Kwacha
Hong Kong	Dollar (H.K.)				

Appendix 4

The Banking and Financial Dealings Act 1971 established the following days to be bank holidays in England and Wales:

Easter Monday

The last Monday in May

The last Monday in August

26th December, if it is not a Sunday.

27th December in a year in which the 25th or 26th December is a Sunday.

The following days are to be bank holidays in Scotland:

New Year's Day, if it is not a Sunday, or if it is a Sunday then the 3rd January.

2nd January, if it is not a Sunday, or if it is a Sunday then the 3rd January.

Good Friday

The first Monday in May

The first Monday in August

Christmas Day if it is not a Sunday, or if it is a Sunday then the 26th December

Index